THE  TIMES

Brief Letters to the Editor

Introduced by
Robert Thomson
Editor of *The Times*

TIMES BOOKS

HarperCollinsPublishers
77–85 Fulham Palace Road
Hammersmith
London W6 9JB

The HarperCollins website address is
www.**fire**and**water**.com

First published 2003

Reprint 10 9 8 7 6 5 4 3 2 1 0

ISBN 0 00 716647 8

British Library Cataloguing in Publication Data
A catalogue record for this book is available from the British Library

Text compilation and design by Clare Crawford

Printed and bound in Great Britain by Clays Ltd, St Ives plc

Introduction

A newspaper is only as good as its readers, and *The Times* is fortunate to have an intelligent audience whose tastes, as the letters in this volume testify, range from philosophy to nomenclature and secateurs (as well as our own non sequiturs). Witty writing takes time and imagination, and it is clear that correspondents to our newspaper have thought long and hard about their subjects and their sentence structures. It is always intimidating for a newspaper editor to receive a missive from a reader whose knowledge of a subject dwarfs that of the paper's own specialist reporters. And it is always a pleasure to have a written conversation with a clever and amusing correspondent. We owe our readers a great debt.

Robert Thomson,
Editor, *The Times*,
London, 2003

Brief Letters
2002

Too rich a diet

From Mr Neville Denson

Sir, May I share my new year resolution with you? I think I'd be more likely to stick to it if it were out in the open.

I have resolved to have kind thoughts every time I see a photograph of Jamie Oliver, rather than the angry, negative ones I have now.

I'm sure he's a lovely person. But I see his face more than my own. Must we be confronted by his youthful exuberance every time we switch on television, pick up a newspaper or turn the pages of a magazine?
Yours sincerely,
NEVILLE DENSON,
St Bees, Cumbria. December 28

Poor panning

From Mr A. A. Bullimore

Sir, Recognising that toilet design is not exactly rocket science, why is it that it seems beyond the wit of man to create lavatory pan and cistern geometry which allows the seat and lid to remain securely in the upright position without the hazard of it all coming crashing painfully down?
Yours faithfully,
A. A. BULLIMORE,
Felixstowe. January 3

From Dr Don Taylor

Sir, It is my experience that the chances of the toilet seat being a "snapper" are considerably increased if the residents of the house are all female.
Yours faithfully,
DON TAYLOR,
Southampton. January 4

From Mr James Williams

Sir, I have been involved in making wooden lavatory seats for 25 years and often come across the phenomenon of the falling seat; so much so that we provide a special cranked pillar to overcome the problem.

Some years ago I had in my possession a fine Edwardian seat that had heavy lead counterweights on the back so it remained permanently in the up position. This necessitated care in sitting and, more particularly, in getting up.

This arrangement would not suit the large number of people who are adamant that the seat should be put down after use. Last year we were commissioned by a client to paint on the top of the seat the badge of Sunderland Football Club and on the underside Chelsea's. Her husband is a Sunderland supporter and I understand it has had excellent results.
Yours faithfully,
JAMES WILLIAMS
(Director, Tosca & Willoughby Ltd), Aston Rowant, Oxfordshire. January 5

From Sir Donald Sinden

Sir, Some years ago I visited a builders' merchant to complain about a new lavatory seat which would not remain in the vertical position.

"Oh, you've got one of them, have you?" said the man behind the counter.

"Yes. Is there anything I can do about it?"

"Oh yes, Sir."

"So what do I do?"

"Jump well back!"

He later sold me two hinge extensions which corrected the fault perfectly.
Yours faithfully,
DONALD SINDEN,
London WC2. January 7

Medium and message

From Mr Roger C. Bryan

Sir, Your instructions at the bottom of your letters page (January 3) are noted. However, when does a letter by telephone cease to be a letter and become a telephone call?
Yours faithfully,
ROGER C. BRYAN,
Bristol. January 3

Art and artists put to the test

From Mr Don W. Steele

Sir, A point worth noting is that the Turner Prize competition is barred to those aged 50 and over. This ban is presumably based upon the assumption that no one in their later years is capable of lifting a few bricks or changing a lightbulb.

I feel it is more likely, though, that someone pointed out that gullibility tends to decline with the coming of maturity, and they wish to play safe.
Yours faithfully,
DON W. STEELE
(Director), The Association of Retired and Persons Over 50, London SW1. January 2

Cloning concern

From Mr Kevin Martin

Sir, I was alarmed to read about Dolly the sheep's infirmity (report, January 5).

My late father suffered from arthritis. Am I to conclude from this that he must have been cloned?
Yours faithfully,
KEVIN MARTIN,
Shefford, Bedfordshire. January 5

Odds and ends

From Mr Peter Maguire

Sir, An acquaintance of mine had a box labelled "pieces of string too short to be of any use".
Yours faithfully,
D. P. MAGUIRE,
Chichester. January 7

From the Reverend John Ticehurst

Sir, Clearing a house after the death of a 90-plus widow, I found in an old oak chest an assortment of potentially useful items, all neatly labelled with Indian ink on tiny luggage labels, in paper bags, including: cups without handles; cup handles; curtain rings; rusty curtain rings.

Now that's what even my wife would call thrift. I think.
Yours &c,
JOHN TICEHURST,
Wareham. January 9

From Mrs F. S. Gibbs

Sir, Soon after my grandmother's death we were much amused to find among the odds and ends in her dressing-table drawer a bottle labelled "Might Be Aspirin".
Yours,
JEAN GIBBS,
Sidmouth, Devon. January 11

The price of happiness

From Mr John Braid

Sir, Money may not buy happiness (report, January 9), but neither does poverty.
Yours sincerely,
JOHN BRAID,
Inverness. January 9

From Mr David Bevan

Sir, Personal experience and much lengthy reflection on the lives and times of others suggests that the problem with happiness is that it does not bring money.
Yours sincerely,
DAVID BEVAN,
Geneva. January 11

From Mrs Michelle Pickering

Sir, Anyone who says money can't buy happiness obviously doesn't know where to shop.
Yours faithfully,
MICHELLE PICKERING,
Burnley, Lancashire. January 13

From Mr Archie Thomson

Sir, If wealth does not bring happiness it

allows one to be miserable in comfort.
Yours sincerely,
ARCHIE THOMSON,
Whitby, North Yorkshire. January 10

From Mr W. M. A. Sheard
Sir, I believe that if I am paid a researcher's fee I may be able to prove that people who have food to eat are generally happier than those who do not.
Yours faithfully,
W. M. A. SHEARD,
Grinton, North Yorkshire. January 12

From Mr Graham Roberts
Sir, My son and daughter assure me that I will feel a warm glow of happiness if I keep giving them more money.
Yours faithfully,
GRAHAM ROBERTS,
Colwyn Bay. January 14

Terms of endearment

From Professor David Thomas
Sir, I am a widower aged 57 and I have just met a nice young lady whom I introduce to my friends as "my companion". After much deliberation, I settled upon this introduction because I think it has a degree of grace, dignity and perhaps even an air of mystery about it.

The problem I have is that my children fall about laughing; they think it is weird, oozes senility and destroys any small vestige of the street cred that I might once have had.

At my age, descriptions such as "partner" or "girlfriend" seem inappropriate, and one rakish suggestion that I could introduce her as "my mistress" just gave me a panic attack. Am I doomed to a life of hot flushes?
Yours sincerely,
D. J. THOMAS,
Wolverhampton. January 15

From Mrs Lesley Russell
Sir, Professor Thomas could try introducing his young lady as "my dear friend". Not only does this meet his requirement of grace and dignity, but it continues to keep people guessing. "Companion" sounds as if she pushes his bath chair and writes his letters to *The Times* for him.
Yours faithfully,
LESLEY RUSSELL,
Upavon, Wiltshire. January 16

From Mr P. Motte-Harrison
Sir, I, who am rather older than Professor Thomas, introduce and refer to my younger companion as "my lady".

My family and friends accept this and are free to apply their own interpretation. I have suffered no embarrassment.
Yours faithfully,
P. MOTTE-HARRISON,
Shoreham-by-Sea. January 16

From Mr Derek Thom
Sir, I suggest the phrase "my bosom friend" ("a very dear or intimate friend" – *The Times English Dictionary*).
Yours sincerely,
DEREK THOM,
Cheltenham. January 16

From Mrs Ann Lovell
Sir, My brother in Toronto once told me of the graceful way in which many Canadians referred to their partners. They were introduced as "my intime".
Yours sincerely,
ANN LOVELL,
Burnham-on-Sea, Somerset. January 16

THE HONOURABLE PEREGRINE POMFRET-PLUNKETT AND 'IS KNOCK-OFF

From Mr Bruce Parker
Sir, I have had a similar problem over how to introduce my own nice young lady to friends and others. This was only partly solved when we became engaged as fiancée seems somewhat inappropriate, too, for a man aged 60. However, all will be resolved on February 14 when I will be able to present "my new wife".

Over to you, professor.
Yours faithfully,
BRUCE PARKER,
Winchester. January 16

From Mr Gerald F. Morris
Sir There is a useful word in Scots – "bidie-in".
Yours faithfully,
GERALD F. MORRIS,
Edinburgh. January 16

From Mr Derek J. Allen
Sir, Professor Thomas, lucky fellow that he is, should forget trying to maintain his street cred and panic attacks and embrace tradition.

By introducing his nice young lady as his niece, the terms of their relationship will become immediately apparent to all.

And he may well gain a few Brownie points.
Yours faithfully,
DEREK J. ALLEN,
Chatteris, Cambridgeshire. January 16

From Mr Peter G. Webber
Sir, I sympathise with the dilemma as to how one should introduce a much younger lady companion to others.

On occasions I used to take my hard-pressed secretary to lunch as a thank-you gesture.

I was at pains to say that if our age difference caused any embarrassment, I'd understand. She said that there was no problem. If pressed, she would explain discreetly that I was her grandfather. We still keep in touch.
Yours sincerely,
PETER G. WEBBER,
Ruislip, Middlesex. January 16

From Mr Roger Till
Sir, Unsuspected perils may lurk in terms of endearment.

Many years ago, it is said, the word "woman" had always to be substituted for "lady" in a provincial daily newspaper. Readers were startled by a report of a reception stating: "Lord So-and-So entered with his woman."
Yours faithfully,
ROGER TILL,
Durham. January 20

From Mr Michael Bird
Sir, Some years ago I was the after-dinner speaker at a function in Alabama.

Introducing me to the audience of 300, the chairman ended by saying: "Please extend a warm welcome to our British guest and his – er, um, ahem, er – accompanist." I was half inclined to abandon my prepared text and sing *The Star-Spangled Banner*, with my lady friend at the piano, but thought better of it.

Perhaps in the Deep South people are not so blasé about these things as they are elsewhere.
Yours faithfully,
MICHAEL BIRD,
London SW13. January 24

From Mrs Sarah E. Birkin
Sir, Forty-five years ago, workers on the building sites of Merseyside received in their wages an allowance for "wife or lay-by".
Yours faithfully,
SARAH E. BIRKIN,
Gisburn, Lancashire. January 23

From Mr Nick Phillips
Sir, Professor David Thomas should introduce his nice young lady as his mistress and, combating the insidious puritanism with which we are faced, lead us with rumbustious relish into the 21st century.

I speak on behalf of 64-year-olds, but as non-playing captain: I have the good fortune to be happily married.
Yours faithfully,
NICK PHILLIPS,
Brussels. January 23

From Mr Eamonn O'Gorman
Sir, I always introduce my companion as "my financial adviser".
Yours faithfully,
EAMONN O'GORMAN,
Elstree, Hertfordshire. January 24

From Mrs Jean Martland Binner
Sir, Enough is enough. Now that all the elderly males are cheered by the thoughts of showing off younger girlfriends, could you perhaps raise female morale by telling us how to introduce our toyboys?
Yours faithfully,
JEAN M. BINNER,
Horsham, West Sussex. January 24

Avian aerobatics

From Mrs Margaret Kaplan
Sir, Parrots and budgerigars, it seems, are not the only birds to imitate us. A glider enthusiast told me recently that he is frequently accompanied by feathered escorts copying his manoeuvres. He added that fighter pilots on exercises in the North sometimes see buzzards, ravens and the like showing off their barrel and flick rolls.
Yours faithfully,
MARGARET KAPLAN,
Cheltenham. January 15

From Major P. E. Farrelly
Sir, I fear that Mrs Margaret Kaplan may have misunderstood her glider pilot friend. It is we glider pilots who attempt to emulate the manoeuvres of the birds in order to climb more efficiently in thermals, for we are fortunate enough to fly in their natural element.
It is a truly exhilarating experience to soar with them, but they always out-climb us.
Yours faithfully,
PATRICK FARRELLY
(Chief Flying Instructor, Wyvern (Army) Gliding Club), Upavon, Wiltshire. January 17

From Mr Phillip Coles-Gale
Sir, During the 18 years I spent with the Hong Kong Civil Aviation Department at Kai Tak Airport we would regularly see black-eared kites hovering at the side of the runway waiting to fly into the wing-tip vortices of landing aircraft, where they then indulged in "enforced" aerobatics.
Occasionally a bird would misjudge its height or get too close to the aircraft, suffering somewhat heavy contact with the ground. There would then be several such mishaps whilst the eager replacements were eliminated in "practice sessions".
Yours faithfully,
PHILLIP COLES-GALE,
Holbeton, Devon. January 18

From Mr Peter Hearne
Sir, It is sometimes possible in the French Alps to fly for several minutes in a mixed-pair formation of glider and eagle, whose fear of man and his works has been happily much diminished by effective conservation. The eagle usually insists on being the formation leader, rightly so because it knows best where the next upcurrent is to be found.
I am, Sir, your obedient servant,
PETER HEARNE
(Vice-President, British Gliding Association), Wateringbury, Kent. January 17

Personalised paper

From Mr Robert A. Morley
Sir, With the facility for ordering a year's prepaid supply of *The Times*, it seems a shame not to take full advantage of the flexibility afforded by computers by tailoring each day's delivery to the whims of the recipient.
For example, you could not only save significant quantities of newsprint (particularly on Saturdays), but also do wonders for my disposition, by omitting from my personal copies all reference, however oblique, to football.
I reserve the right to add cricket at some future date.
Yours faithfully,
ROBERT A. MORLEY,
Southport, Merseyside. January 17

Backyard politics

From Mr Nick Locock

Sir, You report (January 17) that US congressmen have warned President Mugabe that the US Government would increase pressure to ensure that next month's presidential elections would not be rigged.

Do any of these congressmen come from Florida?

Yours sincerely,
NICK LOCOCK,
Whitsbury, Nr Fordingbridge. January 17

Sans pareil

From Mr Bryan Marson-Smith

Sir, The other day my wife and I were travelling from Manchester to Euston (first class – very expensive) on Virgin. I asked the attendant if there were any newspapers. "No," he said, then added: "Oh, there might be a *Times*."

Yours faithfully,
BRYAN MARSON-SMITH,
Sevenoaks, Kent. January 17

Time is money

From Mr David Dell

Sir, It took the English until 1752 to adopt the calendar we now use (Gregorian) which most of the Continentals had gone over to in the late 1500s. Even then "Give us back our 11 days" was heard as the then equivalent of "Keep the pound".

Dare one hope that it will not take us 200 years to see sense over a common currency?

I am, Sir, etc,
DAVID DELL,
London W1. January 19

From Mr David R. James

Sir, Mr David Dell suggests that the cry in 1752, "Give us back our 11 days", was an ignorant reaction to an inevitable European standardisation of the calendar.

In fact it was the reaction to an aristocratic scam on the common people of this country. The people had paid their quarterly rentals in advance, expecting 91 days of tenure for their money. However, because of the calendar change, they only received 80 days before the next payment was due. The aristocrats pocketed the difference.

The common people were not so stupid after all. They just lacked the vote.

Yours sincerely,
DAVID R. JAMES,
Kidderminster. January 21

From Mr Ken Gadsby

Sir, Mr Dell compares the cry "Keep the pound" to the 18th-century "Give us back our 11 days".

He will of course be aware that the Government of the day cropped 11 days from the working year, but still expected you to pay the same annual taxes.

A stealth tax worthy of new Labour.

Yours faithfully,
KEN GADSBY,
Nottingham. January 21

From Mr John Rowe Townsend

Sir, Mr Ken Gadsby says the Government of 1752 cropped 11 days from the working year but still expected payment of the same annual taxes.

Not so. The fiscal year 1752–53, which would have ended on March 25 (Lady Day), was extended by those same 11 days until April 5. There it remains, as we are reminded every year with the arrival of our tax forms.

Yours sincerely,
JOHN ROWE TOWNSEND,
Cambridge. January 24

Men of letters still hold sway

From Mr D. L. B. Hartley

Sir, I became aware that most of the Letters to the Editor in *The Times* were from men. I decided to count the letters in 100 consecutive issues of the paper. Between September 18, 2001, and January 12, 2002, you published 1,942 letters on this page; 244, that is 12.5 per cent, were from women.

I classified by subject 100 letters from ladies which appeared between October 3 and

November 21, 2001. The top three topics were: home and family, 18 letters; terrorism and the war, 17; education, 12. Next, with five letters each, came social questions and the arts.

I turned to my copies of the two anthologies. *The First Cuckoo*, scope 1900–1975, contained 271 letters; 26, that is 9.6 per cent, were from women. *The Second Cuckoo*, drawing on 1900 to 1982, contained 458 letters of which 68, that is 14.8 per cent, were written by women.

The figures are surely significant. The male dominance may be much as our Victorian ancestors would expect; but after all that has been said and done in the past century it may surprise many of our contemporaries.

Yours truly,
DESMOND HARTLEY,
Windermere, Cumbria. January 13

From Mr Mike Reynolds

Sir, The statistical exercise conducted by Desmond Hartley reveals that contributions from ladies accounted for no more than 12.5 per cent of letters published by you in the last four months. He finds this surprising.

What we don't know, of course, is how many letters are received from both sexes. From our household the depressing dispatched/published statistic is: my wife 100 per cent; myself around 10 per cent and steadily declining. I was depressed before I read Mr Hartley's letter. Please publish this and redress a shocking micro-imbalance.

Yours faithfully,
MIKE REYNOLDS,
Witnesham, Suffolk. January 22

From Mrs Gilly Hendry

Sir, In a perfect world, most of your published letters would be from me.

Yours faithfully,
GILLY HENDRY,
North Berwick, East Lothian. January 23

From Mr Robert Waddington

Sir, Never having had one of my letters to *The Times* published, should I now write about my home and family and send my correspondence under my wife's name?

Yours sincerely,
ROBERT WADDINGTON,
Ledbury, Herefordshire. January 23

From Mr Charles P. F. Baillie

Sir, The reason is obvious. Men tend to complain, while women just get on with it.

Yours faithfully,
C. P. F. BAILLIE,
Locking, North Somerset. January 22

Guaranteed to last

From Mr Richard Iley

Sir, "(This) Rock Salt," says the label, "is over 200 million years old, formed through ancient geological processes in the German mountain ranges."

Best before 04 2003.

Yours etc,
RICHARD ILEY,
Birmingham. January 19

From Mr Peter Hirons

Sir, I sympathise with Richard Iley in discovering his 200-million-year-old rock salt has such a brief "best before" date.

I recently received a flyer for a radio-controlled wall clock. This states the device is "accurate to within one second in a million years", as it receives "the precise time signal from The Atomic Clock at Rugby".

My initial interest diminished on noticing that the company was only prepared to offer a 24-month guarantee.

Yours faithfully,
PETER HIRONS,
Rochester, Kent. January 22

From Mr Dan Lyon

Sir, Peter Hirons should have done more than note that his million-year clock was only guaranteed for 24 months.

When buying a massive (and correspondingly expensive) container crane for Preston Docks in the 1970s I was assured by the aggressive salesman that it would be a high-profile tribute to German engineering for the next 20 years.

When I commented on the 12-month warranty in his standard contract, I was immediately rewarded with an unconditional guarantee to match his words.

The crane, and its guarantee, lasted longer than Preston Docks.

Yours faithfully,
DAN LYON,
Preston. January 29

Sober advice

From Mr Mike Maddison

Sir, I recently visited the land of the free but slightly litigious, where I purchased a well earned cold beer. The label read: "Consumption of this product may cause intoxication. If affected do not attempt to drive or operate heavy machinery."

Yours faithfully,
MIKE MADDISON,
Spaxton, Somerset. January 29

The march of time

From Mrs Maureen Plant

Sir, During a visit by my 13-year-old granddaughter, I noticed among her array of cosmetics a tube of expensive anti-wrinkle cream.

She said that she did not want to look wrinkly when she was my age.

During the past few years I have tried similar products with very disappointing results and, not wishing to disillusion her, I refrained from any further comment.

Yours faithfully,
MAUREEN PLANT,
Nottingham. January 18

Elgin marbles

From Mr W. H. Bagust

Sir, A solution.

Make exact copies of the Marbles and mix them with the originals.

Then from a distance of about 100 feet, roughly the distance one would be from the Marbles if they were in place on the Parthenon, invite a team of Greek experts and

a team of British experts to take turns to select pieces.

It could be part of the opening ceremony at the Olympic Games.

Yours faithfully,
W. H. BAGUST,
London W12. January 22

Inhuman treatment

From Mr P. W. Davies

Sir, Forced to wear headphones to obliterate the outside world; restrictions on visual field; compelled to stay immobile for hours on end, with toilet usage and freedom of movement at the whim of pre-programmed and unthinking personnel? Isn't it time we allowed Red Cross inspections of UK call centres?

Yours sincerely,
P. W. DAVIES,
Liverpool. January 23

Domestic workloads

From Mrs Rosemary Bashford

Sir, "Man About the House" (Times 2, January 23) confirms all that my girlfriends and I either laugh or groan about, depending upon our state of exhaustion. I wonder how many husbands perfected a ploy to ensure they were never asked to help, long before marriage?

My husband, in his salad days, worked for his uncle, a builder. To his chagrin as the junior in the office he was told to make the tea. He made it for a day and then dropped the teapot. It was replaced. He waited a few days longer and dropped it again. When a third teapot had to be replaced, he was relieved of tea-making duties for good.

We have a saying in our family: "It's no good trying the teapot technique . . ."

Yours faithfully,
ROSEMARY BASHFORD,
Whitney-on-Wye, Herefordshire. January 23

Counting sheep

From Mr Oliver Mason

Sir, Researchers tell us that counting sheep

is no cure for insomnia (report, January 24). I have found it effective to recite the names, in alphabetical order, of the 50 states of the US, starting with Alabama.

In my early days I seldom used to get further than Louisiana before dropping off. After much practice, however, I found to my dismay that I was sometimes reaching Wyoming without falling asleep.

I was then compelled to include additionally the capital cities of the states, starting with Montgomery, Alabama, and setting off for Cheyenne, Wyoming. So far the furthest I have reached is, I think, Carson City, Nevada.

Yours,
OLIVER MASON,
Wadhurst, East Sussex. January 24

From Ms Elspeth Evans
Sir, My response to a wakeful husband was to suggest that he do a mental trek around a large department store as a sleep inducer (which worked for me).

After a minute or so, the reply came back: "Elspeth, I've run out of money."
Yours faithfully,
ELSPETH EVANS,
Little Chalfont, Buckinghamshire. January 24

From Mrs Janet Ellis
Sir, Instead of counting sheep, perhaps insomniacs should try talking to the Shepherd.
Yours faithfully,
JANET ELLIS,
Standon, Staffordshire. January 25

From Mrs Pauline Taylor
Sir, Following the early and sudden death of my husband I found that reciting the names of the crews of the *Star Trek* starships *Enterprise* and *Voyager* and the space station *Deep Space Nine* helped me to fall asleep.

How can I now prevent myself from dropping off when I want to watch the programmes?
Yours faithfully,
PAULINE TAYLOR,
Colchester. February 2

From Mr Tony Beadles
Sir, I play an imaginary round of golf at a favourite course.

I make some fine shots, but am always asleep before reaching the fearsome 6th hole, the Himalayas.
Yours faithfully,
TONY BEADLES,
Compton Pauncefoot, Somerset. February 2

From Mr Tim Biddiscombe
Sir, As a cricket fan, I find that the most effective way of encouraging sleep is to imagine that I am a bowler faced with Trevor Bailey. I shuffle up, bowl, Bailey blocks, the ball returns down the pitch to me, I collect it, return to my run-up point, bowl, Bailey blocks. Before the over is completed I am asleep.
Yours faithfully,
TIM BIDDISCOMBE,
Hoylake, Merseyside. February 4

From Mr Alf Hailstone
Sir, Since Mr Tim Biddiscombe's suggestion that we insomniacs imagine bowling to Trevor Bailey, I have dropped off successfully with the number of overs decreasing and my run-up reduced.

Last night I was bowling my fifth ball of the first over when it completely deceived him and his wicket was broken.

I had to get up and make a cup of tea.
Yours faithfully,
ALF HAILSTONE,
Holmer Green, Buckinghamshire. February 13

In praise of trains

From Mr David Barritt
Sir, I write to you from my rail seat on the move. It's the first time I have used the railway for a serious journey for years. I am on my return journey to Brighton direct from Manchester.

The trains have been busy but everyone has had a seat. The trains are clean and have been punctual so far. The staff look smart and have been courteous. The trains are new with all mod cons. The stations (whilst some under repair) have looked good. The ticket cost me £7 each way (50p discount for booking online). I am on a Virgin train (credit where it is due).

Perhaps, despite the recent strikes, the tide is turning?
Yours faithfully,
DAVID BARRITT,
Brighton. January 28

From Mr John Bate-Williams
Sir, Like Mr David Barritt I am writing this letter to you from my train seat. The train collected me on time from Kemble. The smartly attired senior conductor cheerfully sold me a ticket for £27 to London and back, and I bought a decent cup of tea from the buffet car.

We are now somewhere on the main line between Swindon and Didcot. I am able to write this letter legibly because the train has reduced its speed to walking pace. The carriage in which I sit is quiet, undisturbed by any announcement explaining the cause of the delay. It is even possible to look out at the countryside without any of the "blur" associated with high-speed train travel.

As Mr Barritt says, credit where it is due.
Yours faithfully,
JOHN BATE-WILLIAMS,
London EC4. January 31

Party while you can

From Mrs Frances Taylor
Sir, I was organising a small party for a friend's 70th birthday and thought I would buy some "fun" decorations at the local party shop. There was little choice for a 70th birthday party and I asked the young assistant the reason.

I was shocked to be told that it was "probably because most people of 70 are dead by then".
Yours truly,
FRANCES TAYLOR,
London SW10. February 4

From Mrs Sylvia Crookes
Sir, Little choice for 70th birthday parties

in Mrs Frances Taylor's local shop in London? Reeth Post Office, in Swaledale, has a good range of 100th birthday cards.

Optimists believe that is because we are a healthy lot up here. Pessimists hold that the sub-postmaster is too much of an optimist.
Yours (64 next Monday and hopeful),
SYLVIA CROOKES,
Bainbridge, North Yorkshire. February 6

From Mrs Virginia Hunt
Sir, While I was buying a wedding anniversary present in Newport, Shropshire, the lady in the jeweller's shop told me of a customer who had had to come to Newport for a silver wedding anniversary card, having been told there was no call for that sort of thing in Wolverhampton.
Yours faithfully,
VIRGINIA HUNT,
Shebdon, Stafford. February 6

From Mr Martin Davies
Sir, Last year, just after turning 70, I brought my five-year-old granddaughter home for a few days whilst her parents went abroad. We had a fine time together and, at the end, I said: "Tessa, it's been great fun – you must come up on your own again."

"No," she replied. "I can't come again because you will be dead."
Yours faithfully,
MARTIN DAVIES,
Oakham, Rutland. February 7

From Mrs Cicely Hudson
Sir, When I was about 70, several years ago, my granddaughter greeted me with: "Grandma, you're very old. I expect you'll die soon."

"Yes, but perhaps not just yet."

"Well, it's all right. I've got another grandma."
Yours faithfully,
CICELY HUDSON,
Redland, Bristol. February 10

From Mr Bryan Symons
Sir, Mrs Cicely Hudson reminds me of my own young grandson's comment, when I commiserated with him on the death of

the first of his grandparents: "It's OK for you, Grandad, but do you realise I have got to go through this three more times?"

Nice to know one will be missed.

Sincerely,
BRYAN SYMONS,
Chew Magna, Bristol. February 16

From Mr E. A. Machin, QC

Sir, Your recent correspondence on the comments of one's grandchildren prompts me to relate an episode of my own.

I recently tried to explain to my granddaughter, aged 12, what was meant by the generations within a family. I told her that I was her grandfather because she was the daughter of my own daughter. Warming to the topic I explained that if, in years to come, she married and herself had a daughter, then I would become that child's great-grandfather.

"Not for long," she said.

I found this most comforting.

Yours faithfully,
E. A. MACHIN,
Exeter. February 19

From Mr Anthony Chandor

Sir, When his other grandfather died my grandson, aged seven, had just suffered another tragedy and said to me: "What a week! A grandfather and a rabbit."

Yours faithfully,
ANTHONY CHANDOR,
Bath. February 25

The Register awaits

From Mr Bernard Graham

Sir, In my declining years I find it a great comfort to learn that *The Times* will be expanding its obituary section.

Yours faithfully,
BERNARD GRAHAM,
Poole, Dorset. February 6

Week gets longer

From Mr Terry Damer

Sir, Some years ago, when based in Tokyo, I was working late in my office (report,

News in Brief, later editions, February 4) when at around 8pm the phone rang. It was one of my Japanese business contacts. "Ah, Damer-san, you are working late," he said. "Well, Ando-san," I replied, "so are you." "No," he responded, "I'm not working. I'm just being here."

Perhaps this is one Japanese working practice we shouldn't have adopted.

Yours faithfully,
TERRY DAMER,
Reigate, Surrey. February 5

In round numbers

From Mr Richard Fenwick

Sir, When buying a pair of socks from a well-known high street store the other day, I was pleased to see them priced at £4 instead of the usual £3.99.

Knocking the odd penny off a trolley load of groceries may add up to a justifiable saving, but does the price of a TV at £499.99 or a car at £14,995 really fool the customer?

Yours faithfully,
RICHARD FENWICK,
Chobham. February 11

From Mr Steve Traynar

Sir, I always understood that the reason that items are priced at, say, £3.99 instead of a round £4 is that it forces the sales assistant to open the till and register the sale in order to give change, reducing the chance of theft by an unscrupulous assistant.

Yours faithfully,
STEVE TRAYNAR,
Witham, Essex. February 12

Safety PINs

From Ms Sally Bigwood

Sir, Most people will probably find using their father's or mother's birth year as secure PIN numbers a little easier than memorising a new alphabet, as suggested by your science correspondent.

Even better, one can use a memorable year, such as 1066 or 1945. My personal favourite is two years prior to the abolition of the Corn Laws. Such years are secure and

easy to recall. They also stop scientists over-engineering another simple task, and help the police by narrowing plastic-card fraud suspects to historians.
Yours faithfully,
SALLY BIGWOOD,
Wakefield, West Yorkshire. February 9

From Mr David Andrews
Sir, As well as phonetics to remember PINs, favourite melodies can work. If 1 represents the first note of the scale, 8 is the octave higher. So 5887 is Hark the Herald and 1135 is Blue Danube. The only problems are atonality and John Cage's 4' 33".
Yours faithfully,
DAVID ANDREWS
(Director of Music), Harrogate Ladies' College. February 9

From the Reverend S. M. Evans
Sir, Hymn numbers can also be helpful in memorising PINs. Nos 7 and 490 in English Hymnal helped me to remember a PIN I once had.

"Lo! He comes, the King of Love," I would say as I tapped in my PIN; and out He would come with £100 or whatever sum I had requested.
Yours faithfully,
STANLEY EVANS,
Ramsgate, Kent. February 17

From Mr Graham Collingwood
Sir, My favourite PIN, no longer in use, was 8078. This was the result of two consecutive rounds of golf one glorious Sunday many years ago, when I came fifth in the club championship.

Alas, four digits are no longer sufficient to accommodate my current state of play.
Yours sincerely,
GRAHAM COLLINGWOOD,
Marlow, Buckinghamshire. February 18

From Mr Mick Diddams
Sir, The obvious solution for any member or ex-member of HM Armed Forces is to use a part of their service number for a PIN, which I do.

This is a number one never forgets.

Yours etc,
M. DIDDAMS,
Sittingbourne, Kent. February 20

From Dr J. Barrie Raynor
Sir, Why must PINs use numbers?

If the buttons on cash machines had the corresponding letters next to the figures, as many telephones do, then one would have the opportunity to have a PIN (or PIL) comprising a more easily remembered word or set of initials.
Yours faithfully,
J. BARRIE RAYNOR,
Church Stretton, Shropshire. February 22

From Mr Paul Ranford
Sir, Ms Sally Bigwood, having explained her system for remembering PINs, tells us all her "personal favourite". With respect, Ms Bigwood's opinions on PIN security are open to question.

Systematic PIN mnemonics related to family birthdays or historical events, while convenient, are insecure in comparison to a random sequence of numbers, memorised and disclosed to no one. The inconvenience of forgetting a PIN is less than that caused by one being guessed by a third party.
Yours faithfully,
PAUL RANFORD,
Wendover, Buckinghamshire. February 25

From Mrs Christine Clark
Sir, My PIN is my late grandmother's Co-op dividend number, chanted by me before any purchase made on her behalf in the 1940s.

My date of birth sometimes escapes me, but granny's divi-number, never!
Yours faithfully,
CHRISTINE CLARK,
Ryton, Tyne and Wear. February 21

In training
From Father Bryan Storey
Sir, Having read your report praising the virtues of sexual abstinence to enhance sport performances, I'm beginning to wonder if my clerical celibacy was the secret

weapon that surprisingly made me victor of a local tennis tournament last year.
Yours truly,
BRYAN STOREY,
Tintagel, Cornwall. February 14

From Mr Kenneth Beere

Sir, Father Bryan Storey wonders whether his clerical celibacy enabled him to win last year's local tennis tournament.

But what will his flock think if this year he loses?
Yours faithfully,
KEN BEERE,
Arundel, West Sussex. February 16

The imperial fightback

From Mr Angus Lamond

Sir, Following the High Court ruling prohibiting the use of imperial weights and measures for trade in fish and vegetables, should we now expect a swath of prosecutions of all those bookies across the country taking bets on horse races run in miles and furlongs?
Yours faithfully,
ANGUS LAMOND,
St Breock, Cornwall. February 18

From Sir Bryan Thwaites

Sir, Presumably also, it is now illegal to sell a car claimed to be capable of so many miles per hour.
Yours faithfully,
BRYAN THWAITES,
London W1. February 19

Most irregular

From Mr Ian Senior

Sir, There is a new irregular verb whose present tense conjugates thus: I inform; you brief; he, she or it spins; we correct the record; you brief against us; they cause a breakdown of trust.
Your truly,
IAN SENIOR,
King's Langley, Hertfordshire. February 16

From Mr Gareth Child

Sir, Mr Ian Senior's irregular verb was bet-tered some years ago by Bernard Wooley, Principal Private Secretary to Prime Minister James Hacker, who observed: "I give confidential briefings; you leak; he has been charged under Section 2a of the Official Secrets Act." (Jonathan Lynn and Antony Jay, *Yes Prime Minister*, "Man Overboard", Salem House 1988.)
Yours,
GARETH CHILD,
Langley Park, Co Durham. February 20

Wake-up call

From Mrs Alexandra Scott

Sir, If, as reported (February 15), people with just a moderate amount of sleep live longer, is it not simply that they have some reason to get out of bed in the morning? Zest, not rest, is the recipe for long life.
Yours faithfully,
ALEXANDRA SCOTT,
Dedham, Essex. February 18

Play the game

From Mr Patrick Mohan

Sir, Thank you for publishing the rules of curling today. Perhaps it might be a good idea to do the same for the rules of rugby for the interested but mystified such as myself.

They may also be of help to the current professional players.
Yours faithfully,
PATRICK MOHAN,
Henley on Thames, Oxfordshire. February 22

News from Everest

From Ms Jan Morris

Sir, Oh what a disappointment to learn that you knew about the first ascent of Everest, in 1953, several days before the Queen's Coronation, but had kept it quiet in order to let the news coincide with the great event.

The Coronation was on June 2. Hillary and Tensing reached the summit on May 29. On the afternoon of May 30, having learnt the news from them in the Western Cwm, I hastened down through the Khumbu Icefall with Michael Westmacott, reaching Base Camp that night to get a message off to you on the morning of May 3l. It reached you on June 1, to be printed in the next morning's paper.

Now I hear that, having nearly killed myself to get the news to you in time for the Coronation, you knew it already. Who told you?
Yours reproachfully,
JAN MORRIS,
Llanystumdwy, Gwynedd. February 27

From Mrs Hilary Cotter
Sir, I feel for Jan Morris. At the time of the Coronation, I was secretary to A. P. Ryan, then assistant editor of *The Times*. On the afternoon before the great day, he returned from the daily afternoon editorial conference in high spirits.

"We have climbed Everest," he told me, "but you must not tell a soul until it is made public in tomorrow's paper."

I still remember sitting in the train that evening, hugging to myself the news that I knew but none of my fellow travellers did.
Yours sincerely,
HILARY COTTER,
Horsham. March 1

Price of fame

From Mr David Townley
Sir, David Starkey's £2 million deal with the BBC (report, March 4) is a far cry from the days of Lord Reith.

Then, a learned professor, on being told his talk had been accepted for broadcasting on the Third Programme for a fee of £25, was said to have replied thanking the BBC and with words to the effect: "I enclose a cheque for £25."
Yours faithfully,
DAVID TOWNLEY,
Banstead, Surrey. March 5

Life of Riley

From Mr Michael Ball
Sir, Some retired people find the terms "old

age pensioner" or "senior citizen" ageist. Perhaps Alan Pickering has the answer in his statement that "people need to appreciate that you can't work from 25 to 55 and then live the life of Riley to 95".

I would be content to refer to myself as a "Riley".
Yours faithfully,
MICHAEL BALL,
Carshalton, Surrey. March 8

Getting older

From Mr Michael Martin
Sir, On entering a pedestrian subway over the weekend, the none too dulcet tones of a flower vendor were heard calling: "Fifty pence the daffs – fifty pence the daffs."

As I was walking by, he changed to: "Ten bob to you, sir."

Worrying really, as I am not even a pensioner.
Yours faithfully,
MICHAEL MARTIN,
Swindon. March 11

From Mr David Skinner
Sir, I am both a pensioner and disabled. I was sitting on a wall in Tenerife a few years ago, waiting for my wife, while a timeshare salesman asked every passer-by to attend some presentation at his resort. After ten minutes I finally asked the details. He gave me a scornful look and told me that I was too old to bother with.

Mr Michael Martin's insensitive flower-seller would at least have taken his money. To be bothered by timeshare salesmen wastes one's time. Not to be worth bothering with strikes at one's very soul.
Yours faithfully,
DAVID SKINNER,
Coventry. March 13

Test of time

From Mrs Vicki Webb
Sir, Kendal Mint Cake is still a staple part of mountaineers' rations, as Sandra Lawrence said in Food and Drink. My husband

has taken the same bar on every expedition over the past ten years.

Purchased in 1992, it has conquered countless summits in the UK, Europe and Asia and survived avalanches in the Himalayas in 1996, but it remains uneaten.

Originally taken along as part of emergency rations, this treasured bar of Kendal Mint Cake has become an essential part of my husband's kit as a sort of talisman.

Yours faithfully,
VICKI WEBB,
Epsom, Surrey. March 10

From Mr David Sharpe

Sir, At boarding school, in the summer of 1957, I bought a Penguin chocolate bar which for many years lay forgotten in my tuck box. It was rediscovered only when, on marriage, I decided to use the box as a container for tools.

Like Mrs Vicki Webb's Kendal Mint Cake it too became a sort of talisman, now in the pocket of an old raincoat worn on only the bitterest of days while watching football.

For more than 40 years it remained uneaten – until the weekend I lent the coat to my daughter who was heading to the Lake District for a hiking holiday. On her return, handing over the coat, she remarked: "Thanks for the snack, Dad. I hadn't realised Penguin bars have increased in size."

Yours faithfully,
DAVID SHARPE,
Whitefield, Manchester. March 15

From Mr Brian McCabe

Sir, The manufacturers of Kendal Mint Cake and Penguin chocolate bars may have the advantage of preservative techniques not available to the amateur, but we do what we can.

Five of my brothers and a nephew and I contest a family golf competition each September, and it is my custom to provide some of my home-made flapjack as "trail food".

A year or so ago (in March), my brother Paul found some at the bottom of his golf bag, wrapped in tin foil, and ate it without any ill effects upon his constitution.

I don't know how it affected his golf.

Yours faithfully,
BRIAN McCABE,
Liverpool. March 20

Gentlemen's clubs

From Mrs Gill Hardman

Sir, As the wife of the headmaster of an independent school, about ten years ago I visited a St James's gentlemen's club for a fundraising gathering for that school (report, March 14).

On arrival, whilst waiting for the men in the party to deposit their coats, I whiled away a few minutes looking at the news reports as they came through the telex machine.

After only a minute or so I was approached by a porter. "Excuse me, madam," he said, "but ladies are not permitted to loiter in the entrance hall."

Yours faithfully,
GILL HARDMAN,
London SW14. March 14

From Lady Sanders

Sir, The Nuku'alofa Club in Tonga was a male bastion in the 1950s. However, in a liberal moment it was decided that ladies would be allowed to use the reading room once a week to enjoy the newspapers and periodicals. I naively supposed that the concession extended to the adjacent library, but was politely disabused by the club steward.

However, in an example of typical Tongan courtesy and ingenious interpretation of rules, he kindly agreed to pass me any books I required through a side window.

I hardly knew whether to feel insulted or honoured and settled on amused and grateful.

Yours faithfully,
BARBARA SANDERS,
Crieff, Perthshire. March 15

Chew on this

From Mr David Wilkinson

Sir, You report today that "Tests found that

those who chewed gum had a better long and short-term memory than their counterparts..." The "obvious" conclusion is that chewing gum improves memory. Another explanation, equally logical, is that those with worse memories forget to take their gum with them.

We are often presented with studies that show that folk who do A are more likely to experience B. We often conclude that A tends to cause B, whereas in fact it may be that B tends to cause A (or even that A and B tend to be caused by C).

Beware the quick conclusion.
Yours faithfully,
DAVID WILKINSON,
Birmingham. March 14

Singles and doubles

From Dr Eva Wittenberg
Sir, Maggie Pringle (*Times* 2, March 13) promotes the joys of singledom and quotes the "propaganda" for marriage by "various churches, not to mention Jane Austen and Bridget Jones, to make everyone believe that coupledom is not only good, but the only way".

Jane Austen herself remained single and did not by any means always regard the singles as unfortunate. In *Emma* (vol 1, chapter 10) her heroine says:

. . . a single woman, of good fortune, is always respectable, and may be as sensible and pleasant as anybody else . . . it is poverty only which makes celibacy contemptible.

Yours faithfully,
EVA WITTENBERG,
Pinner, Middlesex. March 13

From Mr Gerald Morris
Sir, Many years ago an older friend recounted how the family maid had said to her: "Being a spinster can be very pleasant, Miss, once you've got over the disgrace".
Yours faithfully,
GERALD MORRIS,
Edinburgh. March 19

Selective memory

From Mr Peter Wade
Sir, Your report (March 16) that older men are better lovers was at odds with that by the science correspondent that elderly witnesses are fallible: "Witnesses aged over 60 will pick an innocent person out of a police line-up nine times out of ten when an identity parade does not feature the criminal they have seen."

It may be that elderly people remember having very good sex, but they can't identify who it was with.
Yours faithfully,
PETER WADE,
Colchester. March 18

Shopping and thinking

From Mr Ted Johnson
Sir, You published research results suggesting that shopping stimulates the brain.

I suggest that the study was partial. Had the researchers studied brains shopping in pairs, they would undoubtedly have discovered that for every brain being stimulated by the hope of uncovering something she hadn't even realised that she wanted, the accompanying brain is ossifying at a greater rate, as this letter demonstrates.
Yours faithfully,
TED JOHNSON,
Lymington, Hampshire. March 20

From Mr James Macdonald
Sir, Far from ossifying, as Mr Ted Johnson sadly claims, the brain accompanying the shopper in fact suffers two kinds of stimulant simultaneously – the one, mental arithmetic in silently counting the cost, the second literary, composing the letter to the bank manager.
Yours faithfully,
JAMES MACDONALD,
Taunton. March 23

From Miss Annette Dee Wase
Sir, Mr James Macdonald is rather optimistic in contemplating two thought processes

at the same time while accompanying the shopper.

He should realise his limits, refrain from multi-tasking and concentrate on the necessary thought process involved in saying: "That looks lovely on you, dear! Where do I pay?"

Yours faithfully,
ANNETTE DEE WASE,
London NW6. March 27

Mature reflection

From Mr Roger Napleton

Sir, The *Manchild* television series has dramatically highlighted how some men only reluctantly respond to the passing years. My nine-year-old son said to me at the weekend: "Daddy, when you grow up, can I have your motorbike?" I am 55.

Yours faithfully,
ROGER NAPLETON,
Stonegate, Sussex. March 31

Generation gap

From Mr Julian Corlett

Sir, As if struggling to contend with my mid-life crisis were not enough, recently a school lollipop lady ventured into the rush-hour traffic for me to cross the road.

I'm not sure whether she thought I was in second childhood or entering my dotage; either way, my ego was shattered.

Sincerely,
JULIAN CORLETT,
Scunthorpe, North Lincolnshire. April 1

Stuck for an answer

From Mr Ian Geddes

Sir, Apart from my fingers, I have not yet been able to find anything that actually sticks when I apply "superglue". Am I doing something wrong?

Yours faithfully,
IAN GEDDES,
Kilmarnock, Ayrshire. April 1

From Mr Martin A. Locke

Sir, Mr Ian Geddes complains that the only things superglue sticks together are his fingers. He should try applying a little saliva to each surface before applying the adhesive. This fools the superglue into thinking that it is sticking his fingers together.

Yours faithfully,
MARTIN A. LOCKE,
Shrewsbury. April 2

From Mr Stuart Leon

Sir, I always find that superglue also welds the lid perfectly to the tube.

Yours sincerely,
S. LEON,
Ditchling, West Sussex. April 2

From Mr Roger Bentley

Sir, I stuck the rear-view mirror to the windscreen of my wife's car with superglue. Two weeks later a large crack appeared in the glass, with the result that we needed a new windscreen.

Yours faithfully,
ROGER BENTLEY,
Chester. April 8

From Mr Christopher J. A. Dixon

Sir, On a rare visit to the doctor to show him the little cracks on my fingers left by some imprudent gardening, he asked whether I had a tube of superglue at home.

"Dab it on the cracks," he said, "and they will heal." I did and they did.

Yours faithfully,
CHRISTOPHER DIXON,
Oxted, Surrey. April 5

From Mr Bill Haiselden

Sir, I invariably explain the term "irony" to my classes encountering Jane Austen for the first time by alluding to the brand of gum we used to use in the 1970s.

The bright red labels frequently failed to adhere to the pots.

Yours faithfully,
BILL HAISELDEN,
Redhill, Surrey. April 5

From Mr Graham Breeze

Sir, Since my brand of superglue includes an explicit warning that it is not suitable for bonding car rear-view mirrors, one wonders why your correspondent did so and consequently cracked his windscreen.

Another example of men not bothering to read instructions?

Yours faithfully,
GRAHAM BREEZE,
Hawksworth, Leeds. April 9

Freedom of the press

From Mr R. M. Langton
Sir, Why is it that we hear so very little of the misconduct of newspaper proprietors and editors? Is it because they lead such saintly lives or because dog doesn't eat dog?
Yours faithfully,
RICHARD LANGTON,
London W4. March 30

Life expectancy

From Professor Emeritus D. F. Brewer
Sir, Dr Stuttaford today reports a study from Harvard University which "showed that survival is as dependent on intellectual stimulation in older age as it is on physical exercise".

At the age of 76, would reading *The Times* each day be enough to keep me going for another, say, ten to 15 years?
Yours faithfully,
DOUGLAS BREWER,
Lewes, Sussex. March 28

From Mr Tom Pike
Sir, Twelve years' seniority persuades me to promise Professor Douglas Brewer that he will continue to enjoy *The Times* for several more years. He may, however, find that the mounting cunning of the crossword puzzle setters will begin to defeat his more ingenuous nature.
Yours faithfully,
TOM PIKE,
Beckenham, Kent. April 9

From Mr Eric Hulse
Sir, As a fellow citizen of Lewes, I am happy to inform Professor Brewer that I read *The Times* daily with the *Times 2*

Crossword thrown in, and achieved 90 last September.

My good friend the excellent rector of Streat Church has guaranteed me a free burial if I achieve 100.

I intend to hold him to this.
Yours faithfully,
ERIC HULSE,
Lewes, East Sussex. April 8

Decline and fall

From Mr Graham Rowlinson
Sir, I was surprised that a professor of literary studies should complain that the "Don't drive tired" slogan on motorway signs is grammatically incorrect. Would the professor also object to "Open your mouth wide", "Don't come into the house wet" and "Born free"? And if she won the lottery, wouldn't she die happy?
Yours faithfully,
GRAHAM ROWLINSON,
Redhill. April 5

From Mr N. J. Inkley
Sir, I suppose the headline: "Chelsea show readiness to win ugly" is a whole-team example of the grammatical form: "The boy done good".
Yours,
NEIL INKLEY,
Preston, Lancashire. April 17

Beckham's break

From Mr Colin Reasbeck
Sir, Is this to be the most publicised sporting injury since reports on cricketer Denis Compton's knee kept the nation enthralled 50 years ago?
Yours,
COLIN REASBECK,
Alfreton, Derbyshire. April 11

From Mr Jim Mann Taylor
Sir, "Yes, sport is cruel" (headline, T2, April 12). Can we ban it then?
Yours faithfully,
JIM MANN TAYLOR,
Westbury-on-Severn, Gloucestershire. April 12

23 TRAVELLER'S CHECK

MP's elixir

From Mrs Tamsin Forman

Sir, I am 71. After a bad night (sciatica, intimation of mortality, etc) – I opened a letter at breakfast from my MP, congratulating me on my recent 18th birthday and my right to vote. He wanted to "help me with any problems", and wished me "good luck in my future career".

The joyous news that I am still a teenager instantly ironed out all the wrinkles. I have recovered my zip. I have plenty of problems, but none of them involves my future career.
Yours faithfully,
TAMSIN FORMAN,
Brill, Buckinghamshire. April 16

Sunny outlook

From Dr Tom Venables

Sir, It is almost three weeks since I retired and the sun has shone here every day. Is this an hallucination, is it a reward, or does it mean I should have waited until July?
Yours faithfully,
TOM VENABLES,
Calverton, Nottingham. April 16

NHS funding

From Mr Jack Badley

Sir, An independent healthcare regulator. Ofsick perhaps?
Yours faithfully,
JACK BADLEY,
Royston, Hertfordshire. April 19

From Mr Michael Mounsey

Sir, Ofsick? What about Oftrolley?
Yours faithfully,
MICHAEL MOUNSEY,
Newark, Nottinghamshire. April 21

Be prepared

From Mrs Angela Lister

Sir, I have received in the post a home insurance offer which included fire cover for garden plants.

Do they know something about global warming that I don't?
Yours faithfully,
A. M. LISTER,
Blandford Forum, Dorset. April 22

From Mr Jad Adams

Sir, My insurance company has just sent me notice of a "sum assured payable on the first event of death". Payments on the second event are unlikely to be numerous.
Yours,
JAD ADAMS,
Forest Hill, London SE23. April 22

Traveller's check

From Canon Julian Sullivan

Sir, A trip to space is a snip at £14 million, but how much spending money should one take?
Yours faithfully,
JULIAN SULLIVAN,
Sheffield. April 25

From Mrs Olwen Davis

Sir, I can't answer Canon Julian Sullivan's question as to how much spending money one should take on a £14 million space trip.

I'm too busy wondering what currency it should be in.
Yours faithfully,
OLWEN DAVIS,
Haverfordwest, Pembrokeshire. April 27

From Mr Graham Duncan

Sir, I presume that the old but nonetheless valid advice for travellers is just as appropriate for a space tourist: take twice as much money and half as many clothes as you think you will need.
Yours faithfully,
GRAHAM DUNCAN,
Newbury, Berkshire. April 28

From Mr Robin Rees-Webbe

Sir, Readers seem uncertain as to what currency and how much to take on space travel. It will be difficult to work out the exchange rate, so perhaps the solution is to revert to barter. I am sure Mars bars will be acceptable anywhere in space.

Yours faithfully,
A. R. REES-WEBBE,
Shrewsbury, Shropshire. May 1

From the Reverend Jeremy Fletcher
Sir, Robin Rees-Webbe suggests the Mars bar as a useful currency for space travel. But who would calculate the exchange rate with the Galaxy and Milky Way?
Yours sincerely,
JEREMY FLETCHER,
Southwell. May 2

From Mr Peter Tray
Sir, Apart from minor purchases, eg, pie in the sky, the sheer weight of Mars bars would rule them out for space travel. Better take some plastic. It could be light-years before the slip comes back to Earth.
Yours faithfully,
PETER TRAY,
London N12. May 2

Working and motherhood

From Mrs Yvonne Hodgson
Sir, Isn't it funny that no one discovers how stressful it is looking after children until men try it (report, "House-husbands at high risk of heart attacks", April 25)?
Yours sincerely,
YVONNE HODGSON,
Ninfield, East Sussex. April 25

Thinking ahead

From Mr John Walker
Sir, After reading Dr Stuttaford's article on memory loss I hurried off to purchase some Gingko biloba. I was offered, at exactly the same price and quantity, a choice of taking one three times a day or taking one or two tablets once a day. Fearing a lapse of memory, I chose the latter.
Yours faithfully,
JOHN WALKER,
Staines, Middlesex. April 26

From Mr Ron Dodson
Sir, Mr John Walker prefers to take his memory loss tablets once rather than three times a day.

I fear that leaves the remains of the day to remember whether you have taken them.
Yours faithfully,
RON DODSON,
Stockbridge, Hampshire. April 29

From Mr Anthony P. Moran
Sir, I always ask for my tablets in calendar packs. Before I retired I relied on these to ensure that I took my daily dose. Now, however, I use them to remind me which day of the week it is.
Yours faithfully,
ANTHONY MORAN,
Gosport, Hampshire. May 1

The versatile potato

From Mrs J. L. Seccombe
Sir, In the old days one bought potatoes and then decided how one was going to cook them – roast, bake, mash, chips etc. But then supermarkets divided them with labels such as "potatoes for roasting or baking".

Today I bought a bag of potatoes from a leading superstore that was labelled "a multi-purpose potato".

Have we come full circle?
Yours faithfully,
PETRONELLA SECCOMBE,
Kiddington, Oxfordshire. April 26

From Mrs Janet E. Smith
Sir, I fear Mrs J. L. Seccombe has little cause for optimism about the return of the potato.

I heard a young mother in a supermarket instructing her small son to fetch the potatoes. He sped to the nearby freezer, returning with frozen chips, and was praised for selecting the right ones.
Yours faithfully,
JANET E. SMITH,
St Ishmaels, Pembrokeshire. May 8

Holding on

From Mr Tom Gleeson
Sir, After another frustrating day of being kept on hold while telephoning various

firms, I begin to wonder what would happen if Vivaldi came back to earth with a good lawyer.
Yours faithfully,
TOM GLEESON,
Newcastle upon Tyne. May 3

From Mr J. A. Fendley
Sir, Not only Vivaldi is retained to soothe the impatient telephone caller.
I learnt from my insurance company that my car had been deemed a write-off after the performance of an extended excerpt from *In paradisum* of Fauré's *Requiem*.
Yours truly,
JOHN FENDLEY,
Cirencester, Gloucestershire. May 6

From Mr Vernon Frost
Sir, Firms which use Vivaldi's cheerful and lively music for telephone holding could avoid charges of misleading advertising by using instead *The Representation of Chaos* from Haydn's *Creation*.
Yours faithfully,
VERNON FROST,
London N21. May 6

Stuck for a solution

From Mr Humphrey Squier
Sir, Now that EU directives make manufacturers of, for example, cars and white goods responsible for their disposal at the end of their worthwhile life, what about chewing gum?
Yours faithfully,
HUMPHREY SQUIER,
Rochford, Essex. May 6

From Mr Richard Quin
Sir, Does anyone doubt that if chewing gum manufacturers were made responsible for cleaning up the mess consumers of their product make on our streets, within a year they would have developed a gum that would break down in sunlight?
Yours faithfully,
RICHARD QUIN,
Witham, Essex. May 7

From Mrs Anne Adams
Sir, My husband (he who may not always be right, but is never wrong) insists that chewing gum can be swallowed. Can someone settle this longstanding argument?
Yours faithfully,
ANNE ADAMS,
Bath. May 7

From the Director of ArtWatch UK
Sir, Never mind bearing down on the manufacturers of chewing gum and white goods, how about making the manufacturers of aerosol paints liable for the costs of graffiti removal?
Yours faithfully,
MICHAEL DALEY,
East Barnet, Hertfordshire. May 8

Friends in high places

From Mrs R. W. Warner
Sir, In our post we have received a letter addressed to "St Mary the Virgin, c/o Mr R. W. Warner".
Even I did not realise that my husband, a church treasurer, has such elevated contacts.
Yours faithfully,
CAMILLA WARNER,
Wendens Ambo, Essex. May 4

18 at 16?

From Mrs Caroline Charles-Jones
Sir, I received the following e-mail from my furious daughter who wishes to go clubbing and achieve emancipation: "I don't think you realise one thing. 16 now is A LOT older than it was for you." I feel beleaguered and A LOT older than I did before I had a teenage daughter.
Yours faithfully,
CAROLINE CHARLES-JONES,
Dinas, Pembrokeshire. May 5

Signs of the time

From Mr Tom Corrigan
Sir, A month ago I purchased a pot of cream which purports to reduce "signs of ageing". To date I find no reduction in

baldness, gum-shrinkage, myopia, short-term memory loss, involuntary flatulence or incessant reminiscing about the good old days.

I remain, Sir, yours faithfully,
T. A. CORRIGAN,
Gurney Slade. May 3

A place for Richard I

From Professor Sir John Boardman

Sir, Mr Robert Bennett suggests that the statue of Richard I, "a Frenchman, a tyrant, and a brute", be taken from the Houses of Parliament to the bottom of the Thames.

Better still – give it to Paris, to stand in the Gare de Lyon. This both answers Sellar and Yeatman's remark (*1066 And All That*) that he took his name from the station, as a regular passenger en route to the Crusades, and may recompense the French for our insistence that they disembark from Eurostar at Waterloo.

Sincerely,
JOHN BOARDMAN,
Woodstock, Oxfordshire. May 7

Telesales tactics

From Mr Derek Pepper

Sir, Recently I was offered 30 days free on a health insurance scheme and told the salesman I was sorry, but didn't think I would last another 30 days.

The next day someone rang to offer a last will and testament service.

Yours faithfully,
DEREK PEPPER,
Abingdon, Oxfordshire. May 11

Unkindest cut

From Mr Alex Murray

Sir, As a result of your recent editorial changes, my wife will no longer be able to read this letter after I have cut out the crossword.

Yours faithfully,
ALEX MURRAY,
Plaxtol, Kent. May 14

Manner of speaking

From Mr R. J. Vincent

Sir, Boycott, Bradshaw, Burke and Hare
    (Before one's memory dims)
    Were oft employed, from time to time,
    As useful eponyms.
    This humble, published poet
    Seeking fame among high-flyers
    Requires another eponym
    To nominate for liars.

Yours faithfully,
ROBERT JULES VINCENT,
Andover, Hampshire. May 16

Bread winner

From Ms Carole Zepler

Sir, Fiona Beckett's test reports on seven bread machines (Weekend, May 18) convinced me that the best bread is made by hand and baked in the oven.

Hand-made bread does not have the shortcomings she records with the machines, and I certainly don't have to "cut into chunks rather than slices", for I can cut slices wafer-thin. I get finished loaves in far less time than it takes the machines.

Yours truly,
CAROLE ZEPLER,
Canterbury, Kent. May 20

From Mrs Rose Hogan

Sir, The beauty of the bread-making machine is that it has introduced the man of the house to the kitchen.

My husband is master and controller of this wonderful computerised machine (my friends' husbands likewise).

No fuss, no failure and very little washing up. Brilliant.

Yours contentedly,
ROSE HOGAN,
Tewkesbury, Gloucestershire. May 25

From Mrs Gloria Gillott

Sir, Unlike the husband of your correspondent, my husband gave up on the bread machine immediately he realised that the bread did not come out sliced and wrapped in polythene.

He is, however, master and controller of the newly acquired, dual-cyclone, bagless wonder that vacuums our house.

Yours, very contentedly,
GLORIA GILLOTT,
Girton, Cambridge. June 5

The contented cuckold

From Mr James S. Sutherland

Sir, Your Word Watching expert informs readers that a wittol is a cuckold. The explanation given is that a wittol is "a man who is aware of and complaisant about the infidelity of his wife" (Weekend, May 18).

This, in fact, explains why a wittol is not a cuckold (*cf* John Barth's novel *The Sot-Weed Factor* – "Only the wittol can know he is no cuckold").

Yours faithfully,
JAMES S. SUTHERLAND,
Peebles. May 18

In the pink

From Mr Leonard Feltham

Sir, If red wine is beneficial for the cardiovascular system and white wine is of benefit to the lungs (report, May 21), should we not all be drinking rosé?

Yours faithfully,
LEONARD FELTHAM,
London SW15. May 24

From Mrs Pat McAuley

Sir, If red wine is good for the heart and white wine is good for the lungs, what is good for the liver?

Yours sincerely,
PAT McAULEY,
Dorchester, Dorset. May 25

From Professor Emeritus Roger Irving

Sir, For many years I have been drinking red wine and white wine in roughly equal volumes with a carefree sense of pure indulgence. A sour note has crept in.

The experts have found that wine of whatever colour has beneficial effects on specific organs and ailments: no one really enjoys taking medicine.

Yours sincerely,
ROGER IRVING,
Guildford, Surrey. May 29

From Mr John Steed

Sir, What is good for the liver?
  Bacon!

Yours sincerely,
JOHN STEED,
Bracknell, Berkshire. May 29

From the Reverend Nick Percival

Sir, Someone had to write this, so it might as well be me: I suggest onions.

Yours faithfully,
NICK PERCIVAL,
South Shields, Tyne and Wear. May 29

From Mr David Lightowler

Sir, Moderation.

Yours faithfully,
DAVID LIGHTOWLER,
Ripon, North Yorkshire. May 29

From Mr James Hazan

Sir, Port.

Yours faithfully,
JAMES HAZAN,
London W9. May 29

From Mr Ben Petersen

Sir, Abstinence is good for the liver; it is also, however, ruinous for the soul.

Yours faithfully,
BEN PETERSEN,
Doncaster, South Yorkshire. May 30

Proof positive

From Mr Neil Murray

Sir, A local branch of Barclays once allowed me to withdraw money from my account using as the sole basis for identification my old sweater, which still had a nametape from schooldays sewn into the collar.

As the cashier said with a smile, no fraudster would have gone to that much trouble.

Yours sincerely,
NEIL MURRAY,
Sutton, Surrey. May 23

From Mr Alistair Reid

Sir, My cash card having been inadvertently cancelled whilst visiting my parents, I arranged to withdraw cash from the bank branch used by them.

Offering my driving licence as proof of identity I was told that this would not be required as my strong resemblance to my mother, a longstanding customer, meant that I could only be who I said I was.

Yours faithfully,
ALISTAIR REID,
Chester. May 30

From Mr Kenneth Cleveland

Sir, In the days before cheque guarantee cards, a friend of mine wished to withdraw cash at a branch where he was not known. Unable to produce identification, he asked the cashier to telephone the manager of his own branch.

When he returned he asked: "Excuse me, Sir, but what do you drink when you have a hangover?" On receiving the reply "Worthington White Shield" he cashed the cheque.

I remain, Sir, your obedient servant,
KENNETH CLEVELAND,
Armathwaite, Cumbria. May 26

From Mrs Mary Mathews

Sir, My friend and I proffered our MasterCards in Spain as payment in a department store. When asked for further proof of identity and having no passports with us, I showed my Merthyr Tydfil bus pass and my friend showed her Tesco Club Card.

Both were accepted and the purchases were completed.

Yours faithfully,
MARY MATHEWS,
Merthyr Tydfil. June 5

From Professor Emeritus Brian G. Palmer

Sir, My proof of identity problem was resolved rather differently.

I went into my new bank and attempted to buy foreign currency with a cheque drawn on my account at that branch. To my surprise the teller asked whether I had any proof of identity.

I produced my university library card which bore my name, signature and a photograph. Frown. Had I anything else?

I triumphantly pulled out my new-style driving licence, also complete with photograph. Still a frown but, as I was searching among the many cards in my wallet, she spotted the tip of a Barclaycard.

"That's all right, sir. I see you have a Barclaycard." No, she didn't need to see my signature – she had seen it already on the other cards.

Yours faithfully,
BRIAN G. PALMER,
Henley-on-Thames. June 8

From Mr Christopher Y. Nutt

Sir, In 1903 Caruso made his debut at the Metropolitan Opera House, New York. One story goes that in trying to cash a cheque at a nearby bank he was frustrated by the teller's insistence on proof of identity.

Irritated, Caruso sang at him. He got his money.

Yours faithfully,
CHRISTOPHER Y. NUTT,
Little Abington, Cambridge. June 14

From Sir Rowland Whitehead

Sir, Visiting the British Embassy in Bucharest a few years ago my only proof of identity was a Ronnie Scott Jazz Club membership card, complete with my picture wearing a skydiving helmet. The card was instantly accepted.

Ronnie, as usual, was laconic. "Glad to hear it – most of my members are ashamed of their cards."

Yours sincerely,
ROWLAND WHITEHEAD,
London W4. June 20

From Mr Roger Peers

Sir, When I was asked at the entrance to a US Army camp in Taegu, South Korea, to leave proof of identity with the officer on duty, my British passport was not accept-

able. However, my Bodleian Library reader's ticket was instantly approved.
Yours,
ROGER PEERS,
Beaminster, Dorset. June 18

From Mrs Anne Fisher
Sir, When my husband and I were staying with our son in Washington, we were very keen to see inside the Pentagon. As we did not have our passports with us, our Fife bus passes were accepted as proof of identity.
Yours faithfully,
ANNE FISHER,
St Andrews, Fife. June 19

From Mr Bob Day
Sir, Several years ago, on a business trip to Scandinavia, my colleague forgot his passport. While I was subjected to the usual baleful glare as my passport was thumbed through and stamped, my colleague was waved through several border posts on the strength of his gun licence.
Yours faithfully,
R. K. DAY,
Comberbach, Cheshire. June 23

From Mr B. S. Banks
Sir, I once visited a building society to open an account and tendered my bus pass bearing my photograph as proof of identity, only to have it rejected. Worse than that, when the time came to renew the bus pass it was refused as not being suitable proof.
Yours faithfully,
B. S. BANKS,
Coventry. June 23

Patience of Paxman
From Mr Chris W. Drew
Sir, "I am not a gardener myself. I haven't got the patience," says Jeremy Paxman (report, May 21).
This, from an angler!
Yours,
CHRIS DREW,
Llandudno. May 21

From Mr Tim Williams
Sir, It seems likely that Mr Chris Drew is not an angler or he would know that anglers are not patient people.
They do, however, know how to control impatience. A skill so often demonstrated by Mr Jeremy Paxman.
Yours,
TIM WILLIAMS,
Loppington, Shropshire. May 25

Raw deal
From Mr Michael Ball
Sir, I note (News in Brief, May 23) that the person who streaked in front of Her Majesty has been given a conditional discharge and had his trousers confiscated.
Isn't this counter-productive?
Yours faithfully,
MICHAEL BALL,
Carshalton, Surrey. May 23

Flying visit
From Mrs Madeleine Church
Sir, What are the odds of having one's carpet and upholstered furniture steam-cleaned one day and the next day having a duck followed by a drake fly into the room through an open window, leaving their visiting cards before they could be shooed out?
Yours faithfully,
MADELEINE CHURCH,
Saffron Walden. June 2

From Sir Alistair MacFarlane, FRS
Sir, Mrs Madeleine Church's letter on the odds of having a duck and drake fly into a room which had been steam-cleaned just the previous day raises interesting questions for scientists and philosophers.
A scientific explanation would be to attribute such an unlikely event to a large-scale quantum fluctuation in the brain of one, or both, of the ducks. Quantum physicists usually quantify such events in terms of time, rather than odds. They would say that if Mrs Church were to repeat her clean-

ing and opening of windows indefinitely, a large fraction of the lifetime of the Universe would elapse before her furnishings were again sullied by ducks.

Analytical philosophers would see this as a spectacular instantiation of the concept of bad luck. Although avoiding any calculation of odds, they would be wary of invitations to sit on her sofa, should any windows be open.

Moral philosophers could advise her as to whether she should continue trusting ducks, and if this single event constituted just grounds for the shooting of ducks, both specifically and generally.

Yours sincerely,
ALISTAIR MacFARLANE,
Strathconon, Ross-shire. June 4

From Mrs Veronica Scott

Sir, I was amused to read that Mrs Church's house is called The Folly.

Best wishes,
VERONICA SCOTT,
London W11. June 3

From Mrs Jenny Baker

Sir, One sympathises with Mrs Madeleine Church whose newly steam-cleaned carpet and furniture were soiled by a duck and drake that flew into the room.

Some years ago I peeped into the drawing room just moments before we were supposed to be going way on holiday, to find that two starlings had come down the chimney, flown around the room and expired in the hearth.

They had managed to leave their signature on all four walls, all four curtains, every sofa and chair and, of course, the carpet. And they had obviously been eating berries. And they had knocked over a piece of valuable china and broken a fan which had belonged to my great-grandmother.

To their credit, the insurers paid up every penny it took to reinstate.

Entry via the chimney is now blocked.

Yours faithfully,
JENNY BAKER,
Bishops Stortford, Hertfordshire. June 3

From Mr R. G. Dawson

Sir, It was a lovely spring day, so all the doors were open.

Hearing a kerfuffle in the kitchen we and our two black labradors rushed in to find a cock pheasant. We pushed the dogs hurriedly into the dining room and shooed the pheasant out.

Hearing another kerfuffle in the dining room we went in to find two wildly overexcited labradors and a newly dead pheasant, with the room clad in feathers.

As our daughter observed, we really should have checked that there wasn't a pheasant in the dining room before we put the dogs in there.
Yours faithfully,
RICHARD DAWSON,
Halstead, Essex. June 7

From Professor Mark Macnair
Sir, About 20 years ago we had a visit from a starling which came down the chimney and broke a much-loved pair of Meissen cruets. Since our insurance policy covered damage by animals I contacted the company in order to make a claim. The claim, however, was rejected on the ground that "birds are not animals".

All my biological expertise was to no avail in trying to make them change their minds.
Yours faithfully,
MARK MACNAIR
(Professor of Evolutionary Genetics),
Chudleigh, Devon. June l5

Webbed feat

From Professor Emeritus Robert Spence, FREng
Sir, I have self-diagnosed a disability which, I suspect, is widespread. But I also suggest a cure, so that there may be no need for Dr Stuttaford to burst into print.

I have polysyllabic exhaustion, brought about by quoting web addresses beginning "www". It is unfortunate that the thrice-repeated letter is the only one in the English alphabet with more than one syllable. The choice of two syllables could be regarded as merely unfortunate, but three is downright annoying.

The cure, which I happened upon recently in New Zealand, was to pronounce "www" as "dub dub dub", bringing the syllabic count down from nine to three. However, since "dub" appears in the plural, so to speak, one could reasonably say "dubs", thereby saving another two syllables. But why can't we say just "web", and let that also imply the "dot" that usually follows "www" as night follows day?

The syllabic count is now down from ten to one. By this simple device web-induced polysyllabic exhaustion will present no danger of being a burden on the NHS.
Yours faithfully,
BOB SPENCE (two syllables),
Whyteleafe, Surrey. June 3

Tea strainer

From EurIng Professor Bryan Woodward
Sir, My local council has recently advertised for a "Tea Person" ("relevant training will be given") at a rate of "£4.8033" per hour.

Is this the ultimate in penny-pinching?
Yours faithfully,
BRYAN WOODWARD,
Department of Electronic and Electrical Engineering, Loughborough University, Leicestershire. June 4

Cold comfort

From Mr Martin Davies
Sir, The other day, my wife returned from Iceland (the frozen food chainstore, not the country) with a tub of the company's own-brand raspberry ripple ice-cream. On the label, in capital letters, was the reassuring statement This product has been made in a production area where no nuts are present.
Yours faithfully,
MARTIN DAVIES,
Truro, Cornwall. June l

Grave tidings

From the Reverend Jeff Leonardi
Sir, I have received a community charge letter addressed to "The Owner and/or The Occupier" of our Village Burial Ground.

I am not the former and my family assure me that I am not yet one of the latter, though as a Christian I am surely preparing for it.
Yours sincerely,
JEFF LEONARDI,
Rugeley. June 2

Relatively speaking

From Mr Colin Strickland
Sir, You report today that a number of British tourists were "stranded on the Caribbean island of Antigua".

I can well understand the use of the word stranded in the case of Luton airport or Stansted, but Antigua?
Yours faithfully,
COLIN STRICKLAND,
Canterbury, Kent. May 31

Front-row seat?

From Mrs Amanda Nicholson
Sir, Having failed to keep abreast of the social calendar I was baffled by an aisle in our local Tesco dedicated to Seasonal Toilet Rolls.

What else have I missed?
Yours faithfully,
AMANDA NICHOLSON,
Buckingham. June 6

Name dropping

From Mr C. M. Burgess
Sir, My wife is expecting and we are deciding upon names. In an attempt to stay on the cutting edge of modern naming I have reverted to my DIY handbook.

I feel Fascia has a certain cachet, especially if the first "a" is pronounced as in "back". Other current favourites are Soffit and Cowl.
Yours faithfully,
C. M. BURGESS,
Warehorne, Kent. June 3

Canine caveat

From Dr Martin Davies
Sir, "Dogs on leads please – consecrated ground" on a Cornish churchyard gate set me thinking; and recently I found a longer version in East Anglia. Is there scriptural justification? And are the inevitable avian excreta also profane?

Yours sincerely,
MARTIN DAVIES,
Oakamoor, Stoke-on-Trent. June 6

Joint rule

From Professor John A. S. Abecasis-Phillips
Sir, I have been asked by my bank to complete a schedule of assets and liabilities for myself and my "partner".

Are wives out?
I remain, Sir, your obedient servant,
JOHN A. S. ABECASIS-PHILLIPS,
Okayama, Japan. June 4

Salad days

From Mr J. E. Thomas
Sir, Whilst emptying the fridge in my student accommodation at the end of the academic term, I discovered a head of lettuce labelled simply "Best Before: Thursday".

Dare I risk eating it?
Yours sincerely,
J. E. THOMAS,
Ecclesall, Sheffield. June 3

Golden oldies

From Mrs Jill Curtis
Sir, Mr Michael Bland (letter, June 10) asks "Am I getting old?"

This may be an important question if taking medication. A leaflet accompanying my tablets states dosage for "adults and children over 12 years" or "children under 12 years" or "elderly".

When does one become "elderly"?
Best regards,
JILL CURTIS,
London SW15. June 10

From Mr Graham Babel
Sir, You are still middle-aged when your parents and your children cause you equal amounts of worry.
Yours faithfully,
GRAHAM BABEL,
Telford. June 17

From Mr Ridley Hall

Sir, To answer Mrs Jill Curtis. Individuals ten years older than oneself are elderly.
I have the honour to be, Sir, your obedient servant,
RIDLEY HALL,
Walberton. June 19

From Mr Vivian Vale

Sir, Demonstrably – Old age begins and middle-age ends
When you find your descendants outnumber your friends.
Yours faithfully,
VIVIAN VALE,
Cerne Abbas, Dorset. June 20

From Mr T. Gwyn Evans

Sir, *Chambers English Dictionary* defines middle age as: "Between youth and old age, variously reckoned to suit the reckoner."
Yours faithfully,
T. GWYN EVANS,
Aberdare, Mid Glamorgan. June 27

From Mrs Barbara Naughton

Sir, Middle-aged is when you remember at least three occasions in the past when this sort of correspondence has been published on *The Times* letters page.
Yours faithfully,
BARBARA NAUGHTON,
Wimbledon, London SW19. June 26

Measure for measure

From Mr Gordon Harman

Sir, I read in this month's *Professional Engineer* that a new canal lift in Falkirk lifts the equivalent of 100 adult elephants.

A few hours later I read in *The Times* ("Republic where soccer rules", report, June 1) that a Goliath beetle weighs the equivalent of more than eight mice.

Is there no end to this?
Yours faithfully,
GORDON HARMAN,
Lee, Devon. June 3

From Mr Christopher Grounds

Sir, Mr Gordon Harman has juxtaposed the performance of the canal lift at Falkirk (equal to lifting 100 adult elephants) with the fact that a Goliath beetle weighs more than eight mice.

Now I can't help wondering how many Goliath beetles it would take to scare an elephant.

I honestly see no end to this.
Yours faithfully,
CHRIS GROUNDS,
Mississauga, Ontario. June 11

From Dr A. S. Curry

Sir, When lecturing, I used to contrast a sprinkling of salt to 200 elephants when discussing the relation of a nanogram to a gram. My old friend Professor George Clarke of the Royal Veterinary College used to say: "But Alan, are they Indian or African elephants?"
Yours,
ALAN CURRY,
Reading, Berkshire. June 12

Fever pitch

From Mrs Bruce Parker

Sir, A local garden centre is advertising "World Cup Sheds" for sale. I don't know exactly what these are but perhaps I should invest in one. I could either live in it myself or equip it with a television and victuals for my husband until the world gets back to normal.
Yours faithfully,
SUZANNE PARKER,
Winchester, Hampshire. June 16

From Mr Andrew Stilton

Sir, I do not need a World Cup Shed but we have a children's playhouse in the garden which I intend in due course to make into an Old Buffer's Shed.

I will relocate there when my daughters become teenagers and re-emerge when they become socially acceptable again, around the age of 30.
Yours faithfully,
ANDREW STILTON,
Wolverley, Worcestershire. June 17

From Ms S. Curtis

Sir, Mr Andrew Stilton intends to re-emerge from his Old Buffer's Shed when his daughters become socially acceptable again – "around the age of 30". My father wishes to advise him that he may be there longer than he thinks.

Yours faithfully,

SALLY CURTIS (43 years),

Littleover, Derby. June 20

England and St George

From the Vicar of Lewisham

Sir, The other day in Lewisham High Street I saw a burly Afro-Caribbean man come out of the Lewisham and Kent Islamic Centre and get into his van, of which the rear window was filled with a home-made flag of St George. Multiculturalism indeed: black, Muslim, English patriot. I think he would have passed the Norman Tebbit test.

Yours faithfully,

DAVID GARLICK,

Lewisham, London SE13. June 14

From Mr Richard Smith

Sir, Although I was the only person in my office to display the English flag on St George's Day, I am now being called unpatriotic due to my refusal to watch football matches. Has Mr Beckham now replaced St George as our patron saint?

Yours faithfully,

R. SMITH,

Thatcham, Berkshire. June 19

From Mr Michael Bird

Sir, The idea that Englishmen might favour the Cross of St George over the Union Flag will never catch on. Where's the fun in having a flag about which nobody can complain that it is being flown upside down?

Yours etc,

MICHAEL BIRD,

London SW13. June 20

Eye opener

From Ms Heather Ridge

Sir, You reported on June 15 that "Eye-brows were raised when Ms Malone's mother . . . had a cataract operation".

Was this part of the procedure, or the outcome?

Yours faithfully,

HEATHER RIDGE,

London EC2. June 17

Crime deterrents

From Mr Trevor Trotman

Sir, Can I appeal to the motoring organisations to start a campaign for plainclothes policemen to be sprayed bright yellow?

This would make me far less likely to commit a crime while I was in their view.

Regards,

TREVOR TROTMAN,

London SE25. June 19

From Mr David Boehm

Sir, Our local Crime Prevention Officer has been redesignated as the Crime Reduction Officer. PC rebranding?

Yours faithfully,

DAVID BOEHM,

Lower Slaughter, Gloucestershire. June 25

The ears have it

From Mrs Malcolm Stewart

Sir, Reading your excellent obituary of the Duke of Norfolk (June 26), I was interested to learn that sharply pointed ears are apparently characteristic of a military bearing.

Obviously I made a fundamental error in my choice of nursing as a career some 50 years ago, but it certainly explains my daughters' interest in young men wearing uniform.

Yours faithfully,

BARBARA J. R. STEWART,

Harpenden, Hertfordshire. June 27

Proof positive

From Mr Terry O'Brien

Sir, Some years ago, on our way to an early morning lecture, our student-laden Morris Minor was stopped on the A40. A stern policeman explained that a man suspected of robbing a nearby public house was being sought. We were terrified – not by his lengthy inquisition, but lest he should spot the Guinness beer bottle label standing in for the tax disc on the windscreen.

Questions over, he thanked us for our co-operation and, as we breathed sighs of relief, added: "I'm a Mackeson man myself. Drive carefully, lads."

Yours faithfully,
TERRY O'BRIEN,
Finchley, London N3. June 27

The Church's future

From Dr Ted Harrison

Sir, The loud complaints from certain evangelicals that the appointment of Rowan Williams to Canterbury would split the Church bring to mind the words of the late Lord Runcie (in an address in 1999), who feared that the Church would "soon resemble a swimming pool – with lots of noise coming from the shallow end".

Yours faithfully,
TED HARRISON,
Ashford, Kent. June 29

From Mrs Diana Peschier

Sir, Ruth Gledhill suggests (report, June 29) that a fifth of the clergy may resign over women bishops. Good!

Yours faithfully,
DIANA PESCHIER,
Kenley, Surrey. July 1

Heat of the moment

From Ms Hannah Jefferies

Sir, Your report today on the Royal Opera House's leading lady whose dress was set on fire by an on-stage candle is a classic case of it ain't over till the fat lady sings.

Yours faithfully,
HANNAH JEFFERIES,
London SE22. July 1

Chinese instructions

From Mr Bill Woodruff.

Sir, Last week I bought, for a very reason-

able £5.95, a paper shredder as advertised in your paper. It was made in China and described as a "Hand shredder". Fortunately the size of the aperture precluded this possibility, but another part of the instructions asked: "Please dump the crumble in the box in time." Could Delia Smith help with the rest of the recipe?

What puzzled me most was: "Don't open the machine, change the structure or repair it without permission." From whom do I seek permission? Do I need a licence from Beijing?

Yours in doubt,
BILL WOODRUFF,
Lenham, Kent. July 1

From Mrs J. Barker

Sir, My secateurs, made in China, carry the instruction "ideal for use on shrubs in public parks".

I haven't tested them *in situ* yet.

Yours,
J. BARKER,
Huntly, Aberdeenshire. July 3

From Mr William Reeve

Sir, I once had a bottle of embrocation from China bearing the warning "Do not take inside".

We kept it in the garage.

Yours faithfully,
W. REEVE,
Addlestone, Surrey. July 10

Dressing down

From Mr Bernard Adams

Sir, The letters about university life put me in mind of a story about the late Reverend Meredith Dewey, for many years Dean of Pembroke College, Cambridge.

It was his custom to entertain freshmen to tea in his very pleasant rooms. On one occasion the day turned out to be fine and warm, and the Dean felt that a picnic would be nicer. Having arranged for a hamper to be set up, he realised that it might not be entirely convenient for his guest to be out of town, as he might have appointments to keep.

Dressed by this time in open-necked shirt and shorts, the Dean went to the undergraduate's door and knocked. On hearing "Come in" he put his head round the door and said: "I say, would you like to go for a picnic this afternoon?"

"Sorry," came the reply, "I've got to go to tea with the bloody Dean."

Dewey felt that it was nice not always to be recognised.

Yours etc,
BERNARD ADAMS
(Undergraduate, Pembroke College, 1958-61), Brecon, Powys. July 1

Road hog

From Mr Geoffrey Woodward

Sir, Pork Chop, an 18lb Vietnamese pot-bellied pig (report, June 28) "becomes nervous and irritable after about five hours in the car".

Almost human.

Yours,
GEOFFREY WOODWARD,
Worthing, West Sussex. July 2

Birth control

From Mr C. W. Denton

Sir, I see from your obituary of the wonderful Barbara Goalen that she "produced two children in succession".

Is there some other way?

Yours faithfully,
DICK DENTON,
Leighton Buzzard. July 2

Theatre of the absurd

From Mr Ian Liston

Sir, It is political correctness of the silliest order to change the title of *The Hunchback of Notre Dame* to avoid giving offence (News in Brief, June 28).

With the pantomime season but a few months away it looks as if my company may have to perform *Snow White and the Seven Persons of Restricted Growth* and *Beauty and the Bodily Challenged.*

But what am I to do about the Ugly Sisters in *Cinderella*? And I suppose a Slave of the Ring in *Aladdin* is out of the question?

Yours faithfully,
IAN LISTON (Producer),
The Hiss and Boo Theatre Company, Bolney, West Sussex. June 28

Off with her head

From Mr Steve Buckel

Sir, Would it not have been more appropriate to have cast Baroness Thatcher's statue (report and photograph, July 5) in iron?

Yours sincerely,
STEVE BUCKEL,
Hove, East Sussex. July 5

From Mr Rodney Legg

Sir, There is a public house sign near Wareham in Dorset that features a public figure with a severed head. The lady in its case is Anne Boleyn.

Even without her head, Baroness Thatcher has yet to meet the criterion for usurping her, as the inn in question is The Silent Woman.

Yours sincerely,
RODNEY LEGG,
Wincanton, Somerset. July 5

Double blank

From Mr John Acklaw

Sir, Wanting to renew my road tax licence, I spent all morning trying to recall where I had put my insurance certificate. Upon phoning my insurers I found they had forgotten to send it.

As I am over 60 and my insurers are Saga I suppose the odds were even that one of us would have the memory loss.

Yours faithfully,
JOHN ACKLAW,
North Fambridge, Essex. July 6

Wet blanket

From Mr Vincent Saunders

Sir, Isn't it normally about this time of year

hat a politician stands outside Parliament and announces a hosepipe ban due to the drought?

Yours faithfully,
VINCENT SAUNDERS,
Shepherds Bush, London W12. July 8

From Mrs Ann Green
Sir, My husband and I are not worried about the absence of a hosepipe ban, but as OAPs we would like to know if the Chancellor has proposals for the introduction of a summer fuel allowance this year.

Yours faithfully,
ANN GREEN,
Norwich. July 9

From Mr R. W. Tavender
Sir, In the long drought of 1976, the then Prime Minister appointed a Minister for Rain. It rained shortly afterwards. Might it not be appropriate for Mr Blair urgently to consider the appointment of a Minister for Sunshine?

Yours etc,
R. W. TAVENDER,
Worcester. July 11

From Mr John Oxborrow
Sir, Paul Simons refers to the summer of 1976 (report, July 10). I thought the summer of '76 quite awful. Crops failed and gardens turned brown. Many people seemed to find the heat unbearable. No doubt a number of people contracted skin cancer that year. The water supply was in crisis. Forest and heathland fires raged.

I would prefer something in the middle, but as between 1976 and 2002, give me the latter any day.

Yours faithfully,
JOHN OXBORROW,
Coniston, Cumbria. July 10

From Mr Peter Lamberton
Sir, There is no need to appoint a new minister for sunshine; just appoint Stephen Byers as minister for rain.

Yours etc,
PETER LAMBERTON,
Sheffield. July 12

All at sea

From Mr David Williams
Sir, The captain of HMS *Nottingham* should be treated leniently. On BBC News, on teletext and in your paper today, Wolf Rock at Lord Howe Island has been variously described as being 200, 300, 400 and 500 miles from Sydney. Clearly the wretched thing is mobile and its position unpredictable.

Yours faithfully,
DAVID WILLIAMS,
Burford, Oxfordshire. July 8.

From Mr M. W. H. Howroyd
Sir, What a contrast between Commander Richard Farrington, the captain of HMS *Nottingham*, and our captains of industry. The former bravely and forthrightly faces the world press while the latter hide behind the weasel words of their press officers and the gates of their country mansions.

I hope he makes admiral.

Yours faithfully,
M. W. H. HOWROYD,
St Leonards on Sea, East Sussex. July 9

Single vision

From Mr Stanley J. Blenkinsop
Sir, You report today on the demise of the monocle.

Two years ago you used a letter from me reporting my experiences at the hands of the French police after my monocle was stolen, along with my wallet, by a Paris pickpocket.

When I mentioned the lost monocle, the young policewoman taking details looked at me awestruck and inquired: "Are you a sir or a lord, Monsieur?"

After you published this I had letters from at least 14 small optical firms throughout the United Kingdom saying they still made monocles and would be happy to supply a replacement. I have little doubt that most of them, if not all, are still in business.

Yours sincerely,

STANLEY J. BLENKINSOP,
Macclesfield, Cheshire. July 4

From Miss Margery Elliott
Sir, Some time during the late 1920s, when
I was a child, my father, a dealer in fancy
goods, received an urgent and inexplicably
large order for fake monocles with plain
glass.

Inquiries proved that Sir Austen Chamberlain, a monocle wearer, was soon to address the students of Birmingham University, who wished to be appropriately
equipped to receive him.
Yours faithfully,
MARGERY ELLIOTT,
Harborne, Birmingham. July 4

A breath of fresh air

From Mr Graeme Woolaston
Sir, I note that one of the "pioneering fea-
tures" of the proposed Minerva Tower at
Aldgate will be "fresh air for office workers
through opening windows on temperate
days" (report, July 8). Good Lord, whatever
will they think of next?
Yours faithfully,
GRAEME WOOLASTON,
Stepps, Glasgow. July 8

Sinister subject

From Mrs Eleanor Greeves
Sir, I enjoyed Ben Macintyre's "A sinister
subject . . ." (July 6). When I was found to
be left-handed, kind persuasion from the
age of seven to write with right but continue drawing with left resulted, strangely,
in lifelong ambidexterity for both skills. I
have found it especially useful for drawing
(but have not tested my termite collection
rate). However I find today the OED includes "double dealing" under ambidexter.
Yours faithfully,
ELEANOR GREEVES,
Taunton, Somerset. July 8

Water on tap

From Dr Amanda Hopkins
Sir, Taste tap water (report, July 10)?

The discerning drinker's nose wouldn't al
low him to put tap water near his lips be
cause of the pungent chemical smell, sug
gesting worse in its history than W. C
Fields's copulating fish. I'm sure this smel
is why pets are reluctant to drink wate
freshly poured from the tap.
Yours faithfully,
AMANDA HOPKINS,
Rugby, Warwickshire. July 10

Subject to availability

From Mr Julian Corlett
Sir, I inquired of my local reference librar⬛
as to where I might locate their section o⬛
books on ethics, for a research project I an⬛
involved in. Unhesitatingly, the libraria⬛
replied: "I'm afraid they've all bee⬛
nicked," adding: "Our books on ethics an⬛
morality invariably are."
Sincerely,
JULIAN CORLETT,
Scunthorpe, North Lincolnshire. July 11

Delayed decade

From Mr Martin Hopcroft
Sir, In view of recent financial excesses, ar⬛
these the Naughty Noughties?
Regards,
MARTIN HOPCROFT,
Dunstable. July 12

Know your vegetables

From Mr Guy de la Bédoyère
Sir, Today I stood by the supermarket ti⬛
and waited while two young shop assist
ants, recent alumni of our education sys
tem, discussed what my parsnip might b⬛
in order to ring up the correct amoun⬛
Eventually they concluded it was a leek.
corrected them, and thus they at least wen
home wiser. So, I fear, did I.
Yours faithfully,
GUY DE LA BEDOYERE,
Grantham, Lincolnshire. July 10

From Mr Steve Johnson
Sir, Is Mr Guy de la Bedoyere really sug⬛

gesting that identification of vegetables should be yet another responsibility of the education system?

I concede lettuce could be put under the banner of rocket science, but surely this should be the task of parents or the supermarket in question.

Regards,
STEVE JOHNSON,
Mirfield, West Yorkshire. July 15

From Mrs Fiona Widdowson

Sir, Mr Steve Johnson is no doubt correct that identification of root vegetables is not the responsibility of the education system. May I however offer yet another revealing supermarket encounter?

My husband requested: "A kilogram of your mild cheddar, please."

The young man behind the counter replied: "We're only allowed to sell things in grams or ounces."

My husband responded: "Then you had better make it a thousand grams."

Surely this is considered to be within the remit of the national curriculum.

Yours faithfully,
FIONA WIDDOWSON,
Claines, Worcester. July 16

From Mrs Julie Moores

Sir, Could not the geography syllabus include the recognition of Brussels sprouts, swedes and Jerusalem artichokes? The French syllabus mange tout, petits pois and French beans. Kidney beans could be dissected in biology lessons, whilst responsibility for runner beans would lie with the PE staff.

Regards,
JULIE MOORES,
Pylle, Somerset. July 16

From Mr David Meredith

Sir, In 1985, wishing to make lemonade, I placed ten lemons in front of a holiday student cashier in the greengrocers. Prideful of her newly installed electric till, she rang up the lemons individually at 10p each. I was charged 90p.

Somehow, I hadn't the heart to correct her.
Yours faithfully,
DAVID MEREDITH,
Aberystwyth, Dyfed. July 19

From Mrs Linda Prior

Sir, The young greengrocery assistant looked somewhat perplexed when the long sticks of rhubarb I had placed on the scales protruded over the ends. After a moment's thought she moved the rhubarb so that one end was completely on the scales and then repositioned it so that the other end was on the scales and added the two weights together.

When I objected, her next solution was to ask me to hold the rhubarb vertically on the scales.

She seemed very happy with her solution.
Yours faithfully,
LINDA PRIOR,
Radlett, Hertfordshire. July 19

From Mr Andrew D. Robinson

Sir, Being horticulturally challenged is not just the domain of the school leaver. One middle-aged lady recently returned a bunch of asparagus, claiming that the bluebells had refused to flower.
Sincerely,
ANDREW D. ROBINSON (Director),
D & R Group (Food Distributors),
Castleford, West Yorkshire. July 22

From Mr T. P. Goldingham

Sir, Surely our school-leavers should at least know their onions?
Yours truly,
TIM GOLDINGHAM,
Maidenhead. July 22

From Ms Susan Pape

Sir, I have just graduated, having spent the last six years studying part-time for a degree and, do you know, parsnips were not mentioned once.
Yours sincerely,
SUSAN PAPE,
Horsforth, Leeds. July 21

Cannabis rules

From Mr Bernard Coughlan

Sir, I guess it can only be a matter of time before someone is arrested for selling an ounce of dope.

Not because it's cannabis, but because it's an ounce.

Sincerely,
BERNARD COUGHLAN,
London W11. July 16

From Mr Stephen McClure

Sir, Could the downgrading of cannabis be considered as an example of joint sovereignty?

Yours faithfully,
STEPHEN McCLURE,
Dungannon, Co Tyrone. July 15

Gibraltar settlement

From Dr J. J. Nicholas

Sir, Some 20 years ago I was working in Gibraltar when there was a partial blockade at the Spanish border. An old Gibraltarian man talked to me about the situation. He thought that the Spanish Government were fools because he believed that instead of making life difficult, if they offered school and university places with bursaries and scholarships to Gibraltarian youth, within 20 years there would be a pro-Spanish middle class and the place would fall painlessly into Spanish hands.

They didn't and there isn't.

Yours faithfully,
J. J. NICHOLAS,
Exton, Southampton. July 16

Slow train to Fishguard

From Mr John S. Cox

Sir, As a railway enthusiast who has lived in South Wales for over 70 years, I was interested to read (report, July 10) about the London to Fishguard express which First Great Western has now seen fit to abandon owing to falling demand.

However, I am mystified by the claim that the distance travelled in the early days was 210 miles compared with 270 miles today.

Where have the extra 60 miles come from?

Yours sincerely,
JOHN S. COX,
Newport. July 11

From Dr Paul Hannah

Sir, It seems unlikely that the original report (July 10) of a London Fishguard journey of 210 miles would ever have been correct.

As the crow flies, Fishguard is 207 miles from Paddington and the rail route is nowhere near a straight line.

Yours sincerely,
PAUL HANNAH,
Chinnor, Oxfordshire. July 18

From Mr Patrick White

Sir, My copy of Bradshaw for 1910 may offer a partial explanation for the missing 60 miles in the London to Fishguard rail journey.

The timetable for Paddington to Fishguard shows a distance of 209 miles against Fishguard Harbour. The table for the return journey shows 286 miles against Paddington.

The difference is due to a note at the head of the first table which indicates "Miles from Swindon". The reason for this is that the table shows no details for stations between Paddington and Swindon, they being covered by the mainline London-Bristol table.

I still can't account for the remaining 17.

Yours faithfully,
PATRICK WHITE,
Warrington. July 24

Too stressed to eat

From Mr John G. Francis

Sir, After examining my cholesterol profile my doctor has told me that I should avoid eating cheese, butter, cream, eggs, liver and many other fatty and cholesterol-rich foods. Now I am told (T2, July 15) that I should not eat pasta, rice, bread or sugar.

For heaven's sake, someone please tell me what I am allowed to eat, before all this stress causes me to have a heart attack.
Yours sincerely,
JOHN G. FRANCIS,
Saxmundham, Suffolk. July 15

Reds under the beds?

From Mr L. E. Hudson
Sir, On July 15 your broadcasting section for this region described a TV programme as

How the KGB filmed their unsuspecting victims in uncompromising situations.

It's no wonder they lost.
Yours uncompromisingly,
L. E. HUDSON,
Exeter. July 16

Old words anew

From Mr John Nugee
Sir, Recently my nine-year-old son announced that his favourite activity was 'swell".

Crikey! This was considered a hopelessly old-fashioned word even in my schooldays. I wonder what other words from the past are about to reappear for a new lease of life?
Yours etc,
JOHN NUGEE,
New Malden, Surrey. July 16

From Mr Martin Griffith
Sir, Quaint words that the youth of today might resurrect and use?

How about "After you" or "Where is the back of the queue?"
Yours faithfully,
MARTIN GRIFFITH,
London EC4. July 23

Buzzing the Bard

From Mr Donald G. MacLean
Sir, The best place in London to spot helicopters seems to be from in front of the stage of Shakespeare's Globe Theatre.

I counted 17 during Sunday's frequently disturbed matinee performance of *Twelfth Night* and feel this must be something of a record.

I wonder if the Mayor of London has the power to make this a no-fly zone?
Yours faithfully,
DONALD G. MacLEAN,
Milton Keynes. July 22

Noms de plume

From Mrs Gilly Hendry
Sir, Our eldest is celebrating her 21st birthday by throwing a party and I have obeyed her instructions to address the invitations to her friends by the names they call each other. Sensitive parents, look away now.

For pretty Elizabeths, Susannahs, Carolines and Antonias I invariably wrote Bizzy, Soz, Caz and Teddy; in the case of the boys, the Alexanders, Jameses, Freddies and Henrys became Sydney/Ginga, Jamsie/Jimbo, Frank and, again, Teddy. And as to what they do to surnames . . .
Yours faithfully,
GILLY HENDRY,
North Berwick. July 17

Talk of the devil

From Mr David Wilson
Sir, According to your leading article today, Satan understands Welsh. Is that as a native speaker or an adult learner?
Yours faithfully,
DAVID WILSON,
Bridell, Cardigan. July 23

From Mr Gwyn ap Thomas Harrison
Sir, Mr David Wilson asks whether Satan understands Welsh as a native speaker or as an adult learner.

Almost certainly the latter; it was inevitable that Satan would have to learn the language, as how otherwise would he be able to follow what God says when He speaks in His native tongue?
Yours faithfully,
GWYN ap THOMAS HARRISON,
Porthaethwy. July 25

From Mr Erich Steiner

Sir, Satan may have got an "A" for Welsh, but this did not help him to follow what God said.

God speaks Yiddish.

Sincerely,
ERICH STEINER,
Exeter. July 29

Integrity in peril

From Mrs Veronica Goulder

Sir, How apposite that you should lead on the subject of infidelity in marriage (T2 and leading article, July 22) when the stock markets are reeling from the effects of dishonesty in business.

I don't believe that lack of personal integrity is any more sustainable than lack of corporate integrity – both eventually lead to deep confusion and generate instability, both personal and social. Webs are by their natures fragile, and deceit weaves the most fragile of all.

Yours sincerely,
VERONICA GOULDER,
Denmead, Hampshire. July 22

From Mr Jamie Wring

Sir, After infidelity, can we next expect "Thieving: the Top Ten tips"?

Yours faithfully,
JAMIE WRING,
Bristol. July 22

US war on Saddam

From Mr R. J. Cretan

Sir, You report that US Vice-President Dick Cheney "wants to use the end of Saddam's regime as a platform for wider reforms in the region".

Well, wider oil platforms, anyway.

Yours faithfully,
RICHARD CRETAN,
St Paul, Minnesota. July 18

Nelson's purse

From Commodore Malcolm Shirley, RN (retd)

Sir, The former curator of the National Maritime Museum rightly questions the provenance of Nelson artefacts, in particular the bloodstained purse containing a number of coins.

As most naval officers know, like the monarch admirals rarely carry money; mundane financial matters are dealt with by flag lieutenants or subordinates.

Indeed, many admirals of today seem never to have any cash on them when it's their round.

Yours etc,
MALCOLM SHIRLEY,
London SW8. July 23

From Lieutenant-Colonel J. G. Wishart (retd)

Sir, Unlike Commodore Malcolm Shirley I have never met an admiral but I can vouch for the fact that when in the company of generals I have found that, irrespective of the lack or otherwise of cash in their pockets, their signatures alone are sufficient to buy a round of drinks.

Yours sincerely,
J. G. WISHART,
Milton of Balgonie, Glenrothes. July 26.

Better red than dead

From Mr Justin Coleman

Sir, A shire council in Brisbane is painting all koalas killed by motorists bright red and leaving them by the road as a warning.

Would it not make more sense to paint the creatures before any potential accident?

Yours faithfully,
JUSTIN COLEMAN,
Cambridge. July 25

Not-so-near miss

From Mr Chris Taylor

Sir, An asteroid is on course to collide with Earth in 2019 (report and leading article, July 25) – but the experts say not to worry, their calculations are probably wrong.

Perhaps we should know about those they believe will miss us?

Yours faithfully,
CHRIS TAYLOR,
Lincoln. July 26

From Mr Stephen Williams

Sir, In view of the lack of urgency shown by the Department for Environment, Food and Rural Affairs over the recent foot-and-mouth outbreak, is it too late to let them know that I might be hit by an asteroid in 2019, and ask for advice as to what I should be doing about it?
Yours etc,
STEPHEN WILLIAMS,
Saffron Walden, Essex. July 25

Action this day

From Rear-Admiral J. P. W. Middleton, RN (retd)

Sir, After 48 years of fairly continuous employment, I have just retired.

My working colleagues ask incredulously: "What are you going to do?" My retired friends seek to reassure me: "I've never been so busy."

This preoccupation with activity seems a singularly British trait. In Italy, I feel sure, a similar announcement would be greeted with cries of "Bravo! Is your hammock comfortable? Is your cellar sufficient?"

Personally, I do not plan to overdo it in retirement. However, I might try a few more letters to *The Times.*
Yours faithfully,
PATRICK MIDDLETON,
Chilmark, Wiltshire. July 24

From Mr Brian Bartram

Sir, Rear-Admiral J. P. W. Middleton set out the difference between retirement in Italy, with its laid-back culture, and retirement in Britain with its keep-busy culture. My Italian wife and I recently decided to try Italian retirement.

There were concerts in the piazza and in the restored abbey and castle, art and sightseeing of prehistoric, Greek, Roman, medieval and more modern attractions, the beach, excellent food and wine, friends and relatives etc, to cope with.

We have had to come back to London for a rest.
Yours faithfully,

BRIAN BARTRAM,
Southgate, London N14. July 28

Emergency address

From Mr Michael Bird

Sir, In sharp contrast to the patient who complained that an ambulanceman had called him mate (report, later editions, July 26), my last conscious act after dialling 999, and just before slumping to the floor, will be to clutch to my bosom a large sign:

"Dear ambulance driver, Call me Sir, mate, love, ducky or Your Majesty as you wish – but get me to the hospital on time!"
Yours etc,
MICHAEL BIRD,
London SW13. July 26

From Mr Eduard Fuller

Sir, Were I ill enough to require the services of an ambulance I believe I should welcome any term of endearment, although I can understand why Mr Alan Drake, the Lancashire ambulance education and training officer, might object to being called "duck".
Sincerely,
EDUARD FULLER,
Gillingham, Dorset. July 26

From Dr J. Darling

Sir, I am pleased when ambulancemen address me with a term of endearment: they often do.
Yours faithfully,
JANIE DARLING,
South Molton, Devon. July 27

Lessons in integrity

From Mr Sebastian Santa-Cruz

Sir, In Chile we have spent the last 25 years learning how to run enterprises "the Anglo-Saxon way" in a serious effort to escape the tarred Latin American image of corrupt practices exemplified by the behaviour of the region's larger and richer countries.

With dismay we now learn that the great corporate US has been spending a long time

learning how to cheat and steal the Latin American way.
Yours sincerely,
SEBASTIAN SANTA-CRUZ,
Santiago, Chile. July 24

Paper trail

From Mr Neil Kennedy
Sir, My wife reaches pensionable age this year. Consequently, this summer has largely been spent filling in forms.

Despite having twice submitted passport photocopies, as requested, duly signed by a solicitor, she has, so far, received three letters, stating that she will not receive her due benefits, because she does not have a birth certificate which, in a lamentably uncharacteristic lapse of efficiency, was not issued to her, in the Japanese internment camp, where she was born.

I am optimistic that British efficiency will eventually prevail.
I remain, Yours truly,
NEIL R. KENNEDY,
Althorne, Essex, July 26

The new Simpsons

From Mr Stephen Schick
Sir, In the report (July 22) that the Duke and Duchess of Devonshire are prepared to break the law by allowing hunting on their land it is mentioned that the duchess is one of the Mitford sisters. Alongside this report is another with the headline "Search for eccentric family to rival the Simpsons". Is any further search really necessary?
Yours faithfully
STEPHEN SCHICK,
London SW3. July 22

Foods of the world

From Mr Tom Parker
Sir, The label on the front of my jar of Dijon mustard says, reassuringly, "Produit de France". The one on the back reads "Imported in RSA by Patleys (Pty) Ltd, 68 Whitworth Rd, Heriotdale, Johannesburg".

I bought the jar in my local Tesco.
Is this what is meant by globalisation?
Yours faithfully,
TOM PARKER,
Sutton Courtenay, Oxfordshire. July 28

From Mr Michael Banister
Sir, I recently won a raffle prize of a case of wine. The front labels on the bottles say it comes from California (no particular district specified) but the back labels say it was bottled in Italy.

I can report that it does not seem to have travelled well.
Yours faithfully,
MICHAEL BANISTER,
Solihull, West Midlands. July 30

Tory attitudes on sexual preference

From Mr Philip Levy
Sir, The crunch time for tolerance in this country will be when gays and lesbians can openly admit they are Conservatives.
Yours sincerely,
PHILIP LEVY,
London EC4. July 30

Marathon men

From His Honour Judge Michael Baker
Sir, You report on the slowest marathon time in the history of the Commonwealth Games – three hours, 30 minutes and 20 seconds. However, the competitor, Jamie Donaldson of the Norfolk Islands, should take heart. He will have given pleasure and satisfaction to many past and present marathon runners. If a thing's worth doing, it's worth doing badly.
Yours faithfully
MICHAEL BAKER
(London Marathon 1984 – three hours, 28 minutes and 11 seconds),
St Albans, Hertfordshire. July 30

Also known as . . .

From the Reverend Janet H. Fife
Sir, On my arrival here two years ago I

opened a new account with a gas supplier, carefully spelling out my name and title. Accounts arrived addressed to "Mrs J. Face". It took four letters from me to get the name (but not the title) right, at which point I gave up.

Recently I changed to a different supplier and promptly got a letter from the old one, asking me to reconsider. It was addressed to "Dear Occupier". I replied saying that their continued inefficiency in the matter of my name was one of the reasons for my leaving them.

Yesterday I received another letter inviting me to pay my (now non-existent) bills by direct debit. It was addressed to "Mr Pend Incomplete".
Yours,
JANET H. FIFE,
Macclesfield. July 28

From Mrs A. Barbara Ensor
Sir, I once received a brochure from a respectable travel company, the envelope of which was addressed to "Mrs Out to Lunch Ensor".

I still don't understand it.
Yours faithfully,
A. BARBARA ENSOR,
Thurleigh. August 1

From Dr Edward Young
Sir, The Reverend Janet Fife has my sympathy. I recently received from my insurance company, in an envelope marked "Private", a letter which began "Dear Dr Private Edward Young". Two days after phoning to point out the mistake, I received the following reply in the post:
We note that your name is now Dr Edward Young, not Dr Private Edward Young. All our records will be updated once you confirm this for us in writing with a certified copy of your driving licence or the appropriate identification.

After Janet Fife's experiences, I am hesitant about continuing this dialogue.
Yours sincerely,
EDWARD YOUNG,
Earley, Berkshire. August 2

Rare confessions

From Mr Michael J. C. Wilson
Sir, Does nobody confess their guilt any more?

I was brought up in a world where villains would (allegedly) say: "All right guvnor; it was a fair cop." Nowadays it seems that, like Jill Dando's killer (reports, July 30), every convicted person protests their innocence, and that the legal system has let them down.
Yours faithfully,
MICHAEL J. C. WILSON,
Market Weighton, York. July 30

From Dr Robert M. Bruce-Chwatt
Sir, I recently received some advice from an old lag as a "thank you" for the cigarette that I had just given him: "Never admit anything, always deny everything and always make counter-allegations".

Fortunately I have, so far, not had any use for this counsel.
Yours etc,
ROBERT BRUCE-CHWATT
(Forensic medical examiner),
Richmond-upon-Thames. August 3

George's hepatologist

From Mr Brian Ingham
Sir, How appropriate that George Best's physician, Professor Roger Williams, should, according to your report today, be Director of the Institute of Herpetology (the study of, among others, newts).
Yours faithfully,
BRIAN INGHAM,
Eggleston, Co Durham. July 31

Keep Frinton star-free

From Mr David R. Ball
Sir, It's not "dull, conservative Frinton-on-Sea" that has changed since the 1920s (Weekend, July 27) but the common perception of what is "stylish and smart". Compare your photographs of Douglas Fairbanks and his wife Mary Pickford, who owned a house there, with today's stars.

The last sentence says it all: ". . . can anyone imagine this town . . . seeing the likes of Brad Pitt and Jennifer Aniston popping down for a paddle?" That is why it remains such a pleasant and popular place in which to live.
Yours faithfully,
DAVID R. BALL,
Frinton-on-Sea. July 30

History quiz

From Mr John Peter Hudson
Sir, I enjoyed your history quiz (T2, July 31), but the answer to "When was Magna Carta signed?" is "never". It was, of course, sealed in 1215 on behalf of King John, who may well have read French, but is not known to have been able to write and, in common with most, though not all, lay people of high status at the time, is unlikely to have known Latin.
Yours faithfully,
JOHN PETER HUDSON,
Middleton Stoney, Oxfordshire. July 31

A question of faith

From the Reverend John Latham
Sir, A survey allegedly shows women clergy to be a bit dodgy on the belief front (report, July 31). If you observe who did the survey ("the traditionalist think-tank Cost of Conscience") one can hear the unspoken message: "And what can one expect, dear boy? Not really up to the job, are they?"
 Enough of this mischievous, divisive, sexist swiping, for God's sake!
Yours sincerely,
JOHN LATHAM,
Market Harborough, Leicestershire. July 31

From the Reverend John Hartley
Sir, When you leaked the name of the new Archbishop of Canterbury, I told a female colleague, to which she replied: "Ah, but you can't believe what you read in *The Times*."
 I deduce that women priests are, as you

report, more sceptical than their male counterparts.
Yours sincerely,
JOHN HARTLEY,
Bradford. August 1

Disparate measures

From Mr Paul Downham
Sir, I was alarmed to read your description of the Silverpit meteor crater off the Yorkshire coast (report and graphic, August 1) as one and a quarter Canary Wharfs deep and 330 buses across. Surely a feature like this should be measured in the more traditional unit of football pitches? In any event, when you use buses for widths, it is well known that you must measure heights in Nelson's Columns.
Yours faithfully,
PAUL DOWNHAM,
Huntingdon, Cambridgeshire, August 1

From Mr Derek Dainton
Sir, 330 London buses? Even under Ken Livingstone's transport plan, this many in one place stretches the imagination.
Yours faithfully,
DEREK DAINTON,
Findon, West Sussex. August 1

Telephone paternity

From Mr Mark Solon
Sir, My 14-month-old son, Hugo, now calls all telephones "Daddy". Does this indicate that I am working too hard?
Yours faithfully,
MARK SOLON,
London EC1. August 2

Beyond the pale

From Dr Alan B. Shrank
Sir, Last week my wife went to Marks & Spencer to buy some strawberries. Packets marked "British" had a Union Flag symbol but those marked "Scottish" had no flag.
 Today my sister tried to board a Ryanair flight from Stansted to Glasgow, and was

refused because she did not have a passport. Her driving licence was also refused as a means of identification.

Has secession actually taken place?
Yours sincerely,
ALAN B. SHRANK,
Shrewsbury. August 1

At cross purposes

From Mr Mark Thomas

Sir, A law student who represented himself has obtained £30,000 from Wolverhampton University after alleging that the teaching on his law course was not up to scratch (report, August 1). Surely a paradox?
Yours faithfully,
MARK THOMAS,
Ware, Hertfordshire. August 2

Quite sure?

From Mr Michael I. Gee

Sir, In his review of *Don Giovanni* (August 1) Robert Thicknesse refers to "inter-gender relations". Is that something new, or just a new name for an age-old concept?
Yours faithfully,
MIKE GEE,
London NW3. August 1

I'm in the sauna

From Mr Rowlinson Carter

Sir, Entering the sauna at the local leisure centre recently, I joined a woman who was trying to use her mobile phone. Is no haven safe from these things?
Yours faithfully,
ROWLINSON CARTER,
Lewes. August 3

From Mr Steven Pollard

Sir, Perhaps the lady using her mobile phone in the sauna when Mr Carter came in was trying to alert security.
Yours,
STEVEN POLLARD,
Pertenhall, Bedfordshire. August 6

Rodent confidence

From Mr R. G. Pringle

Sir, The steady increase of the rat population (News in Brief, August 1) is reassuring.

Despite indications to the contrary, Britain is not a sinking ship.
Yours faithfully,
R. G. PRINGLE,
Shrewsbury. August 1

From Mrs Ann Mitchell

Sir, A novel method of reducing the rat population was reported from Jakarta in 1986 (*The Times*, July 3, 1986). A village chief in West Java was charging couples ten dead rats to get married and 25 for a divorce. Rightly, a marriage was cheaper than a divorce, but both might have been difficult for the squeamish.
Yours faithfully,
ANN MITCHELL,
Edinburgh. August 7

Cyclists and motorists

From Mr John Butterworth

Sir, Instead of the European Commission insisting that motorists are made responsible for all accidents involving cyclists (report, later editions, August 5), would it not be preferable to ensure that all cyclists have their own insurance, as well as lights that work and are visible front and back.
Yours faithfully,
J. D. BUTTERWORTH,
Esher. August 5

Butchers' signs

From Ms Jennifer North

Sir, In Who Said What (Weekend, August 3), you mention a butcher's sign relating to *Watership Down*: "You've read the book. You've seen the film. Now try the stew."

Several years ago, a delightfully illustrated version used to hang in our Chelsea butcher's window: "You've read the book, you've seen the film, now eat the cast."
Yours faithfully,

JENNIFER NORTH,
London SW1. August 4

Stars in their eyes

From the Reverend R. Wood

Sir, Jonathan Meades (Comment, August 3) wonders how Dave Davies of The Kinks came to be David Davis, the former chairman of the Conservative Party. I was surprised that Alan Clark's diaries made no mention of his years as Allan Clarke with The Hollies.
Yours faithfully,
RON WOOD (Not the Rolling Stone),
Salisbury, Wiltshire. August 3

A good walk spoiled

From Sheriff Neil Gow

Sir, Although most US Presidents since the First World War have been golfers (report, August 6), not all have been top-class players. Standing on the first tee while playing in a charity exhibition match with partner Bob Hope, President Gerald Ford had to smile when the comedian quipped to the waiting press gallery: "The President won't announce which course he's playing until he's hit his first shot".
Yours sincerely,
NEIL GOW,
Prestwick Golf Club, Ayrshire. August 6

Membership query

From Mr F. E. B. Witts

Sir, What is the difference between "a member of the public" and "a member of the general public", and who is a member of neither?
Yours faithfully,
FRANCIS WITTS,
Cheltenham. August 7

From Canon Donald Gray

Sir, Francis Witts is mystified as to when the public become general. The late Derek Nimmo told me his mother and a friend once arrrived at Chester Cathedral for evensong and discovered it was to be an army occasion. Confronted by a stern military personage, Mrs Nimmo's companion apologetically explained they were merely "general public". The announcement earned them a smart salute and the prompt allocation of a front row seat.

Derek opined that it was a good job they had not told him they were "private persons", or who knows to what remote and dark corner of the church they would have been assigned.
Yours faithfully,
DONALD GRAY,
Stamford, Lincolnshire. August 12

Unwanted information

From Mrs Jane Cullinan

Sir, My husband's habit of reading aloud to me snippets from his newpaper whilst I am trying to concentrate on my own was extremely irritating.

It was, however, a day at the beach compared with his latest habit – reading aloud the error messages from the computer screen.
Yours faithfully,
JANE CULLINAN,
Padstow, Cornwall. August 5

From Professor Ian M. Mills, FRS

Sir, My wife, who usually shares the feelings of Jane Cullinan when I read aloud to her snippets from *The Times*, was nonetheless delighted when I read aloud to her Mrs Cullinan's letter.

This shows the fickle nature of women.
Yours faithfully,
IAN MILLS,
Reading. August 12

From Mrs Dorothy Goldman

Sir, Far worse things may await Mrs Jane Cullinan and the wife of Professor Ian Mills than their husbands' habit of reading snippets from *The Times* to them.

In response to my request that he stop doing so, my husband now underlines, annotates and even occasionally cross-references items.

This letter appearing should give him a field day.

Yours faithfully,
DOROTHY GOLDMAN,
Cowbeech, East Sussex. August 14

From Mrs Christine Farrow

Sir, Mrs Cullinan should be thankful she has only one set of interruptions to contend with. I am bombarded with snippets from my teenage daughter and son as well as my husband.

The thing to do is enlarge the subject with a nice discussion. There will soon be no further trouble.

Yours faithfully,
CHRISTINE FARROW,
Christchurch, Dorset. August 14

From Mrs Lesley Russell

Sir, My husband finds my chuckling and quietly nodding, and then not reading out the snippet which has caught my fancy, much more irritating.

Yours,
LESLEY RUSSELL,
Upavon, Wiltshire. August 14

From Mr Andrew Wolfin

Sir, Imagine my unwilling listeners' surprise when they discover that today's newspaper snippet that I choose (irritatingly) to read aloud should come from my own letter!

Yours faithfully,
ANDREW WOLFIN,
London NW4. August 16

From Mr A. J. Killoran

Sir, My partner used to listen when I read out snippets from the paper, but now just makes one of three "Hmm" sounds.

The first, "Hmmm?" on a slight crescendo, I take to mean "What's that?". The second, a short, even-toned, barked "Hm" means "Really?/I agree/Dreadful!/How could they?" etc. The final "Hmmm" is a descending tone and indicates "How funny/Well I never" etc.

As I do not feel the pearls I cast are fully appreciated in this way, I now cut out the amusing items and post them to my parents. Of course, I have no idea if they read them.

Sincerely,
A. J. KILLORAN,
Bristol. August 20

Sign of summer

From Mr Charles Hennessy

Sir, Visitors to this country confused by the weather patterns may care to be reminded of a helpful formula: it is summer in England when there is no "r" in the month.

Yours seasonably,
CHARLES HENNESSY,
London SW7. August 10

Lorna McDoone

From Mr R. J. Carlyon

Sir, T2 Films Choice (August 12) refers to *Lorna Doone* as R. D. Blackmore's ripping yarn about "class war and land feuds in 17th-century Scotland", noting that the production "sacrifices authenticity for spectacle".

How does it achieve this? By filming it on Exmoor, perhaps?

Yours sincerely,
R. J. CARLYON,
Somerton, Somerset. August 12

From Judge Roger Cooke

Sir, *Lorna Doone* may not have been set in Scotland but the story certainly had Scottish connections. The Doones were believed to be a Scottish "extended family" who migrated to a remote part of Exmoor in the 17th century. The name Lorna is said to have been invented by R. D. Blackmore with deliberate echoes of the country of Lorne in the West Highlands.

Yours faithfully,
ROGER COOKE,
London W1N. August 15

Testing cricket

From Professor Norman Hammond

Sir, As I watched the dramatic end of the

Test match at Trent Bridge today, with a cheerful and cheering crowd backing both India and England, it struck me, not for the first time, that Lord Tebbit is wrong: the true mark of Britishness is backing any cricket team with civilised enthusiasm.
Your obedient servant,
NORMAN HAMMOND,
Cambridge. August 12

From Mr John Hess
Sir, Who can blame the Trent Bridge faithful for deserting their seats during the on-off Test match? Watching international cricket has been spoilt by oversensitive rulings by umpires on when to stop play because of bad light.

It is time to use floodlights for the five-day game to guarantee uninterrupted play. Surely the fans and broadcasters would welcome such a move.
Yours sincerely,
JOHN B. HESS,
Nottingham. August 11

Easy terms for lawyers

From Mr Peter Harding-Roberts
Sir, You report that the Lord Chief Justice wants to modernise legal language, removing Latin terms. However, he cannot think of a modern term for doing a case "pro bono".

Perhaps he would like to consider calling such cases "freebies". That is what we have always called such work in my practice.
Yours faithfully,
PETER HARDING-ROBERTS (Solicitor),
Cardiff. August 12

Weather or not

From Mr Andrew A. Fyall
Sir, I am always puzzled by the section of The Weather which is headed "Hours of Darkness". It then lists "Sun rises" and "Sun sets". Am I missing something?
Yours faithfully,
ANDREW A. FYALL,
Bronwydd, Carmarthen. August 13

Easy terms for lawyers

From Mr Douglas Youngson
Sir, I may have the answer to the puzzle raised by Mr Andrew Fyall. As has been remarked before in these columns, The Times weather map on a suitably sunny day shows the sun seeming to cast a shadow. This is perhaps why the hours between sunrise and sunset are referred to as "Hours of Darkness".
Yours,
DOUGLAS YOUNGSON,
Prestwick, Ayrshire. August 15

From Mr Barry Knight
Sir, When are you arranging for the sea state "calm" to be removed from your weather maps? I've yet to see it feature in your forecasts – it seems to be only for ironic effect.
Yours faithfully,
BARRY KNIGHT,
Gillingham, Kent. August 16

From Ms Sonia Francis
Sir, This correspondence reminded me of comments by an American guest of mine. "I don't know why you British waste so much time debating the weather," he said.

"You only need to use one short forecast and it would cover everything."

The forecast? "It might rain."

Yours, with umbrella always packed,
SONIA FRANCIS,
Isleworth, Middlesex. August 17

From Mr Michael Hindley

Sir, One of my early flying instructors advised me to view all forecasts with suspicion. Meteorology, he pointed out, can be affected very badly by the weather.
Yours faithfully,
MICHAEL HINDLEY,
Andover, Hampshire. August 21

From Mrs Sylvia Crookes

Sir, Our brass band were to play in the Friary Gardens, Richmond, at 3pm last Sunday "or if wet in Town Hall".

At 2.30 it was cloudy; at 2.45 it drizzled. The euphoniums and drums gathered in the gardens but I, with the other horns and the cornets, opted for the town hall, some 300 yards away.

At 2.55 the sun came out.

You need to be able to sprint, to play in a band, in an English summer.
Yours,
SYLVIA CROOKES,
Bainbridge, North Yorkshire. August 21

From Mr Brian Lewis

Sir, You report that the Safeway supermarket group is paying up to £100,000 a year for accurate weather forecasts to aid stock control. Does this mean that the rest of us are being given second-class weather forecasts? If so, it explains a lot.
Yours sincerely,
BRIAN LEWIS,
Bicester. August 22

Vote for nobody

From Mr Alex Folkes

Sir, Great! If a ballot paper included a "none of the above" box (report, August 13) I could vote for nobody rather than just a nobody.
Yours faithfully,

ALEX FOLKES,
London SE15. August 13

Capital idea

From Lord Brightman

Sir, The Bank of England wants inflation to rise to 2.5 per cent (Business, August 14). Can some financial expert explain to me the difference between inflation at 2.5 per cent and clipping the coinage by 2.5 per cent, the punishment for which formerly included being hanged, drawn and quartered?
Yours faithfully,
BRIGHTMAN,
House of Lords. August 14

King or saint?

From Mr Larry Belling

Sir, August 16 is the 25th anniversary of the death of Elvis. It is also the Feast Day of Saint Rock. Is this just a coincidence?
Yours sincerely,
LARRY BELLING,
London W1. August 15

Boys and A levels

From Professor Emeritus Philip Stott

Sir, Do no boys achieve A levels these days? I have trawled today's press for pictures of a lad celebrating his grades, but have found only a sorority of success. *The Times* has no fewer than nine young ladies perusing their passes. I did uncover one cartoon of a spotty youth – failing!
Yours faithfully,
PHILIP STOTT,
Gravesend, Kent. August 16

Football posters

From Ms Alison Smith

Sir, While I was very pleased to receive a copy of the gargantuan Premiership poster which accompanied Saturday, August 10's *Times*, it has proved difficult to accommodate within the minuscule office space which I share with six football-loathing colleagues.

Perhaps in the future the Premiership should be reduced in size.

Yours faithfully,
ALISON SMITH,
Galashiels, Selkirkshire. August 13

Bumper crop

From Mr Frederick Percival Brown

Sir, This year was an exception for we had no frost in spring. On my 25-year old, 20ft-high Victoria plum few leaves grew, but after flowering – the blossom was profuse – the plums developed in unbelievable masses. They are now beginning to turn purple, and hang as thick as grapes in pendulous masses up to three and four feet long.

One by one the branches have snapped under the weight, and hang by half the bark's width, yet somehow the sap still flows and the plums are still enlarging.

Should the tree survive it will need pruning back to approximately 10-ft high, when, and if, the plums ripen sufficiently to be picked and eaten.

Yours sincerely,
F. P. BROWN,
Salisbury, Wiltshire. August 18

From Mr Gerard van Dam

Sir, Mr Frederick Brown may not need to wait to harvest his fruit. I once had a Victoria plum tree and found birds were pecking lumps out of the still unripe plums. In desperation I picked them all and put them in bowls. They ripened perfectly and were delicious.

Yours faithfully,
GERARD van DAM,
Oxford. August 19

From Mr Antony Crookston

Sir, Gerard van Dam's success in ripening prematurely picked plums offers a ray of hope with regard to the Chinese Duck Pears which I bought eight weeks ago at a leading supermarket marked "Display until 25 June".

Two months later they are still as hard as cannonballs.

Yours faithfully,
ANTONY CROOKSTON,
Waterlooville. August 23

Divine intervention

From Mr James Young

Sir, "I was well bored" is described as a "soap opera solecism" (report, August 17). I was reminded of the almighty (literally) howler in Matthew xvii, 5 (Authorised Version) when a voice from Heaven introduces His "beloved Son, in whom I am well pleased".

Yours faithfully,
JAMES YOUNG,
London N1. August 18

Islamic rallies

From Mrs Olga E. Lockley

Sir, I was surprised to learn that the Islamic rally planned in London for August 25 had been refused permission by the Greater London Authority on the grounds that it could cause offence to Jews and homosexuals.

Are people who do not fit into either of these categories precluded from being caused offence?

Yours faithfully,
OLGA E. LOCKLEY,
Preston. August 13

Advice for tIDS

From Dr Julia Matthews

Sir, The breakaway Conservatives want to call themselves the "Start Again Party" (report and Comment, August 14): self-styled Saps seems very suitable.

Yours etc,
JULIA MATTHEWS,
Bexleyheath, Kent. August 19

Stormy days

From Mrs Sally Pinfold

Sir, Richard Morrison's recollection of the

sunny South East may well be accurate ("The year we lost our cool", Weekend, August 17), but in Warwickshire banks of black clouds were building up on Saturday, August 28, 1976. By late morning it was blustery, by midday it was raining. I remember it well as it was my wedding day.

I wondered at the time if it was an omen. A number of years later, receiving my decree absolute on a sunny day, I reflected that it probably was.

Yours faithfully,
SALLY PINFOLD,
Leamington Spa, Warwickshire. August 19

From Mrs Julie Graham

Sir, I read with some amusement the letter from Mrs Sally Pinfold about the probable omen of marrying on a wet day and receiving a decree absolute on a sunny one.

I married on September 3 (the date war was declared) and received my decree absolute on May 8 (VE Day).

Yours faithfully,
JULIE GRAHAM,
Withington, Manchester. August 23

100 great Britons

From Mr R. B. L. Fitzwilliams

Sir, Michael Gove gives a generous reception to the BBC's poll of the 100 greatest Britons (report, August 22). Yet apart from Lloyd George he omits the inadequate selection of politicians. Margaret Thatcher is obviously included but Tony Benn, Aneurin Bevan and Enoch Powell hardly belong in a list which stretches back to Alfred the Great.

Gladstone and Disraeli, the political giants of the 19th century and Pitt the Younger, whose exertions helped save us from Napoleonic invasion, ought to be automatic choices but are unaccountably absent.

George Bernard Shaw once said "I despise Shakespeare when I measure my mind against his . . ." yet is excluded, preference being given to Boy George and Aleister Crowley. If GBS was alive he'd turn in his grave.

Yours faithfully,
RICHARD B. L. FITZWILLIAMS
(Editor, *The International Who's Who*, 1975–2001),
London NW11. August 22

From Mr Robert Richardson

Sir, You report that "Chaucer and J. K. Rowling . . . are the only writers on the list" of the top 100 Britons.

Jane Austen, Shakespeare, Dickens and Tolkien were presumably included for their legendary stamp collections.

Yours faithfully,
ROBERT RICHARDSON,
Old Hatfield, Hertfordshire. August 23

From Mrs Marjorie Papworth

Sir, Why is there no mention of Harold Wilson in your list of great Britons? His introduction of the Open University must have brought more happiness and sense of achievement to more people than under most other Prime Ministers.

The Open University embraces all religions, races and abilities and gives a second chance to anyone who cares to take it. Why are not all those who have taken this second chance voting for Harold Wilson?

Yours earnestly,
MARJORIE PAPWORTH,
Godalming, Surrey. August 24

From Mr David Diprose

Sir, What does it say about BBC viewers that the 1st Duke of Marlborough fails to appear in their list of 100 greatest Britons. If I were the BBC, I would not boast about this list.

Yours faithfully,
DAVID DIPROSE,
Exeter. August 26

From Detective Constable Simon Muggleton

Sir, Why no mention of Air Chief Marshal Lord Dowding?

Without him there would be no list.

Yours faithfully,
SIMON MUGGLETON,
Lewes, East Sussex. August 24

One in the public eye

From Mr Andrew Love

Sir, I do not know which I find more depressing: that David Beckham believes that his story is worth telling; that someone deems it to be worth £2 million (report, August 22); or that, when published, it will undoubtedly be a bestseller.

Yours,

ANDREW LOVE,

Pocklington, East Yorkshire. August 22

Unreliable workmen

From Mr Thomas Fleming

Sir, Having wasted another day waiting for a tradesman to do highly paid work in my home, I was struck by the need for a list of unreliable workmen.

If supported by reports from dissatisfied customers, it would help people to avoid wasting time and money on tradesmen who do not turn up and do not carry out the work they are paid to do. I suggest that such a list should be displayed in public libraries.

Yours faithfully,

THOMAS W. FLEMING,

Warminster, Wiltshire. August 23

From Mr Chris Gatter

Sir, As a tradesman I fully support Mr Thomas Fleming's suggestion about lists of unreliable workmen.

Will he also support another list to be displayed in public libraries giving details of customers who are rude, untidy, bad and late payers, and those unable to distinguish between a good and a bad piece of workmanship?

Yours faithfully,

CHRIS GATTER,

Budleigh Salterton, Devon. August 26

Humans welcome

From Miss Christine Moulie

Sir, A friend of mine sent a fax to a hotel in the French Pyrenees, asking if his dog would be allowed to stay at the hotel. The reply was to the effect:

I have been a hotelier for 25 years. I have never seen a dog steal an ashtray or a spoon, or burn the sheets with a cigarette. I never had to call the police for a dog being drunk and disorderly and a dog has never been rude to the staff. That's the reason why I always welcome dogs.

PS. You, too are welcome, should you decide to accompany your dog.

Yours faithfully,

CHRISTINE MOULIE,

London NW6. August 24

Children's cookery

From Mrs Juliet Raynes

Sir, Mr Malcolm Richardson suggests that the poor diet of US children is being adopted by US parents. In France children are expected to follow an adult diet.

My child has a four-course lunch at school. A typical menu might comprise grated carrot vinaigrette; chicken cordon bleu with rice and green beans; Camembert and bread; and pear.

My daughter is three.

Yours faithfully,

JULIET RAYNES,

Paris. August 23

Sitting comfortably

From Mr R. J. Jones

Sir, I have noticed that as soon as someone reaches 50 they always emit a satisfied sigh when sitting down. This doesn't seem to happen with pre-50-year-olds.

Yours faithfully,

ROBERT JONES,

West Malling, Kent. August 26

From Mr Neville Denson

Sir, I fear Robert Jones is mistaken. The sigh that over 50s emit when sitting down is not satisfied but wistful, since you feel you could be doing this for the last time and may never rise from the sitting position.

Yours sincerely,

NEVILLE DENSON,
St Bees, Cumbria. August 28

From Mr Bernard Norris
Sir, I hope Mr Jones lives long enough to agree with me that the over-70s sigh even more contentedly when we stand up.
Yours faithfully,
BERNARD NORRIS,
Storrington, West Sussex. August 28

From Mrs Deborah Atkinson
Sir, I must disagree with Mr Jones. Everyone in our family, including our 18-year-old son, emits a satisfied sigh upon sitting down.
   However, it is only the over-50s in the household who emit a painful wince upon rising from their seat, and then perform their first few steps bent double.
Yours faithfully,
DEBORAH ATKINSON,
Southport, Merseyside. August 28

From Mr Trevor Openshaw
Sir, Having identified the "satisfied sigh" syndrome at 50, Robert Jones should be aware that it will be joined, in a few years, by the "undignified grunt" condition when one tries to get up again.
Yours faithfully,
TREVOR OPENSHAW,
Ferndown, Dorset. August 28

From Mr Nigel Denton
Sir, There was I, at the advanced age of 55, thinking that the fact that I could get up from an armchair without using my hands was a sign of youth.
Yours faithfully,
NIGEL L. DENTON,
Littlehampton, West Sussex. August 28

From Mr Robert Dolan
Sir, I may be old before my time.
   Not only do I tend to sigh upon sitting down, but a similar sound is often to be heard after the first sip of a cup of tea.
Yours etc,
ROBERT DOLAN (Age 21),
Urchfont, Wiltshire. August 28

From Mr Gordon Skilling
Sir, The satisfied sigh in sitting is as nothing compared to the sob as the wife asks you to do something just as you pass the point of no return.
Yours aye,
R. G. SKILLING,
Guildford, Surrey. August 28

Longer shelf life

From Mr Peter Maskell
Sir, You report (Business, August 26) that more copies of the Ikea catalogue will be distributed this year than of the Bible. But there are already billions of copies of the Bible in homes throughout the world and, unlike the catalogue, it will not be out of date in a year and require replacement.
Yours faithfully,
PETER J. MASKELL,
Solihull. August 26

Single yolks

From Mrs P. C. Bloncourt
Sir, How did eggs manage to escape decimalisation? Living alone, four a week would suit me but no supermarket here sells them loose.
Yours faithfully,
P. C. BLONCOURT,
London W4. August 28

From Mrs Daphne Shillingford
Sir, Mrs P. C. Bloncourt has trouble buying loose eggs. Perhaps she could find a farmers' market. Here in Wells I can buy three or four eggs per week at a fair price per egg. My daughter, who lives in South London, has the same friendly service from her local farmers' market.
Yours faithfully,
DAPHNE SHILLINGFORD,
Wells, Somerset. September 1

Callers waiting

From Mr Dougall Clark
Sir, I have just spent a morning being told by charming ladies that their companies

appreciate my business, that they are very busy but they will answer my call as soon as possible. Why can't the banks, insurance firms, travel companies and all who employ these ladies alter their systems to tell their callers where they are in the queue?

We could then decide whether it was worth waiting and, if we did, would be in a much better temper when our call is eventually answered.

Yours faithfully,
DOUGALL CLARK,
Taunton, Somerset. August 29

From Mr John Chambers

Sir, It is certainly helpful when a telephone call handling system announces your position in the queue. When I learnt that I was 14th in the queue for immigration advice I decided to wait, as I had something else to do while waiting. By noting the times when I moved up the queue I could build up a picture of what was happening at the other end.

I inferred that there was only one person answering calls, that they gave as much time as needed to each caller, that they dealt with one call taking over 35 minutes (or took a break), and that, on average, they handled seven calls an hour. However, after two hours, when I was first in the queue, I also discovered that some telephone systems automatically terminate calls after two hours to limit charges when, for example, callers have left the phone off the hook. An expensive lesson.

Yours faithfully,
JOHN CHAMBERS,
Tadworth, Surrey. September 4

Keeping in touch

From Mr Rodney Bennett-England

Sir, Driving from Sloane Square, SW1, to World's End yesterday (about a mile), I counted 23 people using mobile telephones. Nine were motorists at the wheel, six mothers with prams, two cyclists, five pedestrians (two on zebra crossings) and one a bus conductress standing on the

platform and holding the rail whilst she nattered.

Who said the art of conversation is dead?
Yours faithfully,
RODNEY BENNETT-ENGLAND
(Honorary Treasurer), The Chartered Institute of Journalists, London SE16. August 23

America's isolated stance against Iraq

From Mr Tony Wilson

Sir, If Donald Rumsfeld wishes to associate President Bush's position over Iraq with Churchill before the Second World War he might reasonably expect some support from the UK some time in 2005.
Yours faithfully,
TONY WILSON,
Sheffield. August 29

The right wine glass

From Professor David Weitzman

Sir, You report this morning that merlot from a bordeaux glass appears to taste mellower than that from a Martini glass because of the effect of greater oxidation in the former receptacle, and explain this in terms of the larger surface area with which the wine comes into contact with air.

Despite the early hour, I have just now poured a goodly measure of a modest merlot into a Martini glass and measured the area of the top surface. I then transferred the contents into a typical bordeaux glass and again measured the surface area. The bordeaux measurement was, in fact, smaller than the Martini by 23.5 per cent.

I might add that, at this time of the day, I could detect no difference in mellowness between the two glasses.
Yours sincerely,
DAVID WEITZMAN,
Cardiff. August 29

From Mr Gary Watts

Sir, What tosh regarding the demise of the much maligned yet supremely elegant and romantic wide coupe champagne glass.

Anyone who leaves champagne in the glass long enough for the bubbles to diminish is clearly not taking the matter seriously and should be barred from drinking it.
Yours,
G. L. WATTS,
High Wycombe, Buckinghamshire. August 29

French lessons

From Mr H. L. M. Walker

Sir, Whilst my wife (1953 O-level French, fail) happily bargains with French market stallholders, I (1953 A-level French, pass) can only stand by muttering "No, tomatoes are feminine" or "You should be using the subjunctive!"

I was even able, when paying the bill at a small hotel, to say beautifully and accurately in French: "Had we not been awoken at 3am by the dustcart, it would not have been necessary for us to have raided the mini-bar for a bottle of water."

Unfortunately I had to rely on my wife to understand the reply: "Sorry, but it is still going to cost you 50 francs."
Yours faithfully,
H. L. M. WALKER,
Saffron Walden, Essex. August 29

On their mettle

From Mr Jonathan Caine

Sir, You repeated (leading article, August 28) the cliché that Led Zeppelin were "heavy metal pioneers". While it is undoubtedly the case that they inspired a generation of musicians, and fans, to compare them with today's heavy metal bands is a travesty.

In fact Zeppelin can hardly be described as heavy metal at all. Their music embraced such a divergence of styles – blues, hard rock, funk, folk, jazz and even reggae – that it defies categorisation or labelling.

As for *The Song Remains the Same*, a cursory listen to the track which gave its name to the film reveals more subtle guitar changes in a few minutes than most "heavy metal" bands could manage in a lifetime.

Led Zeppelin were, and remain, the greatest of all rock bands.
Yours faithfully,
JONATHAN CAINE,
Dulwich, London SE21. August 29

From Mr Keith Pickett

Sir, I agree that Led Zeppelin cannot be considered a heavy metal group, although I do detect a whiff of elitism in your correspondent's remarks on the skills of heavy metal guitarists. The first flowering of heavy metal as we know and love it must surely be on Black Sabbath's self-titled 1970 debut album.

If all philosophy is merely a footnote to Plato, then all heavy rock music is the same to Black Sabbath.
Regards,
KEITH PICKETT,
Brighton, East Sussex. September 2

From Mr James Fielding

Sir, I must dispute Keith Pickett's claim that Black Sabbath were the founders of heavy metal music.

I recall that the term was used several years before their debut, by a journalist who described the music of Jimi Hendrix as "sounding like heavy metal falling from the sky".

My apologies for being such an anorak.
Yours faithfully,
JAMES FIELDING,
Edinburgh. September 12

Looking for omens

From Mr Henry Thompson

Sir, I read your headline, "Airlines 'indifferent' to problem of lost luggage" with a sense of foreboding as I waited for my flight to Moscow and duly found on arrival that my suitcase had been left behind in Paris.

Could you repay me with a more auspicious headline on my return to the UK? "64-year-old bachelor Yorkshireman tipped to win top Premium Bond prize", perhaps?
Yours faithfully,
HENRY THOMPSON,
Moscow. August 29

Parental pride

From Mr Chris G. Green

Sir, Writing to an American friend, I inquired about her twin 16-year-old daughters. She replied that they are "ranting, self-absorbed, hormonal bags of protoplasm. Procreation sucks."

Isn't it reassuring to know that children are universal?

Yours faithfully,
CHRIS G. GREEN,
Broughton, North Yorkshire. September 1

Management skills

From Mrs Elizabeth Clarke

Sir, I correctly completed all the questions in the management aptitude test (Business, August 26) without the aid of a calculator (too lazy to go upstairs and find one).

Does anyone want to employ a 49-year-old personal tax adviser as a senior manager?

Yours faithfully,
ELIZABETH CLARKE,
Sheffield. August 26

Slow going in London

From Mr A. C. Anchors

Sir, Given that it is now quicker to walk than to drive in Central London (report, August 28), can we expect to see the resurgence of the sedan chair?

Yours sincerely,
TONY ANCHORS,
Didcot, Oxfordshire. August 31

From the Reverend Bernd Koschland

Sir, If the sedan chair will be quicker than driving in London, will it be liable for congestion charges?

Yours faithfully,
BERND KOSCHLAND,
London NW4. September 3

Back to the future

From Professor Emeritus Philip McNair

Sir, Many readers will have been intrigued by your revelation (The Register, August 30) that Byron and Shelley were "discussing Darwin and evolution" on holiday beside Lake Geneva. Was this uncanny prescience on their part, poetic licence, or a sage appreciation of Charles Darwin's grandfather Erasmus and his *Zoonomia* of 1794–96?

Yours faithfully,
PHILIP McNAIR,
Cambridge. August 30

What's in a name?

From Dr Neville Flavell

Sir, In my 30-plus years in teaching I learnt to expect trouble of some kind from any boy with an unusual or offbeat forename.

Contrary to the suggestion in your leader today, however, I never found the same correlation between outlandishly named girls and antisocial behaviour. A Euphemia was just as good as a Jane.

Yours faithfully,
NEVILLE FLAVELL,
Sheffield. September 2

Joy unconfined

From Dr Peter Cameron

Sir, I am accustomed to waiters telling me to enjoy my meal, but recently things entered a new phase. I bought a winter coat in the sales, and as I was leaving the shop the assistant called out: "Enjoy your coat!"

Fortunately I hadn't been buying pyjamas – or worse.

Yours faithfully,
PETER CAMERON,
Birnam, Dunkeld. September 2

From Mr Geoffrey Adams

Sir, When being served in a restaurant, I prefer to be instructed by the waiter to enjoy my meal rather than, as seems the modern custom, hear the phrase "There you go!"

Yours faithfully,
GEOFFREY ADAMS,
Cirencester, Gloucestershire. September 4

Pet name

From Mr Keith Richardson
Sir, On today's front page Roger Boyes writes of the killer whale seeking human company: "Willy, whose real name is Keiko . . ." Surely not?
Yours faithfully,
KEITH RICHARDSON,
Epsom, Surrey. September 3

Outlook fair

From Mr David Booker
Sir, I purchased a rain gauge whilst on holiday recently in Shropshire. Printed on the packaging are the words "Ideal for outdoors".
We have had no measurable rain in the past month.
Yours in anticipation,
DAVID BOOKER,
Bognor Regis, West Sussex. September 1

Cricket commentary

From Mr Malcolm Shirley
Sir, As England does battle against India at the Oval, it is reassuring to see that the famous ground's council, Lambeth, recognises our great cricketing heritage with a street called Bedser Close.
It is a pity therefore that on a nearby building, proudly named Wisden House, there is a large sign ordering "No Ball Games".
Yours faithfully,
MALCOLM SHIRLEY,
Kennington, London SW8. September 4

Mayor's security

From Mr Nicholas Lloyd
Sir, Ken Livingstone says that he feels safer in New York than London (*Evening Standard*, September 3). Perhaps that is because no one knows him there.
Yours sincerely,
NICHOLAS LLOYD,
London N1. September 3

Cars and the Ark

From Captain James T. Lord (RN)
Sir, The front-page photograph today of the Jaguar car being loaded on to HMS *Ark Royal* reminded me of when the previous Ark Royal was on her sea trials in 1955.
As the sub-lieutenant in charge of the gunroom officers (24 midshipmen), I took my own 1923 Rolls-Royce on board for the Mediterranean deployment. The car was an early "Twenty" model with an unusual – for the period – saloon bodywork designed for a lady driver rather than a chauffeur. Although it was the smallest Rolls-Royce made it weighed in at 2 tons, requiring the 3-ton truck slings to embark it.
It created quite a stir, bursting with young men, in the narrow main street of Gibraltar.
Yours faithfully,
JAMES LORD,
Hambledon, Hampshire. September 3

From Mr B. R. Battersby
Sir, Captain Alan Massey is continuing a naval tradition by taking a 3.2 litre Jaguar aboard HMS *Ark Royal*, for the use of senior officers during shore visits.
Admiral Sir Raymond Lygo tells in his biography *Collision Course* (The Book Guild, 2002) how his Austin A30 saloon (bought for £45) was taken off the frigate *Juno* at Chatham when he relinquished command of the ship in 1969.
As he sat in the car alongside, the ship's company lifted it bodily and bore it the length of the jetty at the double. Sir Raymond then drove away to take command of the *Ark Royal*, the largest ship ever to serve in the Royal Navy.
Perhaps Captain Massey's crew should practise weight-lifting to enable them to give him a similar send-off in due course.
Yours faithfully,
BRIAN R. BATTERSBY,
Macclesfield, Cheshire. September 7

From Mr Derick Walker
Sir, How could the sun have ever set on an empire where sub-lieutenants went to sea

accompanied by their personal vintage Rolls-Royces?

I am reminded of a story told me by an accountant from a similar era. While he was on the audit of a small, failing engineering company, one of his firm's trainees turned up on the first day of this, his first job, in a bright red Jaguar sportscar. He was promptly told by the audit manager that it was not in keeping with the image that the firm wished to portray.

He returned the following day in a Bentley saloon, telling the manager that he hoped it was considered appropriate, because it was the only other car he had.

Yours faithfully,
DERICK WALKER,
Hadlow, Kent. September 6

From Squadron Leader Michael Brown, RAF (retd)
Sir, One of the *Ark Royal*'s official vehicles in the early 1960s was a Citroen 2CV which I saw carried ashore, painted in its full Royal Navy livery, as an underslung load by one of the ship's helicopters.

It was then driven, with some panache, around RAF *Khormaksar* in Aden by the briefly shore-based naval aviators. No Rolls-Royces or Jaguars for them.

Yours faithfully,
MICHAEL BROWN,
Market Rasen. September 10

From Commander Christopher Welland, RN (retd)
Sir, Whilst serving in the aircraft carrier HMS *Eagle*, I witnessed the officer responsible for all flying operations' redundant ancient Morris Minor being launched into the Indian Ocean.

It was a most dramatic event and although certain parts fell off on to the catapult track, the main body made it to the deep – surely a unique testimonial to British engineering.

Yours faithfully,
CHRISTOPHER WELLAND,
Old Bosham, West Sussex. September 10

From Rear-Admiral J. P. W. Middleton
Sir, As a sub-lieutenant in the 1950s I took my Royal Enfield 250cc motorbike around the ports of the Mediterranean courtesy of HMS *Camperdown*, a Battle class destroyer. To get it on board I became friendly with a variety of crane drivers. An amiable chief stoker let me keep it within the double skin of the funnel with his hoses.

Submarines had less space, but an engineering lieutenant acquaintance kept a Corgi folding motorbike (as used by the Paras) in an unused torpedo tube, until the torpedo instructor conducting routine maintenance inadvertently discharged it into the deep.

Yours sincerely,
PATRICK MIDDLETON,
Salisbury, Wiltshire. September 14

From Mr I. P. S. Proud
Sir, In 1971 a WRAC captain stationed in Malta had a small Fiat car which was well beyond economic repair. She had brought it to the island duty free, but if she were to dispose of it locally, she would have to pay local duty on the car, and it was obviously not worth taking it back to the UK.

Fortunately the solution steamed into Grand Harbour in the shape of HMS *Ark Royal*. She was invited to the ship's cocktail party and happened to mention her problem to her hosts.

A few days later her Fiat made its last journey to the dockside and was craned onto the flight deck. Once out of territorial waters, the car was attached to the flight catapult and launched out to sea. With the incident duly logged the young captain had evidence that the car was disposed of outside Malta and avoided her tax liability legally.

Yours faithfully,
I. P. S. PROUD,
London W5. September 16

Education gap

From Mrs Jennifer Temple
Sir, Gratifying though it is to read that 66 per cent of ten to 12-year-olds can spell

"battle droid" (report, September 4), it would be more pleasing still if one of them could tell us over-50s what it means.
Yours faithfully,
JENNIFER TEMPLE,
Northampton. September 4

Closet chauvinism

From Mr K. J. Frith

Sir, You report (September 5) that a flatpack wardrobe with sensors to instruct customers how to assemble it has been created "for clumsy men incapable of doing it themselves".

Does this imply that women have no interest in, or are useless at DIY? Or perhaps it suggests that women are sufficiently competent that they have no need of such techno-gimmicks when faced with the simple task of assembling furniture.
Yours sincerely,
K. J. FRITH,
Southampton. September 5

From Mrs Judith A. White

Sir, I don't want a wardrobe which talks to me. I want a wardrobe which will listen to me, so that when he tells me to fit the last screw into the last hole, I can tell him: "But there are no screws left!"
Yours faithfully,
JUDITH A. WHITE,
Ely, Cambridgeshire. September 6

From Mr Edward Bugler

Sir, My only problem with wardrobes that tell me how to assemble them will be if they speak in the same language that the printed instructions are written in.
Yours faithfully,
EDWARD BUGLER,
Farnborough, Hampshire. September 7

1901 Census slips

From Mr Donald Brett

Sir, The Public Record Office's 1901 Census online, now partially available again as a test site, continues to provide amusement.

My grandfather, a Corn and Flour mer-
chant (clearly written in the actual Census page), appears in the transcription as a Cow and Flow merchant. Something to do with milking machines, perhaps?
Yours sincerely,
DONALD BRETT,
Amersham, Buckinghamshire. Sepember 4

Joy and doubts

From Mr Geoffrey Adams

Sir, Having, after 40 years of trying, achieved the lifetime ambition of having a letter published in *The Times*, I am suddenly plagued by awful doubts.

Is it possible that, like A levels, it's becoming easier?
Yours faithfully,
GEOFFREY ADAMS,
Cirencester. September 5

From Mr Noel C. Bramley

Sir, Mr Geoffrey Adams's success in these columns after 40 years of trying clearly illustrates not that it is becoming easier, but that it is done alphabetically.
Yours sincerely,
NOEL C. BRAMLEY,
Faversham, Kent. September 9

From Mr Francis P. Xavier

Sir, If submissions are subject to alphabetical scrutiny and Mr Geoffrey Adams had to wait 40 years to have a letter accepted, what chance do I have?
Yours despairingly,
FRANCIS P. XAVIER,
Raleigh, Essex. September 11

Sharp-dressed Scots

From Mr Brian Parker

Sir, The possible relaxation in the policy of confiscating sharp objects from airline passengers (report, September 6) will be welcome news to well-dressed Scotsmen.

Earlier this year I was on a flight to Rome in the company of appropriately attired Scottish supporters going to the Italy versus Scotland rugby match. Shortly before departure the captain of the aircraft announced that the supporters' kilt pins posed an unacceptable hazard and had to be collected and secured in a sealed bag before the flight could proceed.

Although take-off was delayed by half an hour, the Scotsmen treated the incident with immense good humour and their pins and dignity were restored on landing.

Yours sincerely,
BRIAN PARKER,
Dartmouth, Devon. September 6

Clothes of all nations

From Mrs Celia Gardner

Sir, My recent autumn shopping expedition to two well-known British stores in Chester produced the following manufacturing data:

Trousers	made in Morocco.
Skirt	China.
Blouse	Malaysia.
Twin set	Thailand.
Jumper	Macao.
Canvas shoes	Indonesia.
Leather shoes	Italy.
Pants	Egypt.
Suitcase	France.
And finally, socks	UK.

Yours faithfully,
CELIA GARDNER,
Aberystwyth. September 5

From Mr Nigel P. G. MacLean

Sir, Following Mrs Celia Gardner's recent shopping experience, I am proud to say that, with the exception of some of my shirts (India), the manufacturing data for my mail order company's range of menswear reads:

Trousers	England
Sweaters	Scotland
Leather shoes	England
Tweeds	Scotland
Socks	England
Boxer shorts	England
Ties	Ireland
Belts	England.

I only regret that as yet I have nothing manufactured in Wales.

Yours sincerely,
NIGEL P. G. MacLEAN
(Managing director), Edward Piers, Market Harborough, Leicestershire. September 11

Plump sparrows

From Mrs Ann McMeikan

Sir, Wishing to help my friendly sparrow population through their much publicised decline in numbers, I have been filling bird feeders with copious amounts of sunflower seed kernels. Twenty of the laziest, fattest sparrows you could wish to see now sit in a row on my fence, relaxing in the sun and chattering happily.

Unfortunately, two were too slow to avoid a local sparrowhawk and I am beginning to have concerns for the health of the rest, despite my purchasing the sunflower seeds from a health food shop.

Am I killing them by kindness?

Yours reservedly,
ANN McMEIKAN,
Haywards Heath, West Sussex. September 9

Eating habits

From Mr Colin Bridger

Sir, I have always expressed amazement to my wife that our two small granddaughters eat broccoli as if they were eating chocolate. I mentioned your report on overcoming children's food fads (September 10) to her, expecting a discussion on the merits of the scientists' theories, only to learn that she had told our grandchildren that if they didn't eat their broccoli they would grow up to be like their grandad.

Yours faithfully,
COLIN BRIDGER,
Camberley, Surrey. September 10

From Ms Roz Denny

Sir, I was once demonstrating a delicious vegetable stir-fry recipe from my children's cookbook in a large food store. A little boy about seven years old was standing in front of me mesmerised by the colours, smells and sizzling.

I spooned a portion into a bowl and handed it to him for tasting. He was about to tuck in when his mother rushed up, snatched away the bowl and said: "He won't like that – it's got vegetables in it."
Yours sincerely,
ROZ DENNY,
London SW6. September 12

A brief address

From Sir Antony Jay

Sir, I am a victim of computer abbreviation by my bank.

My wife and I receive a monthly statement of our joint account addressed to Sir Antony Jay and Lad, giving our postman a seriously misleading impression of my domestic arrangements, and I now find I am paying an annual subscription to Friends of the Ear, adding otophilia to my other eccentricities.
Yours faithfully,
ANTONY JAY,
Langport, Somerset. September 11

Enclosed separately

From Mr Richard O'Hagan

Sir, Following Mark Mason's tirade against verbiage (T2, September 12), can I make a plea to my fellow lawyers to cease using the phrase "we enclose herewith"?

A new nadir was reached today when the documents concerned actually arrived later and in two separate parcels, thus fulfilling neither condition.
Yours faithfully,
RICHARD O'HAGAN,
Reading. September 12

Bendy buses

From Mr Mark H. Levy

Sir, Bus companies could save themselves the investment in new bendy buses, which must take up a lot more road space than the double-decker, by spending instead on something which would avoid the added cost of new ticket machines, save the drivers' time in ticketing, improve journey times and provide help and security to passengers.

This thing is called a bus conductor.
Yours faithfully,
MARK H. LEVY,
Knutsford, Cheshire. September 10

From Mr Michael D. Green

Sir, The new long and low bending London buses may be a good idea.

But how are we to describe the height of things in the future?
Yours faithfully,
MICHAEL D. GREEN,
Dawlish, Devon. September 14

From Miss Christine N. Reeves

Sir, Michael Green's arithmetic gives me cause for concern.

Height is measured in Nelson's Columns and length in London buses or, in future, half buses.
Yours faithfully,
CHRISTINE N. REEVES,
London, SW15. September 17

Music for children

From Mrs Jacqueline Frampton

Sir, We have always taken our four children to concerts and our youngest, at 14, still comes with us once a month to the Royal Festival Hall.

Despite being deeply into heavy metal and various shades of black, she quite happily rattles her chains and studs in time with the music.
Yours sincerely,
JACQUELINE FRAMPTON,
Leigh-on-Sea, Essex. September 15

Money allergy

From Mr David R. Robinson

Sir, For years now, handling coins and notes (report, September 12) has caused me to sweat profusely, tremble spasmodically and, on occasions when large sums are involved, foam at the mouth.

Perhaps the scientists could explain why

this only happens when parting with money, and not when receiving.
Yours faithfully,
DAVID R. ROBINSON,
Westerham, Kent. September 12

From Mr Alan Noble
Sir, I suffer from the same allergy experienced by David Robinson when parting with money. Remarkably, neither my wife, daughter nor newly teenaged son are affected by these withdrawal symptoms.
Yours faithfully,
ALAN NOBLE,
Worsbrough. September 16

From Mr Rodney Miskin
Sir, It isn't just the physical parting with cash that triggers allergic reactions.

The same feeling of fear and trembling occurs when virtually dispensing cash online via the internet, whether it's to a bookmaker, the Inland Revenue or an investment fund manager (especially when the firm levies a charge upfront, even before your cash has been put to work for you).
Yours sincerely,
RODNEY MISKIN,
Hastings, East Sussex. September 17

Cheap Knights in London

From Mr Antony Crookston
Sir, Like – I suspect – others who have recently had a letter published in your newspaper, I have received a mailing from the Honorary Scribe to Court No 1 of the Order of the Mediaeval Knights of London. He tells me that the Grand Chamberlain has invited me to join the order.

While appreciative of the honour, I am surprised that a 49-word letter to *The Times* about Chinese Duck Pears – together with a cheque for £25 to be sent to an address in SE13 – is enough to entitle me to be "dubbed a knight". The entry requirements for orders of chivalry are clearly less stringent than in the days of Sir Bartholomew Burghersh and Sir Gaston de Foix.
Yours faithfully,

ANTONY CROOKSTON,
Waterlooville. September 12

From Mr Alan Witt
Sir, I did not receive a mailing from the Order of the Mediaeval Knights of London but, following the publication of my first and only letter in *The Times* some years ago, I received a letter addressed to Sir Alan Witt. It requested money and came from Malawi.

With the publication of this second letter, might I expect elevation to the peerage?
Yours faithfully,
ALAN WITT,
Ashford, Kent. September 18

Down on the farm

From Mrs Catriona Cook
Sir, As a breeder of Oxford Sandy and Black pigs, I can assure you that Orwell was correct in identifying pigs as the most intelligent farm animals (report and leading article, September 12).

Some years ago, I took a sow to a two-day exhibition, planning to leave her in the pen provided overnight while I slept in the trailer.

Unfortunately, Gertrude's pen was sited between stands for home-made fudge and organic lettuces. Fearing that these would be too great a temptation during the night I shared the trailer with her. Thereafter, whenever I was gardening next to Gertrude's field, she would come to the gate for a noisy conversation. Our night together had resulted in a lifelong friendship.
Yours sincerely,
CATRIONA COOK
(Chairman, Oxford Sandy and Black Pig Society), Scarborough, Yorkshire. September 13

From Dr Ian Olson
Sir, Back in the 1960s our transplantation team had every good reason to credit the old country adage, "dogs look up to you, cats look down on you, pigs is equal".

Our experimental pigs would crowd up

front obligingly to have their ear labels read – while one of their number ate the data clipboard held at your back.
Yours faithfully,
I. A. OLSON,
Aberdeen. September 17

Early morning Ashes

From Mr Douglas Barker
Sir, I well remember that dark November morning in 1946 when I switched on my bedside wireless to hear that Donald Bradman had scored a century and MCC were being put to the sword.

Fifty-six years on it appears likely that I shall not be able to hear the news from Brisbane on BBC Radio. Progress?
Yours,
DOUGLAS BARKER,
Nottingham. September 12

From Mr Leslie Rowe
Sir, I, too, remember waking on the blackest of mornings in the winter of 1946-47 to learn on the wireless that in the first innings of the second Test Bradman and Barnes had each scored 234 runs.

Mr Douglas Barker, who seems to have enjoyed such misery in the first postwar series overseas, is now unhappy that the BBC is not to broadcast a commentary on the Brisbane Test this year. He must be a masochist to want to undergo this kind of torture again - unless of course he is an Australian.
Yours faithfully,
LESLIE ROWE,
Thurso, Caithness. September 18

From Mr Ken Broad
Sir, Douglas Barker complains that though he was able to pick up BBC Radio news of MCC's defeat by Australia in 1946 he will not be able to do the same this year - and asks if this is progress. It certainly seems like it to me.
Yours sincerely,
KEN BROAD,
Newport, Shropshire. September 17

Lyrics made clear

From Mrs Fiona Anderson
Sir, I have been deaf since an illness some 18 months ago. I can no longer hear music but provided that I am familiar with the piece that is being played or sung on television I can still hear the music in my brain and enjoy it.

The only drawback I have discovered is the subtitling system which I use for watching television. This has revealed to me that some of the lyrics of my favourite songs are absolute nonsense.
Yours sincerely,
FIONA ANDERSON,
Flecknoe, nr Rugby. September 16

Puzzling offer

From Dr Richard Sharp
Sir, I have today received an offer of car insurance from Lloyds TSB. This includes an invitation to receive their offer in large print or Braille.
Yours meldrewly,
J. R. C. SHARP,
Montrose, Angus. September 14

Vehicle servicing

From Mr Stuart Thompson
Sir, How reassured I am to hear the Retail Motor Industry Federation condemning the sex-related differential in levels of motor vehicle servicing (report, September 18).

The poor service (including overcharging) experienced by 51 per cent of women surveyed, compared with only 33 per cent for men, is evidently creating concern that some garages believe women to be more easily fooled than men. I do hope the industry heeds the warning by Mr Matthew Carrington, the federation's chief executive, against such discrimination so that my wife and I can look forward to being fleeced on an equal basis in future.
Yours etc,
STUART THOMPSON,
Shamley Green, Surrey. September 18

Citizen's watch

From Mr John Smart

Sir, I shall attend the forthcoming country-side rally through our city's streets to observe whether the participants stick to the paths and take home their rubbish.

Yours,

JOHN SMART,

London SW16. September 19

Text education

From Mrs Beryl Wakefield

Sir, I was amused to see the headline "R U 2 OLD 2 TXT?" in T2 (September 18). I have before me an entry in my schoolgirl autograph book dated February 1943 which reads:

2Ys U R

2Ys U B

I C U R

2Ys 4 ME

We were there first.

Yours faithfully,

BERYL WAKEFIELD,

Lichfield, Staffordshire. September 18

Stone Age killing

From Mrs Anne Mort

Sir, Why does research now tell us that the Stone Age iceman "was killed by a rival hunter's arrow" (report, September 17)? Could he not have been the victim of "friendly fire" on a hunting expedition?

Yours faithfully,

ANNE MORT,

Belfast. September 17

The dancing years

From Mr N. H. Bovey

Sir, On Sunday I marked my last day as a septuagenarian with a party. On Monday I celebrated my first day as an octogenarian with another party. I commend the principle.

Yours faithfully,

N. H. BOVEY,

Lutterworth, Leicestershire. September 17

From Mr John Appleyard

Sir, Like Mr N. H. Bovey I marked my last day as a septuagenarian with a party and my first day as an octogenarian with another party – but then I was born on Boxing Day, so it has become something of a habit.

Yours faithfully,

JOHN APPLEYARD,

Irby, Wirral. September 21

Eating on the beat

From Police Sergeant Andy Sigee

Sir, As a serving police officer I have no doubt that free or discounted fast food for police officers will increase their public visibility (report, September 18). My wife, however, is more concerned with the direction in which it might increase my personal visibility.

Yours (currently at 11 stone),

ANDY SIGEE,

London SW11. September 20

End of AA phone box

From Mr Peter Batty

Sir, The AA is, alas, closing the last of its phone boxes. When I joined the BBC in early 1958, as a young film director on *To-night*, the powers-that-be at Lime Grove used various means to communicate with us in emergencies when we were out "on the road". If they knew roughly where we might be, they used to persuade the AA, who luckily were devotees of *Tonight*, to put placards in front of their boxes in the neighbourhood in question to ask us to ring in. This was in the days before motorways, let alone mobile phones.

I remember being quite chuffed driving with a film crew in the Midlands and seeing for the first time a big chalked sign in front of an AA box: "Batty BBC".

Yours faithfully,

PETER BATTY,

Kingston, Surrey. September 19

From Squadron Leader John R. Mann MBE, BSc, RAF (retd)

Sir, During the low-level navigation phase

of my jet pilot training in the 1970s at the RAF College, Cranwell, my flying instructor chose AA boxes almost exclusively as virtual targets. Clearly marked on Ordnance Survey maps, unique, easily identifiable, but visible only from close quarters, they were the ideal test for a budding Vasco da Gama.

I was awarded points for each AA box to which I accurately navigated. On one occasion I collected a bonus when, having "hit" the target, we turned and noticed a gentleman relieving himself behind the box.

Some years on, as a flying instructor myself, I used the AA box for testing my students' skills – the more modern, smaller boxes making life for them rather more difficult.

Yours faithfully,
JOHN MANN,
Southport, Merseyside. September 19

And vice versa?

From Canon Julian Sullivan

Sir, "They f*** you up, your mum and dad" (T2, September 18).

Well yes, there is truth in that, but I'd like to see some research into the destructive effects of children on their parents:

A wise child makes a glad father, but a foolish child is a mother's grief (Proverbs, x, 1).

Yours faithfully,
JULIAN SULLIVAN,
Sheffield. September 19

Not so sad

From Mr Walter Williamson

Sir, SAD (seasonal affective disorder, Medical Briefing, September 19) is surely a matter of individual perception.

Dr Stuttaford invokes Tennyson, but in describing autumn Keats is more to the point: "Season of mists and mellow fruitfulness".

The boredom of summer, with its heat, flies, humidity, noise and interminable sporting events, is over. September ushers in sunshine with a golden glow, and hedgerows ripe with blackberries. Concert halls,

opera houses and evening classes reopen; cosiness returns to the domestic hearth.

Truly a period of joy and rebirth.

Yours sincerely,
WALTER WILLIAMSON,
Rye, East Sussex. September 20

A fraction older

From Mr N. J. Inkley

Sir, I have become intrigued as to where I might have been for the first six months of my life. I have received a document from the agency of a leading insurance company which says of me: "Age next birthday: 70.5".

My wife, however, is interestingly quoted as 71.0.

Yours,
NEIL INKLEY,
Walton-le-Dale, Lancashire. September 23

From Mr Nick Buswell

Sir, Mr N. J. Inkley may be 71.5 next birthday but at least he had only one place of decimals to worry about.

In a notice (of redundancy) I recently received, my employers informed me that amongst the calculations used when computing my terminal pay were: age, 56.89 years; length of service, 3.36 years.

I look forward to returning to full-time employment before my 57.0 birthday on Friday.

Yours faithfully,
NICK BUSWELL,
Horley, Surrey. September 29

From Mr E. J. Hart

Sir, May I be permitted to share in Mr Nick Buswell's sanguinity for his returning to full-time employment prior to his attainment of 57.0 years?

However, should his new post be with Argyll and Bute Council he could find its paymasters similarly reluctant to round off. A recent press advertisement for a Reserve School Crossing Patroller offered £5.1893 per hour.

Yours very truly,
E. J. HART,
Helensburgh, Argyll and Bute. October 2

From Mr John Green

Sir, A few weeks ago, at the age of 79.4, I visited the local branch of my building society to transfer funds. I was told their computer recorded me as dead – although none of my close family had noticed it.

My presence, with proof of identity, carried no weight.

Two weeks later the computer managed to revive me.

Yours faithfully,
JOHN GREEN,
Muswell Hill, London N10. October 5

Wiped off the map

From Mr Charles Hopkins

Sir, I'd be a bit upset if I spent £400,000 on genetic mapping to find out how I might die (Sunday press review, September 23) – and then got hit by a bus.

Yours faithfully,
C. HOPKINS,
Norwich. September 23

From Mr Adrian Hack

Sir, If I spent £400,000 on genetic mapping to discover how and when I might one day die I already know what the report would say.

Dear Mr Hack, We are sad to inform you that when she discovers how much money you have just wasted your wife is 99 per cent certain to kill you.

Regards,
ADRIAN HACK,
Headington, Oxford. September 26

Royal letters

From Mrs Marta Inskip

Sir, I think it is great that the Prince of Wales writes to government ministers about matters of public concern. If they give his letters some consideration that is good, and if they don't that makes him the same as all the rest of us, which is good too.

Three cheers for the Prince!
Yours faithfully,
MARTA INSKIP,
Bath. September 25

From Mr Oliver Chastney

Sir, In order to curtail the excessive correspondence by the Prince of Wales, the Prime Minister would do well to bring to his attention a letter to these columns (February 4, 1970) concerning Charles's great-grandfather:

Sir, King George V, approached by a friend who hoped that a word from His Majesty in the right quarter would solve a difficulty, said: "My dear fellow, I can't help you! You'd better write to *The Times*." (*The First Cuckoo*, George Allen & Unwin, 1981).

Yours faithfully,
OLIVER CHASTNEY,
Norwich. September 25

Slice of long life

From Joseph Munday

Sir, I noticed that the "hundreds and thousands" cake decoration which Mum was using appears to have a "best before" date of February 4, 2214, some 212 years into the future.

How do the manufacturers know? How can I be certain that I will be around to complain if the taste is a little stale on February 3, 2214?

Still, Mum's cakes never last that long anyway.

Yours faithfully,
JOE MUNDAY (age 13),
Kingsbridge, Devon. September 24

Speed cameras

From Police Constable Mark White

Sir, I was admonished at work for daring to suggest that we have speed cameras on the roads of Sussex. Apparently there are none, although we do have a number of safety cameras.

I guess I'm not a very PC PC.
Yours faithfully,
MARK WHITE,
Felpham, West Sussex. September 26

The silly season

From Mrs Joan Atkins

Sir, I came back after a month out of the country to find a primrose in flower in my garden; yesterday I narrowly avoided being knocked over outside my front door by the next-door cat in hot pursuit of a squirrel; and in *The Archers* Jennifer is still blissfully unaware of Brian's exploits.

Will the silly season never end?

Yours faithfully,
JOAN ATKINS,
Cambridge. September 25

From Mrs Jean MacGregor

Sir, I was appalled to read Joan Atkins's letter concerning Brian's exploits in *The Archers*.

Suppose Jennifer reads *The Times*?

Yours faithfully,
JEAN MacGREGOR,
London N10. October 3

Modern manners

From Lady Garden

Sir, On a short, crowded Tube journey, I have just witnessed five separate instances of people offering a seat to someone standing. Each resulted in a smiling, gracious exchange. I am not sure if I should be cheered that the age of courtesy is not dead, or dispirited that signs of it are noteworthy.

Yours faithfully,
SUE GARDEN,
London NW3. September 27

From Lieutenant-Commander Philip Barber, RN (retd)

Sir, I was interested by Lady Garden's observations on displays of courtesy while travelling on London Underground.

Could it be that, following the countryside march and our subsequent good humoured Tube journey back to our coaches, some of our natural rural consideration for others rubbed off on our town "cousins"?

Yours faithfully,
PHILIP BARBER,
Atherstone, Warwickshire. October 1

From Mr Richard Evans

Sir, While travelling on the London Underground recently with a small suitcase, a walking stick and a heavy limp, I had my suitcase gently removed from my hand on three occasions and carried up steep stairs. One of the kind helpers was American, one was English and one Chinese. All three were ladies.

Yours faithfully,
RICHARD EVANS,
Evercreech, Somerset. October 1

From Mr Richard Williams

Sir, Perhaps what Lady Garden has observed is the contagious quality of rare outbreaks of well-mannered behaviour.

Yours faithfully,
RICHARD WILLIAMS,
Stapleton, Bristol. October 1

From Mr Michael Haigh

Sir, I do not think it unusual to be relieved of the burden of carrying one's hand luggage in London.

What was unusual about Mr Richard Evans's experience was that in each instance it was returned.

Yours faithfully,
MICHAEL HAIGH,
Wooburn Green, Buckinghamshire. October 4

From Mr Julian Yell

Sir, A few years ago, returning from a meeting in London, a colleague and I encountered a young mother attempting to get herself, a baby and two suitcases on to a train at Paddington station.

My colleague offered assistance, which she gratefully accepted, but to his great surprise she handed him the baby and loaded the cases herself.

Yours faithfully,
JULIAN YELL,
Thatcham, Berkshire. October 4

Edwina Currie's diaries

From Mr Bruce Shaxson

Sir, The fact that John Major's love for another woman was the one event in his life

of which he was most ashamed indicates stunning egotism. I would have thought that he should be rather more ashamed of coupling the ratification of the ignominious Maastricht Treaty with a vote of confidence in his leadership.
Yours etc,
BRUCE SHAXSON,
Grayshott, Surrey. September 28

From Mr Ralph Berry
Sir Moralists may well debate whether John Major's affair with Edwina Currie or the exchange-rate mechanism policy for which he bore supreme responsibility was the more worthy of shame.
Yours faithfully,
RALPH BERRY,
Stratford-upon-Avon. September 28

From Mr Richard Biddlecombe
Sir, Will John Major now be offered his own national radio show?
Yours faithfully,
RICHARD BIDDLECOMBE,
Glastonbury, Somerset. September 29

From Mr David Boushel
Sir, Perhaps I can clear up one misunderstanding about "back to basics"; the "basics" referred to were instincts rather than values.
Yours faithfully,
DAVID BOUSHEL,
Elm Park, Essex. September 30

From Mrs Maureen Nyazai
Sir, I always suspected it but now I know: Edwina Currie is a bad egg.
Yours faithfully,
MAUREEN NYAZAI
(Conservative councillor, Waverley Borough Council), Godalming, Surrey. September 30

From Mrs Margaret Hunter
Sir, Keep a diary – and someday it'll keep you (Mae West).
Yours faithfully,
MARGARET P. HUNTER,
Easingwold, York. September 30

From Mrs Frances Stott
Sir, Among all the correspondence in your columns arising from the revelations of the affair between Edwina Currie and John Major, there has been plenty of adverse comment directed towards the protagonists in this sorry matter, but not a single word against the supposedly serious, responsible broadsheet newspaper which chose to publish and, like Mrs Currie, profit from her diaries.
I can't believe that there aren't many other readers who share my feelings of outrage. I doubt, however, that I shall see this letter in print.
Yours faithfully,
FRANCES STOTT,
Devizes, Wiltshire. October 2

From Mrs Susan Howden
Sir, There is an old-fashioned word to describe men like John Major.
A man who cheats on his wife and then has the gall to refer to his mistress of four years as if she were the subject of a brief and unimportant fling can best be described as a cad.
Yours faithfully,
SUSAN HOWDEN,
Evercreech, Somerset. October 2

From Miss A. G. Martin
Sir, Our English master at school deplored the trite phrase "Hell hath no fury . . ." claiming that it was the tool of those too lazy to think for themselves.
But I believe even he would have approved the thought which must have sprung to many minds in the case of Mrs Edwina Currie. Except that she was less scorned than gently disentangled.
Yours faithfully,
AUDREY MARTIN,
Gosport, Hampshire. October 2

From Dr Eva Wittenberg
Sir, Lady Archer's surprise at John Major's "temporary lapse in taste" (report and T2, September 30) is not as great as many people's surprise at her permanent lapse in taste.

Yours sincerely,
E. WITTENBERG,
Pinner, Middlesex. September 30

From Mr Michael J. C. Wilson

Sir, Should we accept a more realistic and perhaps French attitude to this matter, namely that it would be unusual if extra-marital affairs didn't occur among politicians?
Yours faithfully,
MICHAEL J. C. WILSON,
Market Weighton, York. October 2

From Mrs Corinna Kershaw

Sir, What is Edwina Currie on about? You don't have to feel shame at the time to feel it deeply later.

For example, I voted Conservative in 1979.
Yours faithfully,
CORINNA KERSHAW,
Godalming. October 3

From Mr Patrick O'B. Baker

Sir, It is to John Major's credit that he says he is ashamed. How refreshing not to hear the usual "I made an error of judgment".
Yours faithfully
PATRICK O'B. BAKER,
Finchley, London N3. October 2

From Dr Vivien Noakes

Sir, Politicians sometimes express disquiet at voter apathy.

If Edwina Currie, who presumably knows, can describe her fellow Members of Parliament (report, October 3) as (to compress her epithets) loathsome, slimy bastards and unpleasant, untalented prats, arrogant, thoughtless, spiteful bitches and rude, pompous, vindictive bullshitters, people who cannot distinguish truth from reality, who are insensitive to others and who are quite simply potty can they be surprised?
Yours faithfully,
VIVIEN NOAKES,
London NW8. October 3

From Mr A. B. Cornwell

Sir, In the window of a well-known Cambridge bookshop is a copy of John Major's autobiography with a card stating: "Half price – not the complete story."
Yours faithfully,
TONY CORNWELL,
Cambridge. October 2

From Mr Martin W. Short

Sir, Autobiography is now as common as adultery and hardly less reprehensible (John Grigg, *The Sunday Times*, February 28, 1962).
Yours faithfully,
MARTIN W. SHORT,
London W11. October 8

Mixed veg

From Dr Nick O'Donovan

Sir, Here on the South Coast, when I go to my local vegetable shop and ask for swede I am given a large, orange-fleshed vegetable. If I ask for turnip I receive a much smaller, whitish vegetable with a green top.

When making the same request for these vegetables when staying at my in-laws' in Middlesbrough, the orange vegetable is proffered when requesting turnip and the smaller green-topped vegetable when requesting swede.

I wonder at which junction of the M1 this nomenclature changes, and why?
Yours faithfully,
NICK O'DONOVAN,
Havant, Hampshire. September 30

From Mr Mark Wilson

Sir, In answer to Dr Nick O'Donovan's query about swedes being called turnips in some parts of Britain, and turnips being called swedes in others, a survey of the company tearoom suggested the border to be Yorkshire, with Nottinghamshire and Cheshire clearly in the "South". Lancashire is divided, with Manchester supporting the South but other areas applying the northern interpretation.

Middlesbrough and Tyneside clearly follow the northern option but the Central North and Cumbria revert to southern ways. On very small samples the Irish Republic

and New Zealand appear to follow the northern pattern while the US opted for southern. Australia is apparently too dry to grow either vegetable.
Yours,
MARK WILSON,
Nottingham. October 1

From Mrs Ruth Parker
Sir, Here in the far South West we receive a large orange vegetable when asking for a turnip. I understand that if you require what in my youth in the South East was called a turnip you have to ask for a "white turnip".

Incidentally, turnip of the orange variety is an essential ingredient of a Cornish pasty.
Yours faithfully,
RUTH PARKER,
Penzance, Cornwall. October 1

From Mr Peter Tray
Sir, Alas, I cannot answer Dr O'Donovan's question. But perhaps he should note that in Northern Ireland the big orange thingy is a turnip, the small whitish one a white turnip, and a swede is the England football coach.
Yours faithfully,
PETER TRAY,
London N12. October 2

From Dr Edward Selby
Sir, Let Brussels decide.
Yours faithfully,
EDWARD M. SELBY,
Middlesbrough. October 2

From Professor Emeritus Edward Garden
Sir, The Swedish turnip (hence "swede") was first introduced into Scotland in the 18th century, and "tatties and neeps" have been an essential gastronomic concomitant to the haggis since then.

I have always understood the word neep to refer indiscriminately to any kind of turnip. It matters not, provided that you have a delicious haggis to go with the vegetable.
Yours,
EDWARD GARDEN,
Inverness. October 1

From Miss Pamela Field-Webber
Sir, To test the North/South vegetable naming theory, I asked my partner – a southerner – what he would call the largish orange vegetable. In line with the theory he responded: "A swede." Asked what he would call the smaller, white-fleshed, purple or green-skinned vegetable, he replied "A small swede."

This may go some way to explaining why after he has been shopping, we eat a limited range of vegetables.
Yours faithfully,
PAMELA FIELD-WEBBER,
Northill, Bedfordshire. October 8

From Mr Alan Collins
Sir, "Vegetable shop" my foot. What happened to the greengrocer's?
Yours truly,
ALAN COLLINS,
Petersfield, Hampshire. October 1

From Mr Paul A. James
Sir, During my childhood on Tyneside we would make a lantern from a turnip on Hallowe'en.

It took an eternity to hollow out the hard orange flesh of the "snadgey" (as we called them) and then carve the ghoulish features. I can still recall the smell as the flame of the night light roasted the lid of the lantern.

Kids these days have it so much easier with the soft, yielding flesh of the pumpkin.
I remain, Sir, your nostalgic servant,
PAUL A. JAMES,
Düsseldorf. October 10

From Mr Keith Virgo
Sir, The answer is to be found in the *Oxford Book of Food Plants*. The turnip (*Brassica rapa*) is distinguished from the swede (*Brassica napus* var. *napobrassica*) by its "root". The turnip "root" is a swollen hypocotyl, whereas that of the swede comprises swollen hypocotyl and lower leave bases. The swede therefore has a 'swollen neck bearing a number of ridges, the leaf scars".

The book further cites turnip "roots" as

being yellow or white and swede "roots" as being purple, white or yellow. The turnip is an ancient vegetable, whereas the swede was introduced in Europe only in the 17th century. If Cornish pasties pre-date this, then their ingredient must be turnip.

Yours faithfully,
KEITH VIRGO,
Newmarket. October 10

From Mr F. W. Taylor

Sir, When I grew up in rural Northumberland a turnip was invariably known as a bagie (pronounced with a long a, like "baygie").

I never knew the origin of this, but now my Swedish-American wife assures me it has to be a contraction of rutabaga, the name by which it is (also universally) known in her home state of Minnesota.

Yours faithfully,
F. W. TAYLOR
Headington, Oxford. October 11

From Mr Peter Stamford

Sir, The swede sounds a more upmarket vegetable in Ontario, where it is called a rutabaga. This name, I believe, is derived from the Swedish dialect rotabagge, meaning "root bag".

Yours truly,
PETER STAMFORD
Port Elgin, Ontario. October 11

From Mr J. F. Holliday

Sir, John Reynolds (1703–79), the pioneering yeoman farmer of Adisham, near Canterbury – and my great (times five) grandfather – was responsible for the inadvertent introduction into the UK of the swede or, as he then chose to call it, "the turnep rooted cabbage", when an incorrect variety of seed from the Continent was delivered to him.

The minutes of the Society for the Encouragement of Arts, Manufactures and Commerce (now the Royal Society of Arts) for November 23, 1768, solemnly recorded:

A motion was made that a Bounty of Fifty Pounds be given to Mr Reynolds for his Intro-

duction of the turnep rooted Cabbage not heretofore made use (of) in this Country, but more especially for his particular attention to the views of this Society by divulging his Discoveries to the World through their means. Agreed to.

Yours,
J. F. HOLLIDAY,
Leeds, West Yorkshire. October 10

Mature students

From Mr Stewart Rigby

Sir, I have recently enrolled as a "mature student" at my local college in order to study Greek.

At the beginning of the first lesson each pupil was given a student handbook. I did not examine mine until I got home. It was then that I discovered a page set aside to "useful telephone numbers".

Finding the first two numbers to be Aids National Helpline and Alcoholics Anonymous removed any sense of maturity I might have had. It just made me feel incredibly old.

Yours faithfully,
STEWART RIGBY,
Prescot, Merseyside. September 30

Every dog has its day

From Mr James Parry

Sir, The Princess Royal and her husband can no doubt take heart that they will be entitled to public funding (formerly legal aid) in defending the allegation of having a dangerous dog (Sunday press review, September 30).

Liverpool Magistrates' Court has advised me that it has granted such an order in relation to one of my human clients, on the grounds that "it is in the dog's best interests" that my client be represented at public expense.

Yours sincerely,
JAMES PARRY,
Gregory Abrams Solicitors, Liverpool.
September 30

Dressed for action

From Mrs Ann Hughes

Sir, Preparing to wash a new sweater and wishing to take all possible precautions, I checked inside for instructions. The label stated: "Please wear dark coloured undergarments for the first few washes."

I am at a loss to know what the consequences may be for having disregarded this instruction.

Yours sincerely,
ANN HUGHES,
Par, Cornwall. October 1

From Ms H. Robinson

Sir, The cleaning instructions in clothing can indeed be revealing. My recently purchased mock sheepskin jacket instructs me to "vacuum regularly".

Yours faithfully,
HILARY ROBINSON,
South Milford. October 2

From the Reverend Brenda Wallace

Sir, If cleaning instructions in clothing are revealing, some descriptions can be confusing. While shopping last week, my clergyman husband puzzled over a display of "three-in-one bras".

Yours faithfully,
BRENDA WALLACE,
Hutton, Essex. October 8

Blair's illuminations in Blackpool

From Mr Alan Millard

Sir, Eric Blair (alias George Orwell) writes in *Nineteen Eighty-Four* about "The Ministry of Peace, which concerned itself with war". Tony Blair, speaking at the Labour Party conference (reports and leading article, October 2), says: ". . . the only chance of peace is a readiness for war".

Are the two Blairs beginning to speak with one voice?

Yours faithfully,
ALAN MILLARD,
Lee-on-the-Solent, Hampshire. October 2

Literary dinner

From Mr Nicholas Utechin

Sir, Will Self (T2, September 27), describing the origins of *The Picture of Dorian Gray*, says: "We have no record of where the dinner took place" when the editor of *Lippincott's* hosted Oscar Wilde and Arthur Conan Doyle at one of popular literature's most productive expense-account meals.

It was at the Langham Hotel which stares proudly up Portland Place in Central London. Doyle was clearly so impressed by the surroundings – and the fact that *The Sign of Four* was accepted there – that he had Captain Arthur Morstan stay there in the self-same book.

Yours faithfully,
NICHOLAS UTECHIN
(Editor, *The Sherlock Holmes Journal*)
Oxford. September 28

Chewing gum litter

From Dr John Atherton

Sir, Derwent May (Thunderer, October 2) doesn't like chewing gum litter. Neither do I. The solution is to tax chewing gum out of existence. If fanatics continue to "chew and drop" the revenue could be returned to councils to clean up the mess.

Yours,
JOHN H. ATHERTON,
Huddersfield. October 2

From the Headmaster of Aldwickbury School

Sir, The answer to the urban plague of chewing gum is to prevent its sale in the first place. Singapore has just such a law and enforces it. It might also help if Sir Alex Ferguson were to switch to something edible.

Yours faithfully,
PETER JEFFERY,
Harpenden, Hertfordshire. October 2

From Mr Bryan C. Diamond

Sir, I have noticed that gum has already considerably disfigured the bright metal

deck of London's elegant new Millennium Bridge, where the blobs nestle securely between the upraised tread strips. The cleaning team confirmed to me that it can be removed only with difficulty. It is unfortunate that a gum-resistant surface could not have been devised for this modern structure.
Yours faithfully,
BRYAN C. DIAMOND,
London NW3. October 2

What's a penny worth?

From Mr Robert Walls
Sir, When I was a child in the 1950s the halfpenny (0.5d) was the lowest value coin and £10 a week was a living wage, a multiple of 4,800.

Now we have the 1p while the equivalent wage must be at least £300, a multiple of 30,000.

Rather than carrying pocketfuls of useless change, would it not make sense to restore the relationship by making 5p or even 10p the smallest coin?
Yours faithfully,
ROBERT WALLS,
Camberley. October 4

From Mr Bob Hale
Sir, Robert Walls was wrong to say that the lowest-value coin in the 1950s was the halfpenny. Even at 52 I can remember using a farthing, which was legal tender until the end of 1960.
Yours faithfully,
BOB HALE,
Fordingbridge, Hampshire. October 5

From Mr Robert Spicer
Sir, I too grew up in the 1950s when it was the farthing that was the lowest value coin. I am having great difficulty in convincing my teenage son that his father lived through a period of history when the pound could be divided into 960 separate coins.
Yours faithfully,
ROBERT SPICER,
Colchester, Essex. October 5

From Mr David Fisher
Sir, The significance of the penny lies in its negative rather than positive value: the pricing points that require giving a penny in change.

Shopkeepers would not want to forgo the millions of fourpences involved in rounding down from, say, £9.99 to £9.95, and conventional retailing wisdom holds that adding the extra penny and charging £10 would lead to a complete collapse of the world as we know it.
Yours faithfully,
DAVID FISHER,
Brighton. October 5

From Mr Michael J. Cansdale
Sir, My father, born in 1904, always reminded me when handing over my "Saturday penny" of the rules of his childhood. My grandfather would only give him his pocket money if he could prove he had spent the previous week's penny in at least four different ways, ie, no more than a farthing on any one item.

He handed down to me his British coin collection, with half-farthings (1/1920) of a pound) and even some third-farthings (1/2880 of a pound). So there's good precedent for keeping the small denominations.
Yours faithfully,
MICHAEL J. CANSDALE,
Wells. October 5

From Mr Michael Banister
Sir, The correspondence about regional variations of the understanding of turnip/swede reminded me of the situation which used to exist in the pronounciation of threepence (3d). Before decimalisation this sum of money was pronounced, as I recall, thrippence in Scotland, threppence in the North and Midlands and thruppence in the South.

These days it seems to be most commonly known throughout the realm as free pee.
Yours faithfully,
MICHAEL BANISTER,
Solihull, West Midlands. October 11

From Mr Geoffrey Bourne-Taylor
Sir, Michael Cansdale is lucky that his father could afford to give him his regular Saturday pennies. In my day the boot was on the other foot: every Saturday, hard-earned paper-round pennies were handed over by me to my father.
Yours faithfully,
GEOFFREY BOURNE-TAYLOR
(Bursar), St Edmund Hall, Oxford. October 15

The Nelson touch

From Mr John Wayman
Sir, While I wholeheartedly welcome the long overdue resumption of beef exports to France, I wonder whether the holding of a high-profile "rosbif" dinner at the George V hotel in Paris on Trafalgar Day (report, October 3) is the most appropriate marketing ploy.
Yours faithfully,
JOHN WAYMAN,
Sudbury, Suffolk. October 3

Anyone for whelks?

From Mr Henry Button
Sir, Blair & Co, according to your headline (Patience Wheatcroft, Comment, October 3), are "barely fit to run a whelk stall". One does not often see whelk stalls nowadays, but the management of them is frequently quoted, usually in relation to politicians, as the nadir of managerial competence.
An inquiry by me in these columns some years ago (July 16, 1976) as to the first recorded use of the expression produced an account of a speech by John Burns in January 1894, in which he described the Social-Democratic Federation as men "who have not got sufficient brains and ability to run a whelk stall".
Yours faithfully,
HENRY BUTTON,
Cambridge. October 7

From Lieutenant-Commander J. H. McGivering, RNR (retd)
Sir, Running a whelk stall is a very complex business, as I know from personal experience as a member of the crew of one here in Brighton.
First we make the pots out of plastic containers with netting entrances and bridles, which our fisherman takes to sea. He has 300-odd pots on the grounds and hauls them daily, weather permitting; the catch is then cleaned and delivered to us, where it is cleaned again, boiled and prodded, the opercula and sacs removed, and given a final cleaning before freezing or going to the stall. All this on the day it is caught and in accordance with hygiene regulations.
The simpler tasks might be within the competence of some ministers, but, generally speaking, I would not even look to them for refreshment in a brewery.
I have the honour to be, Sir, Your obedient servant,
J. H. McGIVERING,
Brighton. October 3

Brakes on Ferrari

From Mr Steve Dawe
Sir, In the quest for a handicap system for Formula One (report, October 7), perhaps some of the drivers could remove their wallets before driving.
The resultant weight loss may increase performance tremendously.
Yours sincerely,
STEVE DAWE,
St Ives, Cornwall. October 7

From Mr Alun Morris
Sir, That noted Labour supporter Bernie Ecclestone need look no further than the tenets of socialism to equalise the outcomes of Formula One races.
A progressive tax and redistribution system for points would prevent anyone getting too far ahead, regardless of talent.
Yours faithfully,
ALUN MORRIS,
Cambridge. October 7

From Mr Phil Elston
Sir, Just putting extra weight on the car shows a lack of imagination.

Having the Ferrari pit crew wear boxing gloves would have the same effect and boost the flagging TV ratings.
Regards,
PHIL ELSTON,
Beckenham. October 8

Verse and worse

From Mr R. J. Vincent
Sir, I am a published and paid poet and my verse, often informed by experience as engineer, soldier, boxer, copywriter *et al*, is usually cheerful and always understandable.

Nevertheless, this coming National Poetry Day and the prospect of much heartbreak, frustration and unrequited love unspoilt by rhyme, scansion or comprehensibility will be eagerly addressed in my constant search for improvement and total acceptability.

I have consequently issued instructions from my garret to the quarters below that I be kept under observation, and for all guns and sharp knives to be placed beyond my reach for October 10 and a few days following.
Yours faithfully,
ROBERT VINCENT,
Andover, Hampshire. October 8

Television hits

From Sir Bill Cotton
Sir, I did not hit Eddie Braben, the writer of *The Morecambe and Wise Show*, with a soda siphon (TV Choice, T2, October 8). My daughter collects them and I treat them as an endangered species.

In the interests of the BBC, I did however hit him behind his writing ear with a Ping 9 iron with which I practised in my office regularly. It had the desired effect. He never wrote for Morecambe and Wise for ITV as well as he did for the BBC.
Yours sincerely,
BILL COTTON,
London SW1. October 9

Post haste

From Mr Bernard Preger
Sir, I believe I have discovered the perfect way to ensure that any letters I post arrive promptly.

I simply disguise them as bills.
Yours sincerely,
B. PREGER,
Bury, Lancashire. October 9

Dogs and children

From Mr T. Knight
Sir, Robin Young (Thunderer, October 8) complains that dogs are accepted at British hotels while children are not. The reason is that the dogs are almost certainly housetrained while the children aren't.
Yours faithfully,
T. KNIGHT,
Oldbury, West Midlands. October 8

She steeped a conker

From Dr John R. A. Duckworth
Sir, Sociologists state that the middle classes are defined by their behaviour.

I came home last night to find my nine-year-old daughter soaking her her conkers in half a litre of balsamic vinegar.

Have we arrived?
Yours faithfully,
JOHN DUCKWORTH,
Hampton Court. October 9

Measure for measure

From Mr Paul Downham
Sir, Congratulations on correctly illustrating the size of the new Marsyas sculpture (graphic, October 9) using 17.5 double decker buses and 0.7 of a Nelson's Column.

However, your comparison with 2.4 Concordes is slightly out, because I recall this earlier work of art being described as seven buses long.
Yours faithfully,
PAUL DOWNHAM,
Huntingdon, Cambridgeshire. October 10

Priceless nanny

From Mr Howard Self

Sir, The increasing necessity for anyone desiring success to "add value" to their chosen organisation appears to have spread from office to home.

On asking a nanny agency recently about their candidates, I was told that a nanny's primary objective is to "add value to the family employing her".

And we thought all we needed was someone to look after children.

Yours faithfully,
HOWARD SELF,
Macclesfield, Cheshire. October 11

Dry cleaning

From Mr Geoffrey Bernstein

Sir, In the cleaning instructions for my son's computer printer, we were given the helpful advice: "Do not immerse this printer in water".

Yours faithfully,
GEOFFREY BERNSTEIN,
London N2. October 12

Bank procedures

From Mr Raj Kothari

Sir, My son, who is 14, recently received a letter from his bank asking him to pick up his new cashcard. Since he is at school this presents some difficulty.

On ringing the bank I was astonished to be told that he would have to write me a letter authorising me to do so.

I was even more astonished to learn that the person I was talking to was in Hyderabad.

Yours truly,
RAJ KOTHARI,
Bridport, Dorset. October 10

From Mr Hugh Jones

Sir, I recently attempted to open a bank account for my son who is 13. The bank official asked my son for two forms of identification. He said the only thing he had was his birth certificate and that he did not have a passport as he was listed on his mother's, therefore was there anything else which would suffice?

The bank official said they would accept a recent utility bill, for example either a gas or electric bill.

We went to a building society.

Yours faithfully,
HUGH JONES,
Cardiff, South Glamorgan. October 17

"Too old" for work

From Mr Richard Bassett

Sir, Perhaps the 56-year-old executive who claims she was sacked for being too old (reports and Thunderer, October 9) should have sought employment in Germany.

I heard the venerable chairman of one of Germany's leading companies being asked whether his very bright *finanzdirektor* might not soon be moving to a position of greater responsibility within the company.

"My dear fellow," he replied, "he is far too young; the man is only 52."

Yours faithfully,
RICHARD BASSETT,
Frankfurt. October 12

Canadians' welcome for the Queen

From Mr Will Lastiwka

Sir, Even in the midst of a frozen wasteland, word has reached us about your concern for the health of Queen Elizabeth (report, October 10).

While this concern for the frailty of the Queen of England is to your credit and, to some extent, justified, please be assured that the Queen of Canada is of much sterner stuff and, I'm sure, finds these autumnal temperatures of little note.

Yours sincerely,
W. LASTIWKA,
Edmonton, Alberta. October 11

In person

From Mr E. W. Lighton

Sir, I see that every Christmas Handel gave

"live" performances of his Messiah (The Register, October 16). But then he would, wouldn't he?
Yours faithfully,
E. W. LIGHTON,
Crewe. October 16

Lie of the land

From Mr Jon Ward
Sir, In appraising the claim that the Lake District is England's finest national park (report, October 15), one should remember the saying ascribed to Will Ritson, one-time landlord of the Wasdale Head Inn. He said that Wasdale has the deepest lake, the highest mountain, the smallest church and the biggest liar (himself) in all England.

It is encouraging that this tradition appears to be being continued by the park authority.
Yours faithfully,
J. D. WARD,
Balcombe, West Sussex. October 15

Not so retiring

From the Reverend Philip J. Swindells
Sir, You report today that Archbishop Hope's planned return to parish work is a radical departure from archiepiscopal tradition. However, it is not without precedent.

A former Archbishop of Canterbury, Geoffrey Fisher, on his retirement as Archbishop became parish priest of Trent, Dorset, from where he harassed his successor in letters to the *Church Times*.
Yours sincerely,
PHILIP J. SWINDELLS,
Sandy, Bedfordshire. October 14

From Mrs Katharine Fewster
Sir, My father, Professor H. J. Rose, retired from the Chair of Greek at the University of St Andrews and, on discovering that there was no mandatory retirement age for junior lecturers, applied successfully for such a post in the Department of English. Finding no satisfactory textbook for the required course (Classical Background for English Literature) he proceeded to write one.
Yours sincerely,
KATHARINE FEWSTER,
St Andrews, Fife. October 19

Self-help

From Mr Hugh Charles-Jones
Sir, Re the Royal Mint's financial losses (Business, October 17), surely the remedy is in their own hands?
I am, Sir, Yours faithfully,
HUGH CHARLES-JONES,
Newport, Pembrokeshire. October 17

Baby carriage

From Mr Tony Killeen
Sir, I was moved almost to tears by the latest television commercial for Virgin Trains, which ends with all the passengers rejoicing in the birth of a healthy baby boy.

Is it true that the mother wasn't even pregnant when she boarded the train?
Yours faithfully,
TONY KILLEEN,
Bristol. October 17

Deflated

From Mr John Featherstone
Sir, A year ago, I sold a batch of blue-chip shares to fund the purchase of a new Korean-manufactured car, normally not a very wise move. A year on, the shares are worth 45 per cent of their sale value. The car is valued at 66 per cent of its purchase price.

Are things really that bad?
Yours faithfully,
JOHN FEATHERSTONE,
Deal, Kent. October 17

Rubbish bag

From Mr William Woodruff
Sir, Full of air with a twisted top? Should the Rubbish Bag which has won its creator

a £30,000 arts award (report, October 18) not have been titled *The Politician*?
Yours,
BILL WOODRUFF,
Lenham, Kent. October 18

Soar points

From Mr Roy Hyde

Sir, "Private school fees will soar by 10 per cent next year" (headline, October 21). Don't be daft. Nothing can soar by 10 per cent.
Yours faithfully,
ROY HYDE,
Cheltenham. October 21

From Mr T. E. Baker

Sir, Mr Roy Hyde objects to private school fees being described as "soaring" by a mere 10 per cent.

He should read the financial pages – where shares have "slumped" and "tumbled" by 2.7 per cent (October 24).
Yours faithfully,
T. E. BAKER,
Ringwood, Hampshire. October 24

From Dr Peter Cameron

Sir, School fees soar by 10 per cent, shares tumble 2.7 per cent.

Fortunately the £20 billion needed by the Chancellor is only to "plug a gap" (Business, October 25).
Yours sincerely,
PETER CAMERON,
Birnam, Dunkeld. October 25

From Dr D. Wilson

Sir, Had one just climbed Everest, a sudden fall of 2.7 per cent would be quite serious.
Yours sincerely,
DONALD WILSON,
Cambridge. October 25

All our yesterdays

From Mr Jon Hildrew

Sir, Back in my day, A levels were a much simpler affair. There were no ambiguous A2 levels, there were no calls for the Edu-

cation Secretary to resign, and there were no mass regrades. No; back in my day, we were simply given a grade and went on our way.

I'm 20.
Yours faithfully,
JON HILDREW,
Nottingham. October 18

Pay for pipers?

From Dr Peter B. Baker

Sir, It is becoming hard to find lawyers to do legal-aided divorce work because, they say, "they get paid less than a plumber on call-out" (report, October 22). Sounds good to me!
Yours faithfully,
PETER B. BAKER,
Ealing, London W5. October 22

JUST A SPOT OF MOONLIGHTING

Big on poetry

From Mr David St John

Sir, You described Lord Byron (T2, October 18) as 5ft 8in and 14 stone but also as 91.73 metres (300ft) and 992.5kg (nearly a ton).

Truly a giant among men.
Yours,
DAVID ST JOHN,
Lostwithiel, Cornwall. October 20

Great Britons

From Mr Clive Moulton

Sir, We clearly are not intended to take Great Britons (report and Play, October 19) too seriously, but what are we to make of a list that includes disc jockeys and some indifferent pop stars but where Gladstone, Wordsworth and Turner do not even make the top 100?

Yours faithfully,
CLIVE MOULTON,
Windsor, Berkshire. October 21

From Mr Trevor Trotman

Sir, Sir Paul McCartney at No 19, Sir Alexander Fleming at No 20. The writer of *Silly Love Songs* and the person whose discovery has saved millions of lives.

What odds could I get that in 50 years' time those positions will be reversed?

Yours faithfully,
TREVOR TROTMAN,
London SE25. October 21

From Professor Neil Jackson, FSA

Sir, A large billboard in York station promoting BBC2's current and rather ridiculous quest for Great Britons shows Shakespeare and Winston Churchill beneath the heading "Writer vs. Fighter".

It struck me that the former, like his contemporary Christopher Marlowe, was quite possibly an ale-house brawler, whereas it was the latter who won the Nobel Prize for Literature.

Yours faithfully,
NEIL JACKSON,
York. October 25

From Mrs Anthea Hardinge

Sir, I'm enjoying BBC Two's *Great Britons* series, but it strikes me that the competition is really between the presenters rather than their subjects.

While conceding that most of the top ten are historic giants who stand on their own undeniable merit, it's not surprising that Jeremy Clarkson's Brunel is so popular, given Clarkson's forceful, enthusiastic style.

Equally riveting was Richard Holmes's Cromwell and I was transfixed and enthralled by Tristram Hunt's Newton. Visually and verbally stimulating throughout, the presenter kept a discreet presence while enriching the list of (amazing) facts with his own interesting and thought-provoking observations.

So are we really judging Isambard, Oliver and Isaac? Or is it Jeremy, Richard and Tristram?

Yours faithfully,
ANTHEA HARDINGE,
Little Bealings, Suffolk. November 20

From Mrs P. J. Macdonald

Sir, The result of the BBC's *Great Britons* poll (report, November 25) reflects a view of the history of Britain which Winston Churchill himself would surely have been the last to endorse.

Yours faithfully,
P. J. MACDONALD,
Deganwy, Conwy. November 25

From Mr Richard Jackson

Sir, What a result! A leader in adversity, an inventive engineer and a beautiful compassionate woman.

Great Britain as perceived by the British, and the world?

Yours faithfully,
RICHARD JACKSON,
Sutton Coldfield, West Midlands. November 24

From Mr Trevor Trotman

Sir, Princess Diana polled twice as many votes as Charles Darwin.

Obviously we have a lot more evolving to do.

Yours faithfully,
TREVOR TROTMAN,
London SE25. November 24

From Major Gordon Darwin Wilmot (retd)

Sir, Who will be remembered world-wide in 1,000 years? It could be Churchill, it could be Wellington, an incredibly brave and able army commander who became Prime Minister. It could be Wilberforce and, less likely, Florence Nightingale, the practical results of whose compassion far outweighed those of Diana, Princess of Wales.

I believe the answer to be Shakespeare.
Yours faithfully,
GORDON WILMOT,
Burford, Oxfordshire. November 26

From Mr William G. Stewart

Sir, *Great Britons* was an important series in one respect. Millions more people will now know who Brunel was, and what his contribution means to engineering, and a lot more about what Darwin and Newton mean, not just to British history but to the history of the world. None of the portraits was by any means perfect but Brunel, Darwin and Newton did have particularly good advocates.

Pop history it might have been, but neither that nor the flawed voting system should detract from the overall success of the series.
Yours faithfully,
WILLIAM G. STEWART,
London SW15. November 27

From Mr Alfred Manders

Sir, When I telephoned my 25p vote for Brunel, the message said that "all the proceeds would go to BBC Children in Need". Now I read (report, November 26) that the BBC proposes to divert £100,000 to a memorial to Sir Winston Churchill.

Which is the greater cause?
Yours faithfully,
ALF MANDERS,
Alcester, Warwickshire. November 27

From Mr Andrew Wolfin

Sir, Is the fact that Princess Diana received twice as many votes as Charles Darwin in the Great Britons poll a case of survival of the fittest?
Yours faithfully,
ANDREW WOLFIN,
London NW4. November 26

From Mr John Godfrey

Sir, Now that the BBC has enjoyed such success with the 100 best Britons, the obvious sequel is the 100 worst Britons.

A particular fascination of the new series would be the not inconsiderable number of names that fall within both lists.
Yours faithfully,
JOHN GODFREY,
Richmond, Surrey. November 27

From Mr R. H. W. Cooper

Sir, Following the result of the BBC's Great Britons poll, a footnote in *Churchill*, Roy Jenkins's acclaimed biography, merits a wider airing:

Nicholas Soames, the eldest child of the Soameses who was therefore brought up on the Chartwell estate, told me an engaging story. When he was about six (circa 1955) he broke through the valet-guard which normally defended Churchill's working room and said: "Grandpapa, is it true that you are the greatest man in the world?"

Churchill said: "Yes, now bugger off."
Yours faithfully,
R. H. W. COOPER,
Ambleside, Cumbria. November 26

Morris and Rossetti

From Mr Charles Spencer

Sir, Marcus Binney's description of Jane Burden as Rossetti's model (report, October 21) is misleading. She was more like his muse.

He and William Morris first saw Jane in an Oxford theatre when they were painting murals in the Oxford Union building. They both fell in love with her. Morris was inspired to paint his only picture, to build the Red House, and even to design her clothes. Rossetti produced a wonderful series of drawings and paintings of her.

Bernard Shaw said he found her boring and stupid, discussing suet puddings. But the lady clearly had intelligence; she married Morris, who had money, and then had an affair with the more romantic Rossetti.
Yours truly,
CHARLES SPENCER,
London W9. October 21

Living at home

From Ms Liz Scott

Sir, Children return to the nest (report, October 21) not just for monetary reasons.

The main attraction is that now children are allowed to have their lover to stay overnight at the parental home. There is simply no incentive to leave to enjoy the pleasures of the flesh when these are available at home, with home cooking and no bills to pay thrown in.

Yours faithfully,
LIZ SCOTT,
Teddington. October 21

From Mrs Susan Starks

Sir, From the economic point of view, it is surely beneficial for children to live at home as long as possible, thus making efficient use of the nation's housing resources, which in turn will take the pressure off rents and house prices.

Financially speaking, parents and children should agree a level of rent that balances household expenses against the children's ability to pay. If the parents do not need the cash, they can put it into a savings account and return it to the children when they eventually move out (which, in our experience, will not take long).

Yours faithfully,
SUSAN STARKS,
London W6. October 26

From Mrs Angela Lynne

Sir, Not everyone now allows their children's lovers back for the night.

We have five daughters and a son, all in their twenties and all living away from home. Home life offers a free bed (single), free food (which they have to cook), free fires (which they have to make), free flowers to pick (which they have to weed) and a free companionable dog (which they have to walk).

At least two or three of the offspring, in varying combinations, come home to this reviving lifestyle every weekend.

Yours faithfully,

A. G. LYNNE,
Attleborough, Norfolk. November 1

From Mr Andrew Wolfin

Sir, In my relatively large (and extremely close) family, we children return to the nest not for monetary reasons, but to conduct our arguments in person rather than on the telephone.

Come to think of it, the appearance of this letter should guarantee a major row over the weekend.

Yours etc,
ANDREW WOLFIN,
London NW4. October 25

Short memory

From Mr R. W. Mellor, FREng

Sir, I phoned my insurance company to report some storm damage. "What storm was that?" was the reply.

Yours faithfully,
R. W. MELLOR,
Chelmsford. October 28

From Mr Malcolm Mackinven

Sir, On reporting storm damage to his insurance company Mr R. W. Mellor was asked: "What storm was that?"

Could it be that the insurance company call centre is on the Indian sub continent?

Yours faithfully,
M. R. J. MACKINVEN,
Chelmsford, Essex. November 1

Quality of copy editing

From Mr Michael Goldman

Sir, Dan Franklin, publishing director of Jonathan Cape, says (report, October 28) that it is impossible to judge whether standards of copy editing in book publishing have declined.

I expect that anyone who was reading books over 30 or so years ago and who has continued to do so will strongly disagree with him. I agree with his suggestion that authors are also to blame, but it is the publishers who must accept responsibility for lowering standards of quality control in this respect.

Yours faithfully,
MICHAEL GOLDMAN,
Blackheath, London SE3. October 28

From Mr Ormond Uren

Sir, Many years ago a Soviet dissident living in exile in Britain pointed out to me that "ugly literals" were unknown in Soviet publishing.

Before publication books would be subject to scrutiny by a series of censors. The censors were highly literate people, so in their quest for subversive ideas they would also pick up and correct any misprints along the way.

Yours sincerely,
ORMOND UREN,
London NW5. October 28

From Mr Philip Vaughan

Sir, I suspect I am not alone in finding wry amusement in the juxtaposition of your cartoon and its deplorable grocers' apostrophe on page 18 today with your third leading article on page 19, wherein you lament "the decline of British publishing standards".

Yours sorrowfully,
PHILIP VAUGHAN,
Reading. October 28

From Mr Joseph Palley

Sir, You denounce book publishers for cutting corners with copy editing and proofreading (leading article, October 28).

Glass houses and stones?

Yours etc,
JOSEPH PALLEY,
Richmond, Surrey. October 28

From Mrs A. H. Powell

Sir, How splendid to read of Doris Lessing taking up the cudgels for standards of perfection in publishing. So often the misuse of a word or an incorrect Latin tag can spoil the wincing reader's enjoyment of an excellent book or article.

For many years I assisted the late R. E. Latham, Editor of the British Academy's *Medieval Latin Dictionary from British Sources.* There could hardly have been a better training ground for an apprentice dragon than typing his green-ink MSS and later dealing with the eyeball-scrunching galley proofs from the Oxford University Press (already scanned by its own "learned reader"). Tedious work and, indeed, "very, very poorly paid".

But it was fascinating, and there was the occasional small accolade from the great man when an overlooked biblical reference was picked up or a quotation restored to its proper section in the text.

Yours faithfully,
AVRIL H. POWELL,
Norwich. November 2

All at sea

From Mr Keith Coleman

Sir, The picture of HMS *Nottingham* being transported back to the UK on the deck of the *Swan* (October 23) reminded me of the severe rebuke I received from a naval officer when I inadvertently called his ship a boat. I was informed a boat was small enough to be carried by a ship.

Oh, that I could meet him now!

Yours sincerely,
KEITH COLEMAN,
Chelmsford, Essex. October 24

From Professor Calum Carmichael

Sir, The late Duncan Forbes of Clare College, Cambridge, once told me that, on a visit to South Uist in the Outer Hebrides, a villager, hearing that Forbes was from Cambridge, said to him: "I am a great seafaring man myself, now tell me a little about the Oxford and Cambridge Boat Race".

Yours sincerely,
CALUM CARMICHAEL,
Ithaca, New York. November 2

From Mr A. J. Colbert

Sir, HMS *Nottingham* was badly damaged when she hit submerged rocks and has just returned after a voyage half way round the world aboard a ship-carrier without further mishap (report and photograph, December 9).

Perhaps in future all our warships should travel this way.

Yours faithfully,
A. J. COLBERT,
Walsall. December 9

The cult of "cool"

From Mrs Sheila Seymour

Sir, Reading "The A-Z of Cool" (T2, October 28) brought to mind Maurice Chevalier singing *I'm Glad I'm Not Young Any More*.

Yours faithfully,
SHEILA SEYMOUR,
Tadcaster, North Yorkshire. October 28

From Mr Dillwyn Miles

Sir, Maurice Chevalier may have sung *I'm Glad I'm Not Young Any More*, but he is also reputed to have said: "I prefer old age to the alternative."

Yours faithfully,
DILLWYN MILES,
Haverfordwest, Pembrokeshire. October 31

From Wing Commander I. S. Headley, RAF (retd)

Sir, My wife and I are less frequently targeted in the street these days by aggressive individuals clutching clipboards. We have concluded that we must be perceived as poor risks for insurers, too poverty-stricken to afford double-glazing, lacking opinions relevant to market researchers, and looking more suited to receiving charity than to offering it. On the other hand, we might just be perceived as a pair of miserable-looking old gits.

In either case, we detect advantages in getting older.

Yours sincerely,
IAN HEADLEY,
Wetheringsett, Suffolk. October 30

From Mr Peter Stamford

Sir, Richard Needham, for many years a columnist on the *Toronto Globe and Mail*, wrote the following about getting older:

As you grow old, you lose your interest in sex, your friends drift away, your children often ignore you. There are many other advantages of course, but these would seem to me to be the outstanding ones.

Yours sincerely,
PETER STAMFORD,
Port Elgin, Ontario. November 5

Dispelling doubt

From Mr Julian Corlett

Sir, I note that the first 20 readers supplying correct entries to the spelling competition (T2, October 29) will receive a copy of the "indispensible" *Times Style & Usage Guide*.

Would it not have been of more use to those submitting incorrect entries?

Sincerely,
JULIAN CORLETT,
Scunthorpe, North Lincolnshire. October 29

Falling expectations

From Mr Bernard Preger

Sir, In the absence of any other good news about the weather, can you reassure me that the reservoirs are now full?

Sincerely,
BERNARD PREGER,
Bury, Lancashire. October 27

Mail and female

From Mrs P. Wilford-Smith

Sir, How's this for junk mail? I have just received a Gillette Mach 3 razor.

Yours faithfully,
PAMELA WILFORD-SMITH,
Ledbury, Herefordshire. October 31

From Mr Alex Galloway

Sir, I am not sure why Mrs Pamela Wilford-Smith regarded her Gillette Mach 3 as junk mail.

It may be indelicate to mention it, but the silky smooth legs of many of my lady friends are no more natural than my smooth cheeks; and in most cases the means of

achieving the result is, I believe, the same.
Yours etc,
ALEX GALLOWAY,
London E14. November 1

Art appreciation

From Mr Marc Cranfield-Adams

Sir, Surely the difference between Kim Howells's paintings (report and photograph, November 1) and those exhibits submitted for the Turner Prize is that one lot have been created by so-called professionals and the other by an amateur. Long live the gentleman amateur.
Yours etc,
MARC CRANFIELD-ADAMS,
Richmond-upon-Thames, Surrey. November 1

From Mr David Hill

Sir, Defenders of the Turner Prize (reports, October 30) are reminding us again that down the years great works of art have sometimes been dismissed initially as fatuous rubbish. It does not follow that everything that appears to be fatuous rubbish must be a great work of art.
Yours,
DAVID HILL,
Marlow, Buckinghamshire. October 31

From Andrew Rutherford

Sir, May I be the first to collect the various comment cards on display at the Tate and enter them for next year's Turner Prize?
Yours faithfully,
ANDREW RUTHERFORD (Aged 10),
London SW15. November 1

Sleep patterns

From Mr Craig Reid

Sir, Simon Crompton ("Sweet dreams", T2, October 28) says that the origin of eight hours as the norm for a night's sleep is not clear but "may be connected to medical opinion during the two World Wars."

Another factor could be the increased regulation of life in the the 19th and 20th centuries caused by industrialisation. Now that mines and factories are fewer, and peo-

ple can work at home and can run their lives more flexibly, the "eight hours a night" could lose its currency and eventually be replaced by the catnap.
Yours sincerely,
CRAIG REID,
Wallasey, Merseyside. October 28

The collapse of the Burrell case

From Mr Collin Rossini

Sir, Does the Queen recall that she promised me a knighthood when I saw her at fête some years back?
Yours,
COLLIN ROSSINI,
Leigh-on-Sea, Essex. November 1

Death at Pooh Corner

From Mrs Pen Jenkinson

Sir, Did the reported research ("Gloom is Good", T2, October 25) measure degrees of optimism and pessimism? Could it be that it is those midway between the "one-note optimist" and the "fully paid-up pessimist" who are most at risk of an early death?

Possibly the truly gloomy attract fewer dependants and needy friends than those of more cheerful disposition. The happy are approachable. They are usually kind and considerate. They offer a shoulder to cry on. Perhaps this permanently wet shoulder contributes to a shorter life?

Eeyores have few confidants. Poohs typify the one-note optimist. Neither is likely to be looked to for moral support. Could the timid little Piglet be the most likely candidate for an early grave?
Yours faithfully,
P. A. JENKINSON,
Scarborough, North Yorkshire. October 30

News in brief

From Mr Gary Best

Sir, What a fortnight. Ulrika revealing, Deayton leaving, Crozier resigning, IDS twitching, the Queen forgetting and Posh escaping. One could forgive the Labour

Government if it had decided it was a good fortnight to bury bad news.

However, I'm sure *The Times* was looking out for that sort of thing.

Yours,
GARY BEST,
Reigate, Surrey. November 4

Trick of the night

From Mr P. W. Arthur
Sir, Having declined to "treat" a few days ago on Hallowe'en, I had eggs thrown at me on my doorstep.

This recent import from America is simply a protection racket wrapped up as an innocent little jape.
Yours faithfully,
P. W. ARTHUR,
Tunbridge Wells, Kent. November 2

From Ms Jennifer Frazer
Sir, I must protest at the almost universal assumption that "trick or treat" is a wholly American custom.

Anyone who had the benefit of a good Scottish upbringing will have regularly gone "guising", dressing up and receiving sweets from neighbours. The fact that the English didn't catch on to this until years later is to their disadvantage.
Yours faithfully,
JENNIFER FRAZER,
London NW4. November 6

From Mr Duncan Broomhead
Sir, While "trick or treat", as we see it today, is heavily influenced by America, there is no need for Jennifer Frazer to feel sorry for the disadvantaged English.

For over 200 years October 31 has marked the beginning of the "souling" season in Cheshire. While the Scottish "guisers" are receiving sweets from their neighbours, the Cheshire "soul cakers" will be performing their local version of the mumming play and, according to the song, they will be requesting ale and strong beer. Cheers.
Yours faithfully,
DUNCAN BROOMHEAD,
Macclesfield, Cheshire. November 7

From Mrs Valerie Lanceley
Sir, I grew up in the 1950s in a small North Yorkshire farming community; it was our practice to celebrate Mischief Night on November 4.

Preparations began during the day when the adults removed garden gates and furniture lest they end up on the bonfire next day, blocked up their letterboxes and made sure pets were safely inside. Formidable old ladies armed with walking sticks would take up position and keep watch behind the curtains.

As night fell we children went mischief-making, but we certainly didn't expect any treats – the object was not to get caught.
Yours faithfully,
VALERIE LANCELEY,
London SW15. November 9

From Mrs Elizabeth Hughes
Sir, In Scotland it was not "trick or treat". Rather, we nervous children had to sing a song or recite a well-rehearsed poem on the neighbour's doorstep – an exchange of treats.
Yours faithfully,
ELIZABETH HUGHES,
London N20. November 10

From Mr Clive Howard-Luck
Sir, The custom of "souling" must have gone back to pre-Reformation times.

A *Dictionary of the Sussex Dialect* shows that, during the souling season, people dressed in black held street collection for Masses for the dead to be said on All Souls Day and subsequent days in November. Later on, house-to-house collections were made for this purpose with the collectors being offered soul cakes (hot spiced buns) and ginger-pop.
Yours faithfully,
CLIVE HOWARD-LUCK,
Hastings. November 12

From Mr Alan Ritchie
Sir, Guising has as much to do with "trick or treat" as busking has to do with armed robbery.

A Scottish guiser will entertain the neigh-

bours with a song, dance, poetry or jokes and hope to be rewarded for their efforts with a sweet or two. But at no point is there the threat inherent in the American custom of trick or treat, which is simply blackmail.
Yours faithfully,
ALAN RITCHIE,
Clarkston, Glasgow. November 12

From Mr David Higham

Sir, I too was brought up in North Yorkshire, and my father used to enjoy Mischief Night enormously, rigging up hosepipe booby traps to spray mischief-makers.

After attending a confirmation class one dark and stormy Mischief Night I attempted to make a contribution by removing the churchyard gate, only to be caught redhanded by the vicar. With Jeeves-like inspiration I explained that I had found the gate already off its hinges and was trying to replace it. I was given sixpence.

If you are still with us, Mr Beswick, I confess.
Yours faithfully,
DAVID HIGHAM,
Chester. November 13

From Dr Euan W. MacKie

Sir, There have been comments in the press recently that Hallowe'en on October 31 is becoming more popular than Guy Fawkes night.

It is true that fireworks went off in this Glasgow suburb in a desultory manner every evening for about a week before November 5, but last night was different. One could almost have believed that a local war had broken out and was raging all evening.

The commemoration of the Gunpowder Plot certainly seems to be flourishing up here.
Yours faithfully,
EUAN W. MacKIE,
Bearsden, East Dunbartonshire. November 6

From Dr Glyndwr Prosser

Sir, I sympathise with the protest of Mr P. W. Arthur against the trick or treat protection racket, but on religious grounds.

My strategy this year was to prepare a brief message explaining the meaning of Hallowe'en and All Saints. This was to accompany a chunky Mini Kit-Kat bar and the offer of a Luke's Gospel.

But nobody came.

My wife and I, though, are enjoying the treats.
Yours sincerely,
G. V. PROSSER (Chartered psychologist),
Woking, Surrey. November 6

From Mr B. M. Marsden

Sir, Jennifer Frazer is mistaken in her view that the English lagged behind Scotland in the custom of trick or treat.

The 1867 diary of the Derbyshire antiquary Llewellynn Jewitt, who lived in the remote Peak village of Winster, states that on several days in the winter of that year several parties of "Guisers" and "Mummers" visited his home and "we had them in the kitchen and gave them refreshments and money".

Though some of the visitors performed well, one group of guisers "were so dull and stupid" that he speedily packed them off.
Yours faithfully,
BARRY M. MARSDEN,
Bingley, West Yorkshire. November 7

Fewer and less

From Mr Michael Bird

Sir, Useful distinctions between "less" and "fewer" can and should still be made (Philip Howard's Comment, October 31).

Is there not a world of difference between an editor asking his columnists to write fewer pedantic articles and asking them to write less pedantic articles?
Yours etc,
MICHAEL BIRD,
London SW13. November 4

From Dr R. C. Bowes

Sir, Michael Bird seeks to distinguish between an editor asking his columnists to write fewer pedantic articles and asking them to write less pedantic articles.

While the former is admirable, the latter

THIS IS AN HISTORIC OCCASION

I'M HERE ONLY FOR THE BEER

fails to observe that pedantry, like pregnancy, cannot be qualified. You can't be "a bit pedantic".
Yours pedantically,
BOB BOWES,
Chewton Keynsham. November 6

From Mr Martin Heddy
Sir, It may be, as Dr R. C. Bowes says, that there are no degrees of pedantry.

Surely, however, an article that contained one instance of pedantry would be a less pedantic article than one that contained, say, five.
Yours etc,
MARTIN HEDDY,
Brighton. November 8

From Mrs Linda Thomson
Sir, I take issue with Dr R. C. Bowes's statement that "pedantry, like pregnancy, cannot be qualified".

During childbirth I was relieved to be ever less pregnant, and now (this letter notwithstanding) I am surely less pedantic than my husband.

Yours faithfully,
LINDA THOMSON,
Oxford. November 10

From Mrs Theo Stegers
Sir, Is it not just a little bit pedantic to say you can't be a bit pedantic?
Yours faithfully,
SALLY STEGERS,
Tidebrook, East Sussex. November 12

Mother's invention

From Mrs Vicky Macnair.
Sir, Who needs a bed that tilts to get reluctant risers up in the morning (report and photograph, November 2)?

What's wrong with the much cheaper "mother wielding a very cold wet sponge" technique? It never failed with my teenage son, and even works during power cuts.
Yours faithfully,
VICKY MACNAIR,
Chudleigh, Devon. November 2

Ups and downs

From Mrs Rosemary Fernandez.
Sir, Among the many problems my husband has to contend with in this modern age is now the fear of disappearing underground if the Urilift pop-up urinal (report and photographs, November 2) malfunctions once he is aboard.
Yours sincerely,
ROSEMARY FERNANDEZ,
Kenley, Surrey. November 2

Diana's butler

From Miss Helen Jones
Sir, Paul Burrell is now not so much a "rock", rather more an irritating piece of grit.
Yours faithfully,
HELEN JONES,
Romsey, Hampshire. November 7

Every cloud . . .

From Mrs Sally Tooth
Sir, I assume that one part of The Weather

on your back page is written for optimists and another for pessimists.

Under Today's Weather, for Greater London, South East England, etc it says: "A dry, bright day is expected, with the best of the sunshine likely in the morning before more cloudy conditions develop in the afternoon." Under the Five-Day Forecast, for London today, it says "Rain".

I am writing this looking out at a cloudless blue sky and bright sun.
Yours optimistically,
SALLY TOOTH,
London SW1. November 11

Bad form

From Mr Nicholas Kieft

Sir, I have received a letter from the Inland Revenue informing me that children's tax credit has been replaced by child tax credit and asking me to complete a form that is 12 pages long.

Fair enough, they need the information, but the accompanying instructions are 47 pages long.
Yours truly,
NICHOLAS KIEFT,
Boroughbridge, North Yorkshire. November 11

Sainted knight

From Mrs T. Browne

Sir, In an RSPB gift catalogue, St Francis of Assisi has been dubbed Sir Francis Assisi.

Is this promotion – or demotion?
Yours faithfully,
T. BROWNE,
Helston, Cornwall. November 11

From Sir Martin Berthoud

Sir, Mrs T. Browne asks whether the dubbing of St Francis of Assisi as Sir Francis in a catalogue constituted promotion or demotion. The latter, surely.

While I was running a charitable trust I was treated over the years to a bewildering assortment of mis-spellings and distortions of my name and title. Highlights were Mr Sir Martin & Co and Sir Martian; but the culmination came when I was addressed as

St Martin. For a second I felt beatified and, yes of course, promoted.
Humbly Yours,
MARTIN BERTHOUD,
Stoke by Nayland, Suffolk. November 13

The monarchy's troubled times

From the Reverend David Ackerman

Sir, Nobody could accuse the media of having a short memory, but your leading article ("A modern monarchy", November 12) suggests total amnesia.

Was it only a few months ago when the success of the Queen's Golden Jubilee confounded the press, which had systematically underestimated support for the Royal Family?

For me the question of the moment is not whether the monarchy has a future but whether the "free" press has one. Surely a privacy law is now more imminent than a republic ever will be.
Yours faithfully,
DAVID ACKERMAN,
Cheltenham, Gloucestershire. November 13

From Mr W. H. Cousins

Sir, The British monarchy is secure: what would the mass media do without it?
Yours sincerely,
W. H. COUSINS,
Upminster, Essex. November 13

From Mr Francis Wilford-Smith

Sir, What worries me most about the current "revelations" is the thought that one day we may wake up and find ourselves with the monarchy we deserve.
Yours faithfully,
FRANCIS WILFORD-SMITH,
Ledbury, Herefordshire. November 13

From Mr Emlyn Whitley

Sir, I have little interest in news of either low-level thuggery or high-level buggery; can't we have more about us lot in the middle?
Yours hopefully,
EMLYN WHITLEY,
Sudbury, Suffolk. November 12

Military measures

From Mr Graham Carr

Sir, Today (report, later editions) you inform us that the missing decoy tank found in Wales is the size of three cars, which I imagine is roughly the size of a tank.
Yours faithfully,
GRAHAM CARR,
Southwell, Nottinghamshire. November 12

Rough ride

From Mr Ronnie Cowe

Sir, I see that the Queen is travelling to the State Opening of Parliament in a "stagecoach" (leading article, November 12).

Is this an economy measure?
Yours faithfully,
RONNIE COWE,
Banbury, Oxfordshire. November 12

Dodgy motors

From Mr Brian Peter Moss

Sir, You list dirty numberplates as being one way of dodging the Central London congestion charge (report, November 13). How about an illegally mounted tow bar?

Recently in a car park I pointed out to a motorist that one of the bolts on his tow bar appeared to have sheared. He politely but unashamedly informed me that the device was not intended for towing a trailer, but was to "fool the speed cameras" by obscuring the number.
Yours sincerely,
BRIAN P. MOSS,
Tamworth. November 13

Watch out

From Mr Ian R. M. Chaston

Sir, Any generalised government warning of danger is of little use without some explicit suggestion for effective action.

You will recall the roadside warning sign, "Beware, Low-Flying Aircraft". As the late, great, Michael Flanders said: "There's not a lot you can do about that . . . take off your hat!"

Yours faithfully,
IAN CHASTON,
London E14. November 13

From Mrs Lesley Gillick

Sir, Mr Ian Chaston mentions roadside warnings. What about the sign denoting rocks falling off mountains? My dilemma has always been whether to drive faster or slower.
Yours sincerely,
LESLEY GILLICK,
Sheringham. November 15

From Mr Andrew Hicks

Sir, Mrs Lesley Gillick is unsure whether to increase or decrease her driving speed when warned of falling rocks. Might I suggest that she closes her sunroof.
Yours faithfully,
ANDREW HICKS,
Streatham, London SW16. November 21

From Mr Ken Broad

Sir, My rule for road-signs is "falling rocks": go fast, "leaping deer": slow down.

The real dilemma occurs in hilly rural areas when, as so often happens, both signs are displayed in close proximity.
Yours sincerely,
KEN BROAD,
Newport, Shropshire. November 25

From Mr Michael Bird

Sir, As one rounds an Alpine bend, the real challenge is to predict the trajectory, not of falling rocks, but of the French or Italian driver coming the other way, having seen the same road-sign.
Yours faithfully,
MICHAEL BIRD,
London SW13. November 26

From Mr D. O. R. Mossman

Sir, I recall a *Punch* cartoon of many years ago which depicted a cluster of four signs at the roadside. They were, in order: Steep Hill; Double Bend; Narrow Bridge; Hospital.
Yours sincerely,
D. O. R. MOSSMAN,
Caterham, Surrey. December 1

Women drivers

From the Reverend Dr Jeanette Meadway

Sir, You report that 98 per cent of convictions for dangerous driving were of men drivers. This means that men are 49 times more likely than women to be convicted of dangerous driving. You report that they are also more likely to kill pedestrians.

Female drivers are twice as likely as men to have a collision in a car park.

The headline above these facts was "Insurance figures prove that women drivers can't park". A more appropriate headline would be "Female drivers get worst press".
Yours faithfully,
JEANETTE MEADWAY,
Woodford Green, Essex. November 10

From Mrs Diane K. Horsler

Sir, Women's lack of ability in parking their cars may need further investigation. My husband recently bumped into another car whilst parking, and apparently that was my fault, too.
Yours faithfully,
DIANE K. HORSLER,
Solihull, West Midlands. November 9

Clergy's employers

From the Reverend W. David Platt

Sir, After nine years as a curate, I became an incumbent in 1972. On my next tax return I entered "God" as my employer.

Soon I received a letter from the Inland Revenue. It was headed, "A case for special treatment."
Yours faithfully,
DAVID PLATT,
Didcot. November 14

From Mrs Gillian Gaisford

Sir, At about the same time as Father David Platt informed the Inland Revenue that his employer was "God", the husband of our cleaner at the vicarage advised them that her occupation was "Servant of the servant of the Lord". It went through without further comment.

Yours faithfully,
GILLIAN GAISFORD,
Knutsford, Cheshire. November 18

Ashes to ashes

From Dr Peter Burton

Sir, Sporting events like the Ashes are about loyalty. How dispiriting then to read your leading article "Not cricket: Ten ways to make the Ashes series competitive": a vein of humour long near-exhausted, now clumsily re-mined. Please either stick up for the players, and/or call for specific changes, or else hold your peace.

England are a decent international side playing the very toughest, and still drawing crowds down there. There was loss of nerve in this match perhaps, but the team deserves support.
Yours faithfully,
C. T. P. BURTON,
London E2. November 13

From Dr R. S. W. Hawtrey

Sir, A well-known prep school, famous for academic achievement, was for many years almost invincible at cricket. In the 1980s its first XI, if they were rash enough to lose a game, would be greeted by an extra Latin prep.

It's worth trying, surely.
Yours etc,
RALPH HAWTREY,
Cambridge. November 12

From Dr C. W. Godden

Sir, I have been a loyal follower of English cricket since childhood but need advice. I have a bookmaker account and prior to flying to Australia at the weekend thought I might place £5 on England to win the series 4–1. To my astonishment the odds of that happening are exactly the same (500–1) as Elvis being found alive.

Shall I go for the double at a quarter of a million to one or be safe and just back Elvis?
Yours faithfully,
CHARLES GODDEN (Member, MCC),
Guildford, Surrey. November 14

From Mr Alastair Stewart
Sir, Perhaps now is the time to introduce Handicap Cricket. A Test match should still comprise four innings: the Australians play one, and England play three.
Yours faithfully,
ALASTAIR STEWART,
Nunnington, York. November 26

From Mr Hugh Sanders
Sir, What a pity the Ashes urn is in no state to travel. Why not reduce it and its contents to new ashes and encapsulate them in a more robust container, which could then be played for annually? This would keep the Australians happy, retain the integrity of the original concept and give us something to play for.
Yours faithfully,
HUGH SANDERS,
Maidenhead. December 5

From Mr Mike Tait
Sir, I think the reason the MCC will not send the famous urn to Australia is that no one in the English cricketing world can be trusted to get the thing out of its cabinet without dropping it.
Yours sincerely,
MIKE TAIT,
Malvern, Worcestershire. December 6

From Mr George Reid
Sir, It can't be long, surely, until the England rugby XV score more than the Test cricket XI.
Yours faithfully,
GEORGE REID,
Edinburgh. November 29

From Dr Dave Allen
Sir, I have been rising early each day to suffer the miseries of the Ashes so I am as disappointed as most and would like nothing more than a strong England side in the future.

I would make one observation about the difficulties of achieving that aim. We introduced many modern sports to the world, we continue to have aspirations in most of them and this spreads our limited talent too thinly.

The Americans have the best idea because they play World Series competitions which exclude all foreign sides outside North America.

England should challenge every nation in the world to a triple crown series, playing one match each of cricket, football and rugby. Only four nations, France, Australia, New Zealand and South Africa, would have any real hopes of winning such a series against us. Such an experience might encourage us to be more positive about our sporting abilities.
Yours faithfully,
DAVE ALLEN,
Department of Creative Technologies,
University of Portsmouth, Hampshire.
December 2

From Dr Stephen J. Lockwood
Sir, As I understand it, England received the Ashes as a memorial to a humiliating defeat delivered by the Australians.

It would seem appropriate, therefore, that they remain in England.
Yours truly,
STEPHEN J. LOCKWOOD,
Colwyn Bay. December 3

From Mr R. A. B. Crowe
Sir, Mr George Reid forecasts that the England rugby XV will soon score more than the England cricket XI.

This has already taken place. The England XV scored 134 points against Romania at Twickenham in November 2001 while the England XI scored 79 runs at Brisbane in November 2002.
Yours sincerely,
R. A. B. CROWE,
Leigh-on-Sea, Essex. December 1

From Mr Roy Wallace
Sir, Dr Dave Allen's idea to improve our standing in the sporting world by challenging all nations to a triple series consisting of cricket, football and rugby, is interesting.

However, a much better idea would be for us to invent a new sport but not tell anyone else.
Yours faithfully,
ROY WALLACE,
Elstree, Hertfordshire. December 5

From Mr Tony Killeen
Sir, Mr Roy Wallace suggests that we need a unique sport we can beat the world at.
Does any other country play Quidditch?
Yours faithfully,
TONY KILLEEN,
Bishopston, Bristol. December 6

From Mr John Welford
Sir, Mr Tony Killeen suggests that Quidditch is a sport at which British teams could beat the world, on the grounds that it is played nowhere else.
Unfortunately, in *Harry Potter and The Goblet of Fire* the final of the Quidditch World Cup is played between Ireland and Bulgaria, with England having been knocked out in an earlier round.
Anyone for bog snorkelling or tiddlywinks?
Yours faithfully,
JOHN WELFORD,
Nuneaton, Warwickshire. December 10

From Mr Stephen Aries
Sir, England's drubbing of Romania at rugby may be considered some form of revenge for the fact that England were trounced by Transylvania 390–10 in the last Quidditch World Cup.
Yours faithfully,
STEPHEN ARIES,
Reigate, Surrey. December 10

From Mrs Christine Laine
Sir, On December 31, 2001 you reported that "the first Muggles Quidditch match was played in a temperature of –15C in Moscow last week".
Another good idea snitched.
Yours faithfully,
CHRISTINE LAINE,
Wrexham. December 11

Bad line
From Mr Charles Hedgcock
Sir, Today the automated voice at National Train Inquiries apologised for the delay in answering, due to "adverse weather conditions".
Leaves on the telephone line?
Yours faithfully,
CHARLES HEDGCOCK,
London W14. November 14

Expensive imports
From Mr Geoffrey Mills
Sir, So our friendly immigration services have let in Turkish crime organisations ("Turkish gangsters blamed for 'Wild West' street battle", report, November 12) as well as Jamaican Yardies, Chinese Triads, Italian Mafia, and the Albanians now said to be running London prostitution.
What space have they left for our native English villains?
Yours faithfully,
GEOFFREY MILLS,
Andover, Hampshire. November 12

Short-changed
From Mrs Joanna Thomson
Sir, Last week I attempted to get a gas heater serviced, an overgrown tree pollarded, my brother's honey imported and to remortgage our home.
Because of bureaucracy and paperwork my only success was in borrowing the money. Is that all that is left for us to do these days?
Yours etc,
JOANNA THOMSON,
Walmer, Kent. November 18

Benefits of age
From Mrs W. Morgan
Sir, Among my husband's 80th birthday cards was a letter from Age Concern advising him of a "Funeral Plan".
Yours faithfully,

WINIFRED MORGAN,
Cardiff. November 18

Postal delay

From Mrs Margaret Dean
Sir, Today in the office I received from the Royal Mail a beautiful box containing a single pink carnation. The card enclosed assured me that flowers and foodstuff dispatched via their network would be safely and freshly delivered next day.

Sadly, the carnation was dead, presumably having been travelling for some days. Should I be grateful that it wasn't a kipper?
Yours faithfully,
MARGARET DEAN,
Torquay. November 14

Royal Family's place in national life

From Mr Andrew Bell
Sir, The Princess Royal has spent the last ten days visiting the British overseas territories of Ascension Island and St Helena.

So remote is St Helena in the South Atlantic that, to accomplish this journey, she has spent two nights in the air and four days on a cargo ship to be on the island for 50 hours. The loyal 5,000 "Saints" are celebrating their 500th anniversary and the Princess Royal's visit doubtless gave much pleasure.

Except for your Court Circular I have read no references anywhere to this royal visit. We can now expect to be treated to square metres of newsprint about HRH, her husband and their misbehaving dog (Law, November 19).
Yours faithfully,
ANDREW BELL,
Helston, Cornwall. November 20

Student stress

From Miss Jayne Mann
Sir, I am a sixth-form student and I would have liked to comment at length about your report "Pupils under constant exam stress" (November 19).

However, as I have to do my art, geography, English and technology homework, prepare a presentation for my silver Duke of Edinburgh's award, work to pay for driving lessons, practise for my out-of-school dance classes, organise my work experience, help around the house and learn my lines for the school play – all so that I can have a fully rounded statement of experience to offer to a university – I'm sorry, but I haven't got the time.
Yours faithfully,
JAYNE MANN,
Abbots Bromley, Staffordshire. November 19

Fighting talk

From Mr Dermot Hunt
Sir, This morning's sports pages contain the following three phrases: "Dave and me messed up all the time" – Frank Skinner; "intellectuals like what we are" Simon Barnes; and "All credit to my caddie and I" – Colin Montgomerie.

Would you agree that only the third one hurts?
Yours faithfully,
DERMOT HUNT,
London W1. November 18

Caught in the act

From Mr Alastair McWhirter
Sir, "Voyeurism is to become an offence" (report, November 20). "TV Choice – *Celebrity Big Brother*" (T2, same day).

Any chance of emergency legislation?
Yours faithfully,
ALASTAIR McWHIRTER,
Devizes, Wiltshire. November 20

Modern masters

From Professor Richard Wilson
Sir, You report that Olafur Eliasson, the artist hired by Tate Modern, has turned a river green in Stockholm. This is nothing new. It happens in Chicago every year, to mark St Patrick's Day, and it is done by city workers.

Also in Chicago there are several pulsing jets in a semi-tropical garden. All day long and every day they intermittently hurl bending rods of water over coffee-drinkers in the garden cafe. It is a spectacular and unusual experience, but nobody has yet thought of hiring Chicago's city plumbers to put on major exhibitions at Tate Modern or anywhere else.
Yours sincerely,
RICHARD WILSON,
Beverley, Yorkshire. November 20

From Mr Michael J. C. Wilson
Sir, Now that the brouhaha over the Turner Prize shortlist has died down, the awards committee might consider taking a leaf out of the National Lottery book.

If the entries fail to provide a respectable example, they should declare a "rollover" for the following year. That would both concentrate minds and counter the negative publicity the recent awards have brought about.
Yours faithfully,
MICHAEL J. C. WILSON,
Market Weighton, York. November 21

Forever England?

From Canon Eric Chard
Sir, "English is not classed as a nationality." So I am advised in my completion of the Criminal Records Bureau's disclosure application form. From now on it appears I am simply British.

Perhaps I should also begin to describe myself as a priest of the Church of Britain?
Yours sincerely,
ERIC CHARD,
Clitheroe, Lancashire. November 18

Pukka patience

From Mr Mike Brown
Sir, Given the fine example of almost saint-like patience that Jamie Oliver has shown so far with his absentee trainees (no money for bus fare, but still can afford cigarettes) in the Channel 4 series *Jamie's*

Kitchen, I am thinking of starting a club with the initials WWJD, standing for "What Would Jamie Do?", to remind me whenever I lose my temper or feel frustrated.
Yours sincerely,
MIKE BROWN,
Trowbridge, Wiltshire. November 20

From Mr Peter Stanley
Sir, Mr Mike Brown extols Jamie Oliver's saint-like patience and suggests starting a club with the initials WWJD, standing for "What Would Jamie Do?" As he probably knows, bracelets have been sold worldwide for more than three years now bearing the same initials but standing for "What Would Jesus Do?"

Does Mr Brown sense a divine calling in Jamie Oliver?
Yours faithfully,
PETER STANLEY (Manager),
Folly's End Church, Croydon. November 24

Tax code secrets

From Mr Derek Rees
Sir, Now that I have retired my tax details have been transferred by the Cardiff Tax Office to the Inland Revenue at Salford.

I have received my new tax code. In the box used to give further information is the following explanation:

IRCC MCR COD CHNG BASED ON ESTPAY FIG FROM IREC CARDIFF

They enclosed a leaflet P3, Understand Your Tax Code. I wonder if there is a leaflet, Undstad ur Txmns abvs.
Urs fayfule,
DEREK REES,
Caldicot, Monmouthshire. November 22

From Mr John Halford
Sir, I presume that Mr Derek Rees's tax details have been transferred from Cardiff to Salford to make room for my tax records to be transferred from Plymouth to Cardiff.
Yours faithfully,
J. W. HALFORD,
Hartley, Plymouth. November 27

Unwanted charity

From Mr Norman Phillips

Sir, Is there a charitable organisation able to make use of unsolicited pens sent to me by charitable organisations?
Yours faithfully,
NORMAN PHILLIPS,
Bidford on Avon, Warwickshire. November 23

From Mr Robin Stevens

Sir, Mr Norman Phillips asks about charitable uses for pens provided by charities.

Look no further than your local church. They are needed in the pews for visitors to complete declarations on Gift Aid envelopes.
Yours faithfully,
ROBIN STEVENS
(National Stewardship Officer), The Archbishops' Council of the Church of England, London SW1. November 26

From Mrs Thelma Shepherd

Sir, Earlier this year our church had a pen collection for a school in Namibia. Eighty were sent and gratefully received.

The pens continued to come in and the next batch are being sent to a school in Ghana that has a link with a local school here. We are assured that they are going to a good home.
Yours truly,
T. SHEPHERD,
Wing, Bedfordshire. December 2

From Mrs Thelma Shepherd

Sir, Rather naively I did not expect, following publication of my letter about our church sending pens to children in Africa, to receive almost 900 pens and many lovely letters.

The pens are now going to Plan International UK in Uganda, one of *The Times* Christmas charities, and to a school in The Gambia. I thank your readers for this interesting experience, but please, no more pens.
Yours truly,
T. SHEPHERD,
Wing, Buckinghamshire. January 4

Educated dress

From Professor Emeritus Bob Spence, FREng

Sir, Mary Spillane's advice concerning lecturers' wardrobes (report, November 21) suggests that she has never presented an extensive course of lectures to a class of lively, intelligent and inquiring 20-year-olds whose principal criterion is whether the lecturers know their subject and can answer questions without waffle.

For my lectures next week, and contrary to her advice, I shall avoid lipstick and black hair (the latter option vanished some years ago), don my filthy laboratory coat that doubles as a board cleaner and retain my longstanding beard. My shirt will not, I fear, be "in this season's colour, plum".

Will my students mind? Not a bit. They certainly know how to present themselves for business interviews without Ms Spillane's advice, and in later years will have fond memories of my Hawaiian shirts and other sartorial eccentricities.

Lecturers do not live on a catwalk; they perform in the real world.
Yours faithfully,
ROBERT SPENCE,
Whyteleafe, Surrey. November 22

Figures of fun

From Mr Andrew Bernard

Sir, Your graphic ("Tanker disaster", November 21) on the loss of the *Prestige* shows that the depth to which it has sunk is 11,500ft, or 3,500m, or "9.2 times the height of the Empire State Building".

The correct Imperial unit for the discussion of height and depth is surely Nelson's Column. That being so, the *Prestige* rests 62.16NCs down. Furthermore, it weighed 81,564 tonnes deadweight, as much as some 11,652 African elephants each of seven tons, and was, at about 800ft, as long as 26.67 London buses (30ft).
Yours faithfully,

ANDREW BERNARD,
Clanfield, Oxfordshire. November 22

I'm on the train

From the Reverend Claire Wilson

Sir, The frequent flouting of the no-mobile-phones rules in railway "Quiet Coaches" makes these supposed safe havens worse in the end for my blood pressure than the rest of the train in which the things are permitted nuisances.
Yours sincerely,
CLAIRE WILSON,
London E4. November 28

Polysyllabic confusion

From Mr Richard Need

Sir, Why does Barbara Roche, the Minister for Social Exclusion and Deputy Minister for Women (report, November 27), want to replace the five syllable word "homosexual" with the 13-syllable expression "orientation towards people of the same sex", when that is precisely what homosexual means?

Can she be confusing the Greek prefix used here (meaning "the same") with the Latin "homo" (meaning man)?
Yours faithfully,
RICHARD NEED,
Cheam, Surrey. November 27

Ticket surcharges

From Mr Stephen Gell

Sir, I recently saw an advert for tickets to a concert taking place next August; the tickets are priced at £35 each, but on top of this a £3.25 booking fee and a £4.70 transaction fee were also required for each booking.

This must qualify as one of the better rates of pay for a job: £7.95 to put tickets in an envelope and post them.
Yours sincerely,
STEPHEN GELL,
Leek, Staffordshire. November 26

From Mrs Vanessa Smith

Sir, Stephen Gell was indeed unfortunate in paying an additional transaction fee over and above the booking fee and ticket price for his concert tickets.

I was delighted on booking tickets to be connected to a real person, rather than a machine telling me to "press 2". At the end of our conversation, somewhat shamed, he added there was an extra 84p surcharge, over and above the ticket price and booking fee.

I was laughing so hard I had him repeat it: "Human assistance fee."
Yours faithfully,
VANESSA SMITH,
Guildford. December 1

Quite a mouthful

From Mr Michael Harman

Sir, "Now that ministers have bitten this bullet, they must swallow it whole" (leading article, November 27).

I look forward to your medical correspondent's comments on this interesting development of an ancient practice.
Yours sincerely,
MICHAEL HARMAN,
Camberley, Surrey. November 27

Real musketeers

From Mr Larry Rushton

Sir, Most great writers refine and develop or, depending on your view, steal from, the works of others. Thus, as the remains of Alexandre Dumas are installed into the Pantheon (report, November 30), we might spare a thought for Gatien Courtils de Sandras.

About a hundred years before Dumas was born he wrote *The Memoirs of M D'Artagnan*, perhaps loosely based on the life of a Gascon soldier called Charles de Batz. Herein one finds a sinisterly beautiful "Milady", secret jewels connected to a royal scandal, and three devoted palace-guard musketeers called . . . yes, you guessed them.
Yours sincerely,
LARRY RUSHTON,
Piddington, Northampton. November 30

Crossword puzzle

From Dr Norman Woffenden

Sir, Recent trends in the issue of prizes for the Saturday Crossword cause me unease.

I struggle to complete the crossword and use dictionaries, a thesaurus, books of quotations, crossword cheat books, encyclopaedia, electronic cheats, my wife, son and daughter-in-law to complete the thing and most weekends am able to send it in. Sometimes my answers are correct, but the lottery of the draw has not led me to win one of the five £20 book tokens so generously given by *The Times* each week.

In the past few weeks the odds have increased against competitors from these isles. Some 20 per cent of these magnificent prizes have been awarded to residents in continental Europe, the Far East and the Americas.

Is this the thin end of the wedge? Are we slowly being excluded?

Yours exasperatedly (but not xenophobically),
NORMAN WOFFENDEN,
Bolton. December 1

From Mr John Spencer

Sir, For some time I was minded to write to you on the lines of Dr Norman Woffenden's expression of anxiety over the (surely disproportionate) frequency with which an overseas address crops up in the list of lucky winners of your Saturday crossword competition. My hand was stayed only by the fear that I would become a marked man. But of course there are marks and marks.

I shall kick myself if I see Dr Woffenden's name this coming Saturday.

Yours perhaps regretfully,
JOHN SPENCER,
Oxford. December 3

From Mr Peter Webber

Sir, I still hold a sneaking regard for an ex-colleague who won your Saturday crossword competition during a postal strike in the early 1980s. He picked our brains, then submitted his correct solution by means of the then newfangled fax machine.

No sense of shame; just a smug expression on his face and the flaunting of his splendid Parker pen prize.

Yours sincerely,
PETER WEBBER,
Ruislip, Middlesex. December 7

From Mr John Lloyd

Sir, I find that as the years advance I get quicker at completing the crossword on my own. Last Saturday I started at 14.00 and finished at 15.10 – a record for me. Either the crossword is getting easier or exposure to the methods of clueing over 28 years renders solutions more easy.

There is a third possibility: I have suddenly become clever. My wife discounted that immediately.

Yours faithfully,
JOHN LLOYD,
Norwich. December 8

From Mr Barry Hyman

Sir, First clue in the T2 crossword on Saturday (Weekend): "Civil War reenactment society". Give up in disgust. Turn to Libby Purves for comfort on page 3 of the same section. First paragraph: "I was in The Sealed Knot."

Can we always get help like this?

Yours faithfully,
BARRY HYMAN,
Bushey Heath, Hertfordshire. December 7

From Mr Don Finkel

Sir, The explanation for the increase in overseas winners of *The Times* crossword competition is that the crossword is now available for online submission via subscription at: www.timesonline.co.uk/crossword

Yours sincerely,
DON FINKEL,
Edgware, Middlesex. December 9

From Mr Frank Woodgate

Sir, Having been the fortunate recipient of one of your wonderful crossword prizes (for 22,175), after many years of trying, I too noticed that recent winners have been emanating from not only the mainland United States, but also the offshore Hong Kong island of Lantau. I decided that exotic foreign stamps were turning the heads of the decision-makers.

More significantly, it seems that increasing attempts are being made to encourage non-Anglophones to enter by incorporating foreign words in the answers. Since my glorious win I have seen, among others, German (*echt*), Italian (*terza rima*) and Spanish (El Niño).

Sacré bleu!
Yours faithfully,
FRANK WOODGATE,
Blackheath, London SE3. December 6

From Mrs Hilary Lainé
Sir, I have noted that, over the years, as the circulation of *The Times* goes up, there is no corresponding increase in the number of crossword prizes offered, so the chances of winning go down. I now do the crosswords for my own satisfaction and enjoyment, keep the answers, and check them if in doubt.

Some 20 years ago, a friend of mine became thoroughly exasperated by her lack of a win in your crossword competition after many attempts. From then on, if she completed the puzzle, instead of sending it in by post, she put the value of the stamp into a jamjar, and after a few years had saved up for her prize, thus bypassing the lottery completely.

Yours
HILARY LAINE,
Crewe. December 3

From Mr David E. A. Michael
Sir, Take heart, correspondents. I have won *The Times* crossword puzzle competition four times but have a zero strike rate with letters to the Editor.

Yours faithfully.
DAVID E. A. MICHAEL,
London SW3. December 6

When I was a lad . . .

From Mr John O'Byrne
Sir, The retirement of Strom Thurmond from the US Senate at the age of 100 (report, December 2) reminds me of a competition run by *The Washington Post* some years ago. Readers were asked to tell youngsters how much harder they had had it in the old days.

The winner was: "In my day, we didn't have Strom Thurmond. Oh, wait, yes, we did!"
Yours truly,
JOHN O'BYRNE,
Dublin. December 3

Degrees of terror

From Mrs G. H. Suttling
Sir, After reading about the smallpox terror alert in Britain I saw this alarming headline in a Norwegian paper: "Drunken moose alert in southern Norway".

Should I cancel my trip to Norway?
Yours sincerely,
G. H. SUTTLING,
London EC4. December 3

From Mr Matthew Wetmore
Sir, Mrs G. H. Suttling should not cancel her trip to Norway, but rather should go as an envoy of the British people to discover what it is about that country that makes a moose turn to drink.

Norway traditionally gives us a Christmas tree. Perhaps we should offer a team of outreach counsellors in return.
Yours faithfully,
MATTHEW WETMORE,
Halesworth, Suffolk. December 5

Firefighters' initiatives

From Mr B. D. Woolley
Sir, The Army saved the day over the foot-and-mouth problem and has bailed us out during the firefighters' dispute. May I suggest that it runs the NHS?
Yours faithfully,
B. D. WOOLLEY,
Sherborne, Dorset. December 3

You don't understand

From Mr D. Barton
Sir, Catherine O'Brien (T2, November 28) tells us that "every generation complains

that their parents don't understand them". Presumably she meant every generation since teenagers were invented in the 1950s.

Before that we were perhaps not so self-absorbed as to expect adults to understand us, so there was no cause for complaint. Rather it was for us to learn to understand, with our parents' help, the adult world which we were shortly to enter.

Yours,
D. BARTON,
Alton, Hampshire. December 2

From Mr David Wilson

Sir, They may complain about it, but surely the last thing teenagers actually want is to be understood by their parents.

Yours faithfully,
DAVID WILSON,
Bridell, Cardigan. December 6

Staying young

From Dr Kirsty Nichol Findlay

Sir, Jessica Lawrence should be flattered at being referred to as a "girl" at the age of 39 (report, "Woman sues over mistakes in her medical records", December 2).

My husband, a large canon of 60, was this year forced to resign from his parish awaiting two knee replacements, which have since been notably successful. He leapt with delight on reading his surgeon's report referring to him as "this lad".

Yours sincerely,
KIRSTY N. FINDLAY,
Hallthwaites, Cumbria. December 2

Royal critics

From Mr Roland White

Sir, It wasn't that many years ago when criticism of the Royal Family was deemed unfair because they were not allowed to answer back.

How times change, and how I bet they wish that was the position today.

Yours faithfully,
ROLAND WHITE,
Felpham, Bognor Regis. December 4

Conspiracy theory

From Mr Christopher Tanous

Sir, Your leading article "Pox and Panic" says that "there will always be a certain set of individuals for whom conspiracy is an attractive theory".

Individuals? Surely they're all in it together.

Yours paranoically,
CHRISTOPHER TANOUS,
Uckfield, East Sussex. December 3

Cherie Blair's flats

From Dr Michael Tansey

Sir, Disproportionate attention is being given to the private business of Mrs Blair in which no law was broken and any error of judgment (which is entirely a matter of perception) is a matter only for those concerned. The fact that this receives any attention at all reflects both the squalid posturing of some of the media and the nature of that segment of the population obsessed with the foibles and weaknesses of celebrities.

Yours sincerely,
MICHAEL TANSEY,
Gamlingay, Sandy. December 8

From Mr Ian K. Lanceley

Sir, The media coverage of Cherie Blair is not to do with the "foibles and weaknesses of celebrities", but has far more to do with the fact that false information was put out by 10 Downing Street, presumably in an attempt to cover up the facts.

Yours sincerely,
IAN K. LANCELEY,
London SW15. December 9

From Mr Denis Jackson

Sir, The stream of allegations made against Mrs Blair can simply be summed up thus: if you cannot successfully attack the Government's policies, or the Prime Minister himself, then await the opportunity to attack his family.

It is a sad reflection on society and an abuse of free speech by the press.

Yours faithfully,
DENIS JACKSON,
Cowes, Isle of Wight. December 10

From Mr Richard Lethbridge
Sir, The House of Commons will debate a government proposal to ban hunting with dogs on the grounds of cruelty.

Would it be too much to hope that a Member might table an amendment to ban hunting with journalists on the same grounds?
Yours faithfully,
RICHARD LETHBRIDGE,
Fulbrook, Oxfordshire. December 10

From Mr Sandy Skinner
Sir, If Mrs Cherie Blair, a private citizen, is indeed making personal use of the 10 Downing Street press office, a public resource, will she be sent a bill?
Yours faithfully,
SANDY SKINNER,
Winchcombe. December 10

From Mr David Bage
Sir, I cannot help thinking that everybody is going a bit over the top in their efforts to have a go at Mrs Blair.

Most of us have got friends who themselves have friends who are not exactly our "cup of tea". More to the point is that we have a Government that is such a compulsive spinner that it can never tell it like it is, even on the odd occasions when the truth would have done little or no harm at all.
Yours faithfully,
DAVID BAGE,
Lynsted, Kent. December 9

From Mr Jonathan Radgick
Sir, I am bemused by the surprise so widely expressed that a person of intelligence and probity such as Mrs Blair should employ a convicted fraudster to act as an intermediary in a property transaction.

Surely anyone who has had the joy of dealing with estate agents and lawyers in a purchase or sale of their property would think that having such a person on their side evens things out nicely.
Yours faithfully,

JONATHAN RADGICK,
Callaly Castle, Northumberland. December 10

From Mrs Elizabeth Bishop
Sir, Caesar's wife must be above suspicion.
Yours,
ELIZABETH BISHOP,
Oxshott. December 9

From Mr Gerald Grainge
Sir, Is Peter Foster Cherie's "star" in the same way that Paul Burrell was Diana's "rock"?
Yours faithfully,
GERALD GRAINGE,
Finglesham, Kent. December 10

From Mrs Caroline Charles-Jones
Sir, In the good old days we used, occasionally, to tell lies; then we were economical with the truth; recently we were misrepresented. Now we have a "misunderstanding".
Yours confusedly,
CAROLINE CHARLES-JONES,
Dinas, Pembrokeshire. December 10

From Mr Christopher Ashton-Jones
Sir, Whilst I would probably not be too upset for my wife to refer to me humorously as one of the "balls in the air" which she is juggling, I would be a little upset if she had not told me at the earliest opportunity of her plan to spend £600,000 of our savings (if we had it) buying two flats.
Yours faithfully,
CHRISTOPHER ASHTON-JONES,
Haslemere, Surrey. December 11

From Mrs Abigail Watson.
Sir, Cherie Blair has done no service to other career women in calling on the sympathy vote by citing the juggling act as a reason for her misjudgment.

The enterprise I work for is employing a firm of lawyers at around £200 per hour to carry out some highly sensitive business. We would be very, very upset to think for one moment that our business could be one of the balls that might be dropped.
Yours faithfully,
ABIGAIL WATSON,
Peterborough. December 11

From the Reverend C. T. Coney

Sir, How is it possible to keep one's family out of the public eye and, at the same time, display them on one's official prime ministerial Christmas card (photograph, December 12)?

Yours faithfully,
C. T. CONEY,
Begelly. December 12

From Mr Wil Malone

Sir, Simon Jenkins describes the press as a tiger. This is true only if you would describe a tiger as a cross between a weasel and a rat.

Yours sincerely,
WIL MALONE,
London N3. December 11

From Dr Brian Long

Sir, If only Tony had mentioned the purchase of the flats to the Queen.

Yours faithfully,
BRIAN LONG,
Chichester, West Sussex. December 12

From Mr Iain Mathieson

Sir, I hope that before Euan departed on his perilous journey Mrs Blair was able, through her tears, to advise him to avoid bad company.

Yours faithfully,
I. MATHIESON,
Doune. December 13

From Mr N. C. Johnson

Sir, There seems to be a need for a new term (media offence?) for misdeeds which are not illegal but which cause the tabloid press to go into a self-righteous frenzy. Extramarital sex by a politician has always been a "media offence"; now it seems that associating with someone who has been in prison is another.

There doesn't appear to be a comparable offence applicable to newspaper proprietors, editors and journalists.

Yours sincerely,
NORMAN JOHNSON,
Farnham, Surrey. December 17

On the wrong foot?

From Mr Mark Studer

Sir, It was amusing to learn that the Latin dictionary used by Vatican scholars translates football as *pediludium*. But for an Italian encyclopaedia to claim Roman origins for our national game (report and photograph, December 6) on the strength of Julius Caesar's legionaries grabbing a sphere of moulded vegetable matter bound together with the hair of young maidens is surely bordering on the pediludicrous.

Yours etc,
MARK STUDER,
London WC2. December 8

Unholy season

From Mrs Dorothy Crane

Sir, I was in a large, busy record store having trouble locating the particular hymn compilation I wanted to buy as a Christmas present. A young assistant apologised for the lack of choice available on display, adding that at this time of year "we tend to have to put all the religious stuff away".

Yours,
DOROTHY CRANE,
Hutton, Preston, Lancashire. December 7

From Mr Thomas Whipham

Sir, Some years ago in a London store I saw cards displayed in two stacks, one headed Religious Cards and the other Christmas Cards.

Yours faithfully,
THOS: WHIPHAM,
London W9. December 10

Boldly going . . .

From Mr David Horchover

Sir, It may be that Sir David Attenborough "isn't exactly a secular saint" (T2, December 6), but he does appear to have superhuman qualities. The same TV review goes on to point out that Sir David has travelled to various locations on this planet, "many of them inaccessible".

Yours faithfully,
DAVID HORCHOVER,
Pinner, Middlesex. December 7

"Catastrophe" looming in Iraq

From Mr James W. Thirsk

Sir, American and British politicians have denigrated the Saddam report without having seen it.

"I never read a book before reviewing it," said the Reverend Sydney Smith, "it prejudices a man so."

But he was only joking.

Yours sincerely,
JAMES W. THIRSK,
Hadlow, Tonbridge, Kent. December 10

From Dr Tony Steele

Sir, I offer a new unit for specious rhetoric which I suggest be called a credule, one full unit being equivalent to the assertion that Saddam Hussein threatens world security.

Sincerely,
TONY STEELE,
Bristol. December 8

Restoration of the city

From Miss Barbara Dorf

Sir, Those of us who love the beautiful city of Edinburgh will offer our heartfelt sympathy for the ruinous fire. By the time planners, architects and developers replace these ancient buildings, the citizens will need even more sympathy. Think of Princes Street.

Yours faithfully,
BARBARA DORF,
London W11. December 9

Crowded stage

From Mr David Ponte

Sir, Are class sizes on the increase? In this year's Nativity play, my niece Lydia will take the role of a blade of grass.

Yours festively,
DAVID PONTE,
London NW3. December 9

From Mr Richard Akroyd

Sir, I think Mr David Ponte may be right about increased class sizes. Twenty years ago my five-year-old son – admittedly a vociferous little boy – announced that he had been cast in his school's Nativity play as The Crowd.

Yours faithfully,
RICHARD AKROYD,
Sheffield. December 11

From Mr David Charles

Sir, Class sizes must be getting bigger. My grandson was given the role of Chief Decoration in his Nativity play.

He was in charge of a jangle of smaller decorations and he got a round of applause when, in an unscripted moment, he had to discipline some of them.

Yours faithfully,
DAVID CHARLES,
Falmouth. December 11

From Mrs Jane Lawrence

Sir, Class sizes aren't necessarily on the increase but primary schools tend to produce Nativity plays that include the entire infant school, possibly numbering several hundred. The sum is greater than the parts and 30 blades of grass are halfway to a lawn.

Although this is broadly the season of the tea towel and dressing gown, we once needed to ask parents to dress their child as a raisin for a class song about figgy pudding. They might have been holding out for the Angel Gabriel, but all took it cheerfully in the Christmas spirit.

Yours faithfully,
JANE LAWRENCE (Retired head teacher),
London SW14. December 13

From Mrs M. A. Clifford

Sir, With more and more four-year-olds now at primary schools, nurseries are finding that the number of children of suitable age for performing in Nativity plays has decreased.

Nevertheless, rehearsals can still prove entertaining; we have one member of our cast who, despite holding a lamb, is convinced

that he is a shepherd's pie, while a soloist insists on singing "a whale in a manger".
Yours faithfully,
MAGGIE CLIFFORD (Principal),
Fledgelings Nursery School, Ramsgate.
December 17

From Mrs Jean Leo
Sir, Class sizes are certainly increasing.
Some years ago our eldest child returned from her infants' school to announce she was to be "a host of angels" in their forthcoming Nativity play.
Possibly that would offer more scope than a blade of grass?
Yours faithfully,
JEAN LEO,
Wroughton, Swindon. December 18

From Mrs Christopher Scholefield
Sir, Blade of grass? In my youngest son's Nativity career he has been a piece of tinsel and a grain of sand.
Yours festively and in the front row every time,
LISA SCHOLEFIELD,
St John, Jersey. December 18

From Mrs B. Madgwick
Sir, I was a mince pie in our school Nativity play, circa 1936. My costume was two circles of brown paper applied back and front. I was happy and satisfied with this part, as were 40 or so other infants. It meant that a wise teacher had skilfully given the whole class a chance to take part.
In that late winter afternoon I was thrilled to hear that my dear Mum had actually seen a sleigh pulled by reindeer crossing the sky as she came to pick me up from school.
I still have that picture in my mind's eye today. We need a little make believe in our lives.
Yours faithfully,
B. MADGWICK,
Taunton, Somerset. December 23

From Mr Julian Thomas
Sir, For this year's round of Nativity plays we are contributing a "Bauble", as well as "The man who tells Mary and Joseph where to go" (the innkeeper).

Last year, we contributed a "King without a present" (a page).
Yours faithfully,
JULIAN THOMAS,
Southsea, Hampshire. December 15

From Mr Adrian Ringland
Sir, My grandson Jack is a snowman in his school's Christmas play.
"What do you have to say?" I inquired.
"I don't talk – I just melt," he replied.
Yours faithfully,
ADRIAN RINGLAND,
Ballygally, Larne. December 15

From Mrs Nicola-Jane Levy
Sir, My four-year-old was not sure whether she was a shepherd or a leopard. This made costumes difficult, and was not resolved when she asked: "Which one eats sheep?"
Yours faithfully,
NICOLA-JANE LEVY,
London N10. December 18

Lost in the smog

From Major Donald Harrison, The King's Own Royal Border Regiment (retd)
Sir, The anniversary of the great London smog (The Register, December 5) reminded me that 50 years ago I took a team from the Royal Military Academy Sandhurst to play badminton against University College London.
Making our way from Goodge Street Tube station to UCL we met an old lady in tears. She had lived in the area all her life but could not find her way home. One of us had to be hoisted up to read the street name, which enabled her to find her directions.
We subsequently started to play badminton, but someone left an outside door open; the smog rolled in, obscuring the other side of the net, and the match had to be abandoned.
Yours faithfully,
DONALD HARRISON,
Hurst Green, Clitheroe. December 8

Santa's helpers?

From Dr Justin R. Daddow

Sir, I have received a letter from British Gas to inform me that an engineer was coming to service our heating system on Wednesday December 25, 2002. They added that they hoped this was convenient.

This led me to wonder if this highly dedicated workforce should consider modernising their working practices. The cessation of routine work on Christmas Day would surely be a convenient (and cost-effective) place to start. Needless to say, we shall not be waiting in.

Yours faithfully,

JUSTIN R. DADDOW,

Bath, Somerset. December 11

Top 100 people

From Dr C. G. Winearls.

Sir, *The Economist* list of Britain's Top 100 people omits the Chief Medical Officer and the NHS Chief Executive but includes the chairman of a tobacco company, the Senior Steward of the Jockey Club, the President of the MCC and the former Director of the Royal Ballet. Message received.

Yours faithfully,

C. G. WINEARLS,

Headington, Oxford. December 9

Princely paupers

From Mr Timothy O'Sullivan

Sir, As a Benedictine monk Cardinal Hume "died" to the world at the time of his profession in 1942. Any allowances or expectations from his family (better described as moderately affluent than "immensely wealthy") were disposed of at that time. His literary estate comprised royalties from his books which, because of his eminence, sold quite well.

With one exception, none of the nine archbishops of Westminster since 1850 has died leaving anything beyond personal effects. The exception was Cardinal Manning, who held £200 in Great Western Railway stock. He bequeathed it to the archdiocese's solicitor, to settle that patient man's fees.

Yours &c,

TIMOTHY O'SULLIVAN,

Winchelsea, East Sussex. December 12

Deck the Tate halls

From Mr John Harvey

Sir, Tracey Emin's Christmas tree (report December 12); a critical appraisal:

Yours faithfully,

JOHN HARVEY,

Rodmell, Lewes, East Sussex. December 12

From Canon Julian Sullivan

Sir, I have written you a letter about this latest example of the folly of conceptual art and sent it somewhere else.

Yours faithfully,

JULIAN SULLIVAN,

Sheffield. December 12

No chat please . . .

From Mrs Pam Tull

Sir, For the past 31 years my husband has held the view that chatting leads to divorce. Having been proved correct by Professor Constance Gager (report, December 12), he is now not chatting with a smug look on his face.

Yours faithfully,

PAM TULL,

Brockenhurst. December 12

From Mrs Margaret Ziegler

Sir, For the past 52 years my husband has held the view that chatting is boring, as did his father before him.

On my first visit to his home, at the second meal that we sat down to, his father put his book on the rest in front of him and said: "I hope you accept it as an honour that we feel we can read at meals with you." My future husband followed suit. A book rest accompanied each place setting.

Yours sincerely,

MARGARET ZIEGLER,

Ringwood, Hampshire. December 14

From Mr William Ziegler

Sir, My mother (letter, December 20) describes her first meeting with my father's family, where reading, rather than conversation, accompanied meals. When my future wife had her first meal at my parents' house she was placed on my father's right. To her alarm he said not one word to her during the meal, but later told my mother that she was a "nice girl". She has often wondered how he knew.

I suspect it was because he felt my mother talked enough for both, a statement borne out when she was asked what they did in the evenings: "I talk and Oliver reads."

Yours faithfully,
WILLIAM ZIEGLER,
Landford, Salisbury, Wiltshire. December 20

From Mrs Jean Gould

Sir, Re non-chatting husbands, what started years ago as "Do you fancy looking at The Times crossword?" has developed into a mealtime obsession. In the unlikely event of our finishing the crossword at lunchtime, in the evening we delve into our stock of carefully hoarded "spares".

My husband tells me that after 45 years of marriage we have run out of words. He may have; I haven't.

Yours faithfully,
JEAN GOULD,
Pinner, Middlesex. December 23

Solid food

From Professor Gareth Williams

Sir, A Bristol hotel's directory of services states that: "Our night porter does a great line in sandwiches using a variety of fillings."

It is comforting to see such a rapid response to the research (report, T2, December 6) highlighting the dangers of dietary iron deficiency.

Yours sincerely,
GARETH WILLIAMS,
Department of Medicine, University Hospital Aintree, Liverpool. December 11

Railway tracks

From Mr Roger M. Thomas

Sir, Someone in the retail department of Virgin Trains must have a sense of humour. Among the items on sale in the "shop" on a Virgin train on which I was travelling recently was a CD by the band Manic Street Preachers. The title? *Forever Delayed.*

Yours faithfully,
ROGER M. THOMAS,
Abingdon, Oxfordshire. December 14

Spirit of Christmas

From Mr T. P. Walters

Sir, The story about the vicar who exploded the myth of Father Christmas (report, December 11) set me thinking. Maybe there was so much upset because Christmas, for most adults as well as children, tends to centre on the tree, with lights, cards, presents, etc, and above all the potent symbol of Father Christmas. In comparison, the Virgin Birth seems ever more remote and most people don't believe in it any more – even, perhaps, some bishops and priests.

Surely the essence of Christmas remains – a family celebrating together the mysteries of loving and giving.

Yours sincerely,
TOM WALTERS,
Harrow Weald, Middlesex. December 13

From Mrs Anne Miles

Sir, Since God created the Universe and everything in it in just six days, Santa's task of delivering presents to Britain's 19 million households on Christmas Eve looks like mere child's play to me.

Yours faithfully,
ANNE MILES,
Bournemouth. December 16

The older place

From Lord Harmsworth

Sir, I have just received a Christmas card

from the newly reformed, largely non-he-
reditary House of Lords. The card is in aid
of Age Concern, *inter alia.*
    Have I missed something?
Yours sincerely,
HARMSWORTH,
Beaminster, Dorset. December 16

Amphibious vehicles

From Mr Paul Rubert
Sir, Would any representative of the British
motor trade care to comment upon your
report (December 16) of the Great Car
Pile-Up at Sea, according to which the
2,900 luxury cars "worth up to £30 million" (about £10,000 each, in other words)
were shown as having list prices in Britain
ranging from £22,000 to £52,000?
Yours faithfully,
PAUL RUBERT,
Stockport. December 16

Christmas hits

From Mr Christopher Hawtree
Sir, Your list of the elements which consti-
tute a hit Christmas record – children's
chorus, sleigh bells, etc (report, December
14) – overlooks one of the most striking effects of all: the cash register at the beginning of Wizzard's magnificent *I Wish It
Could Be Christmas Every Day.*
Yours faithfully,
CHRISTOPHER HAWTREE,
Hove, East Sussex. December 15

Conmen's victims

From Mr Derek Greatrex
Sir, Daniel Finkelstein is too cynical in his
view of conmen's victims (T2, December
11). One night a few years ago I gave an
elderly man a lift on the M6 and lent him
some money, which he apparently needed
to get home. There was no gain for me, except perhaps the hope that someone would
do the same for me if I ever needed it. Of
course I never saw the money again, and
later learnt that he had been working the

same trick up and down the motorways for
several years.
    There are two types of conman. One ex-
ploits people's greed and the other their
good nature. The first type may be dishon-
est, but their victims' motives are none too
admirable either. The second type are truly
evil, because they destroy trust. If I ever
meet someone who really does need the fare
home, I probably won't help them, because
of that one despicable confidence trickster.
Yours sincerely,
DEREK GREATREX,
Caversham, Berkshire. December 12

Royal family trees

From Dr Peter Clapham
Sir, Your item (December 11) on the introduction of the Christmas tree to Britain
states, I'm sure correctly, that we have
George III's wife, Queen Charlotte, to
thank for bringing the practice from Germany. But I would contest the suggestion
that the custom temporarily died out under the "childless" William IV before being
reintroduced by Victoria's Albert.
    Far from being childless, William IV fa-
thered some ten children as Duke of
Clarence by his long-suffering mistress
Dora Jordan. And when William later married Adelaide of Saxe-Meiningen, his Queen
would have been familiar with the custom.
Decorated Christmas trees were said to have
been a common feature in the Royal Household, which abounded with William's children and grandchildren.
Yours festively,
PETER CLAPHAM,
Weybridge, Surrey. December 11

Case for the defence

From Mr Mark Cunningham, QC
Sir, How very unkind of the compiler of to-
day's T2 Crossword to give "Senior lawyer:
type of worm" as the clue for "silk".
Yours faithfully,
MARK CUNNINGHAM,
London WC2. December 17

From Mr David Meredith

Sir, Mark Cunningham, QC, thinks "silk" an unkind answer to "Senior lawyer; type of worm" in the T2 crossword. And there was I thinking the answer was "slow". Silly old me!

Yours faithfully,
DAVID MEREDITH,
Aberystwyth, Dyfed. December 18

American phrasebook

From Dr Larry Martinez

Sir, Mr Philip Howard's Comment column today discusses the Americanisms "meet up" and "meet with".

May I, as a native American, provide some hair-splitting? "To meet" indicates a first-time encounter with someone in a social or professional setting. "To meet with" refers to a prearranged or scheduled prolonged consultation between the parties. "To meet up with" points to a future arrangement "to meet with" the selected parties.

Sincerely Yours,
LARRY MARTINEZ (Associate professor),
Department of Political Science, California State University, Long Beach. December 13

Not even a mouse?

From Mr Tony Walker

Sir, As Father Christmas on our Rotary float recently, I asked one little girl if she had written to tell me what she wanted for Christmas.

She replied: "No, my computer has crashed."

Yours faithfully,
TONY WALKER,
Gerrards Cross, Buckinghamshire.
December 17

The wonderful sprout

From the Countess of Strafford

Sir, Ann Treneman (T2, December 16) paints an unfriendly picture of the sprout. It is a delicious, sweet, nutty creature, asking only for a little care.

The best of all is the home-grown sprout, nurtured with love and tenderness. When ripe and ready, pick and cook lightly, toss with butter, salt and pepper – delicious. Otherwise, chop a handful and throw them into a stir fry. Or shred and mix with red cabbage in a mustardy dressing.

The list is as long as your imagination.

Yours sincerely,
JUDY STRAFFORD,
Easton, Winchester. December 17

From Mr M. Davison

Sir, You report that the people of Diss, Norfolk, buy 54,000 sprouts a week (In Brief, December 17). When my children were young the only way I could get them to eat their greens was to call all vegetables peas. Hence long peas, plump peas, yellow peas, thin peas, etc.

I reckon that in Diss sprouts are called "fat fluffy peas" whereas in West Bromwich (where just 720 sprouts a week are sold) they are called small cabbages.

Yours faithfully,
M. DAVISON,
Grays, Essex. December 17

From Mr Stuart Cormie

Sir, I must join the celebration of the humble sprout. Indeed, it is the only green vegetable I can eat with enjoyment.

As a fan of Indian food too, I look forward to the time when sprout bhaji appears on the menu at my local restaurant. If even spinach warrants this treatment, the sprout's exclusion is unjust.

Sincerely,
STUART CORMIE,
Sherborne, Dorset. December 21

From Mr John Paxton

Sir, When I was about six I received the following letter from Father Christmas on Christmas Day: "If you don't eat your greens I shall not be coming next year."

Yours faithfully,
JOHN PAXTON,
Hardway, Somerset. December 21

Friendly mail

From Mr Barry Walsh

Sir, Ah, the Christmas post. Less junk mail and, in the e-mail era, the pleasure of seeing friends' handwriting.

Can it last?

Yours faithfully,
BARRY WALSH,
London SW14. December 18

From Mrs Sylvia Crookes

Sir, Mr Barry Walsh extols pen and ink against modern methods of communication, but I find computers very useful.

Conscious of my appalling handwriting, I print Christmas envelopes from my database. It spares the postman a headache; and I can remove at a stroke people who have died/fallen out with me since last year.

I e-mail my Christmas message, complete with photo of grandchildren, to all my overseas friends. It saves 68p for each message to the US, to say nothing of saving a tree or two, should they choose not to print off my letter.

Yours faithfully,
SYLVIA CROOKES,
Bainbridge, Wensleydale. December 19

Good news

From Mr Eric Dehn

Sir, Could *The Times* produce a special Christmas Eve edition with no references whatever to Blairs, Bush, bishops or butlers thus contributing to a care-free Christmas Day?

Sincerely,
ERIC DEHN,
Bristol. December 17

Mother's tactics

From Mrs Clare Desai

Sir, This year I have discovered a novel way of hiding my family's Christmas presents. I simply stack them on the stairs, where they immediately become invisible – just like all the other junk that lurks there in the vain hope of being restored to its rightful place by its rightful owner.

Yours sincerely,
CLARE DESAI,
Shepperton. December 18

From Mrs Jane Wilde

Sir, I find the kitchen rubbish bin a safe hiding place for the family's Christmas presents. Only the Bin Fairy on her daily rounds will find them.

Yours faithfully,
JANE WILDE,
Salisbury, Wiltshire. December 20

From Mr P. Chesters

Sir, We stacked the presents in the new shower that we had installed in our ten-year-old son's bedroom.

He took the hint.

Yours faithfully,
P. CHESTERS,
Wallasey, Wirral. December 23

Bat out of hell

From Mr Tim Bloomfield

Sir, The discovery of a greater mouse-eared bat (In brief, December 19) is cause for celebration, the more so as this species was thought to be extinct.

However, 30kg, the weight you quote, is a lot of bat – more like several large turkeys, or my seven-year-old nephew in his Batman suit. Have you any idea of the collateral damage a single 30kg bat could do if it recklessly flew into you one night? Or the type of diet required to sustain such a remarkable animal?

As I hear of no sudden decline in the cat population of West Sussex, I conclude that your report is incorrect.

Yours sincerely,
TIM BLOOMFIELD,
Highgate, London N6. December 19

From the Reverend Brian E. Phillips
Sir, Startled to read that a bat weighing in at 30kg was back I hastened down to our local supermarket, hoping to arrange 30 bags of sugar in a bat-like formation so that I could properly appreciate this discovery.

I left the manager in no doubt that he should take more interest in our wildlife as he escorted me out of his shop. I think he was miffed that even his best turkeys came nowhere near 30kg; even allowing for the added water content, the best he could offer was a mere 15kg.

Yours faithfully,
BRIAN E. PHILLIPS,
Ross-on-Wye. December 19

From Mr Bill Cairns
Sir, If the greater mouse-eared bat weighs some 66lb, as a resident of West Sussex I feel I should stay indoors at night until it is declared extinct again.

Yours faithfully,
BILL CAIRNS,
Chichester. December 19

From Mrs Janis Mason
Sir, Why worry about possible terrorist attacks? Should we not be more concerned about the dangers of meeting with a 30kg bat when it comes out of hibernation?

Yours sincerely,
JANIS MASON,
Scothern, Lincolnshire. December 19

From Mr Godfrey J. Curtis
Sir, Monty, our somewhat overweight yellow labrador, just about weighs 30kg on a good day.

The thought of him equipped with leathery wings and airborne fair boggles the imagination.

Yours,
GODFREY J. CURTIS,
Trumpington, Cambridge. December 19

From Mr Derek Cannell
Sir, No wonder the mouse-eared bat is hiding in a hole in the ground.

It is probably waiting for the results of the airport inquiry to see if there will be a runway big enough to use for take-off.

Yours sincerely,
DEREK CANNELL,
Bangor, Co Down. December 19

From Mr Andrew Blackmore
Sir, My children are struggling with the concept of Santa Claus and flying reindeer. To add 30kg bats to the night skies is pushing their imagination a little too far. A greater mouse-eared bat usually weighs about 30g, not 30kg.

Yours faithfully,
ANDREW BLACKMORE,
Chippenham, Wiltshire. December 19

The biter bit

From Canon A. C. J. Phillips
Sir, I was surprised that wildlife experts in Malawi did not know the technique adopted by Mr Chawinga to escape from a crocodile (report, December 13).

My father, who retired as a mining engineer from Africa in 1930, told me of a man who similarly escaped by biting the crocodile's nose, this being the animal's only soft part. I have regularly passed on this information to others and am glad to have its usefulness confirmed.

Yours truly,
ANTHONY PHILLIPS,
Flushing, Cornwall. December 14

Paper persons

From Mr James Hearnshaw

Sir, Included with my copy of *The Times* today was a very nice Christmas card from my "paper person".

Since a girl's name had been given I assume the person is in fact a paper girl, but I cannot help wondering what politically correct influences have prevented her from using that term.

Yours faithfully,
JAMES HEARNSHAW,
Stopsley, Luton. December 16

From Mrs Patricia Cook

Sir, Our copy of your inestimable paper was delivered with a Christmas card the other day. The card was apparently from "Your Deliverer".

The Second Coming, or just a Christmas good wish?

Yours sincerely,
PATRICIA COOK,
Brookmans Park, Hertfordshire. December 21

Collegiate companions

From Captain P. R. D. Kimm, RN (retd)

Sir, I have just read in a church newsletter of the donkey and "Oxon" in the stable at Bethlehem. Presumably the Cantab will arrive later – among the Wise Men.

Happy Christmas,
PETER KIMM,
Emsworth, Hampshire. December 22

Delaying tactics

From Mr Philip Groves

Sir, In the past difficult matters were "pigeonholed" but still on view for future attention, later they were put on the back burner to be left to simmer but hopefully go cold.

More recently such problems were kicked into the long grass to be lost unless returned to by persistent meddlers. Now we are urged to draw a line and move on.

What next?

Yours faithfully,
PHILIP GROVES,
Rickmansworth, Hertfordshire. December 24

Credit where it's dual

From Mr Trevor Trotman

Sir, "Sir Paul has reversed the traditional 'Lennon-McCartney' credit on 19 tracks" (report, December 18).

I understand that Jerry thought he deserved higher billing than Tom but decided against making an issue of it, in case it made him look a laughing stock.

Yours faithfully,
TREVOR TROTMAN,
Woodside Green, London SE25. December 21

Old man, new man

From Mrs Anita Metcalfe

Sir, I notice in the bathroom that my husband of 34 years has just bought himself an "invigorating deodorant".

I wonder if I shall be able to stand the pace.

Yours faithfully,
ANITA METCALFE,
Northwood, Middlesex. December 23

Double helping

From Father Christopher Hilton

Sir, I consider myself a healthy type, and receive enthusiastically the Government's recommendation to eat five portions of fruit and vegetables a day.

However, is apple and blackberry crumble one portion or two?

Yours faithfully,
CHRISTOPHER HILTON,
Peterhouse, Cambridge. December 27

Resolve undermined

From Mr Brian Synge

Sir, My new year's resolution for 2002 was to say something (other than "good morning") to one person each day. I started on January 3, saying to an Underground employee: "So nice to see such a clean and tidy platform, etc." He said: "If you've any complaints, go and see the governor up-stairs."

On January 4, I was having breakfast in a nearby hotel whose restaurant overlooks the swimming pool; after a longish wait I said to the waiter: "Is the pool heated?" He said: "We are short of staff in the kitchen this morning."

My resolution ended.
Sincerely,
BRIAN SYNGE,
London SW1. December 27

Cricket fantasy

From Sir Robert Sanders
Sir, You suggest (leading article, December 27) that "A 24-pack box of Fosters lager . . . will disturb the concentration of . . . ten (Australian) athletes".

You must be joking, mate.
Yours faithfully,
ROBERT SANDERS,
Crieff, Perthshire. December 27

Not so elementary?

From Ms Susan Pease
Sir, I am concerned about the liberties sometimes taken by film and television with geography.

Last night Dr Watson and Sir Henry Baskerville quite correctly left from Paddington for the West Country. They were then shown travelling east, on an elevated section of track, with a view of the dome of St Paul's in the distance.

Is this artistic licence or a touch of G. K. Chesterton?
Yours faithfully,
SUSAN PEASE,
London NW6. December 27

From Mr E. W. Lighton
Sir, Is Ms Pease not aware of the Hollywood rule that certain places must be underlined by visual tags, eg, Empire State Building and/or Statue of Liberty for New York, Eiffel's Meccano set for Paris?

I was more disturbed by seeing railway passengers in the Sherlock Holmes story alight at Exeter, in the heartland of the GWR (God's Wonderful Railway), from carriages drawn by a shunting tank engine bearing the initials SR.
Yours faithfully,
E. W. LIGHTON,
Crewe. December 30

From Mr W. S. Becket
Sir, Mr E. W. Lighton was deluded by Holmes's knowledge of the railway system. Holmes and Watson did indeed leave London by the Great Western Railway from Paddington but with great cunning travelled in the Weymouth slip coach, which allowed them to detour via Yeovil and proceed to Exeter St David's by a Waterloo-Exeter train of the Southern Railway.

Pass me our old friend *Bradshaw*, Watson!
Yours,
W. S. BECKET
(Traffic manager, British Railways, 1984–89), Deiniolen, Gwynedd. January 1

Watch this space

From Mr John Davies
Sir, I have noted from recent advertisements that wristwatches for men are getting more and perhaps unnecessarily complicated, with several dials, buttons, bezels, etc. I wonder how many need or make use of such gizmos.

So that I may easily note the time of day, my personal preference is for the plainest possible face with two hands and a date window.
Yours sincerely,
JOHN DAVIES,
Prestwood. December 28

From Mrs Catherine Sykes
Sir, John Davies suggests that wristwatches are becoming too complicated, but this is also typical of mobile phones.

When my husband came to change his, he said he would just like to ring people to have a conversation. The assistant seemed very disappointed.

Yours faithfully,
CATHERINE SYKES,
Rowley Regis, West Midlands. December 30

From Mr Michael ONeil

Sir, John Davies expects too much of his wristwatch. I have a plain face Sekonda bought in Warsaw in 1977 for $6; it continues to keep perfect time. On the few occasions that I need to know what date it is, I look at the top of the Letters page.
Yours aye,
MICHAEL ONEIL,
North Shields, Tyne and Wear. January 4

From Mr John Gifford

Sir, In my 65th year I have been given by my son, for Christmas, a combined watch and heartrate monitor for sporting activities so complicated that it has an instruction manual and software to analyse its measurements.

I was flattered until I noted that the fitness rating/age table stops at 65, and that the watch offers advice on what to do "if no heartbeat signal is received for more than five minutes . . ."

Presumably this is meant for others.
Yours faithfully,
JOHN GIFFORD,
Hutton Rudby, North Yorkshire. December 30

From Mr Eric G. Hardy

Sir, Surely the purpose of "wristwatches for men with several dials, buttons, bezels, etc" is that, when worn on a bronzed and hairy masculine wrist, they are a form of display aimed at attracting females of the species. I got one several months ago as a free gift with a mail order purchase and have worn it constantly since.

It may be because I am 84 that all it does for me is to tell the time.
Yours faithfully,
ERIC HARDY,
Surlingham, Norwich. January 8

Imperial lather

From Mr Michael Milner

Sir, First it was 30kg bats. Now it is spiders that are 125mm when in continental Europe, but only in (12.5mm) when they land in the imperial jurisdiction on our shores (report, December 24).

What concerns me and perhaps many of your other readers is, if at in they can jump 2ft, then when back to full size they can possibly, pro rata, attain a distance of 20ft in one go.
Yours faithfully,
MICHAEL MILNER,
Dilhorne, Stoke on Trent. December 24

From Dr D. J. Jordan

Sir, Your recipe for mince pies (T2, December 26) seems enticing. But 80oz of plain flour? Are these pies aimed at the 30kg bats that have so recently excited your correspondents?
Yours faithfully,
DAVID JORDAN,
Defence Studies Department, King's College London. December 27

From Mr Dudley Smith

Sir, We have long been inured to over-enthusiastic sub-editors converting approximate metric measurements to precise imperial equivalents, but a new development has appeared. Your report of ice blocks 10m high helpfully converts this to 32.8ft (later editions, December 31).

Would it not have been better to have expressed this as 32 feet nine and five-eighths inches, for the benefit of those of us not conversant with decimal feet?
Yours faithfully,
DUDLEY SMITH,
London SW20. January 1

2003

Water woes

From Commander Mike Cudmore, RN (retd)
Sir, How cheering, amid all the pessimism about potential flooding, to see a smiling flood victim family with their son Noah (report, December 31).

It reminded me of a public meeting at Ilchester, badly flooded twice in five months, where in a packed and mutinous village hall the chairman introduced the hapless water board official: Mr Moat.
Yours faithfully,
MIKE CUDMORE,
Norton sub Hamdon, Somerset.
December 31

Uncrowded stage

From Mr Peter Semlyen
Sir, I note that school productions these days are fully cast with parts as small as blades of grass meriting an actor each.

The opposite phenomenon is to be noted on the professional stage. In this year's Festival Hall production of *Peter Pan* the entire tribe of Tiger Lily and her warriors is played by one scantily clad actress.

As for the crocodile – this was mentioned but made no appearance. What next, a one-man *Romeo and Juliet*?
Yours faithfully,
PETER SEMLYEN,
Mill Hill, London NW7. December 28

From Mrs Lesley Moule
Sir, Mr Peter Semlyen is right to be worried about a possible one-man *Romeo and Juliet*. Last term, the Year Five pupils at my son's school were enthralled by a one-man production of *Twelfth Night*.
Yours faithfully,
LESLEY MOULE,
Baldock, Hertfordshire. January 4

From Mr Neil Murray
Sir, In the 1970s and 1980s The Smallest Theatre in the World, created by Marcel Steiner, toured the UK.

Its stage and auditorium (which seated one, and doubled as the box office) were mounted in the body of a sidecar attached to a 1950s Panther motorcycle. This wondrous theatre also featured a Sistine Chapel-style frescoed ceiling from which hung a chandelier.

Steiner's repertoire included *A Tale Of Two Cities, War and Peace, Ben Hur* (including the chariot race), and *The Guns of Navarone* (including the scaling of the cliffs and the blowing up of the guns). Steiner died in July 1999, and deserves his place in history (as well as this august page).
Yours sincerely,
NEIL MURRAY,
Sutton, Surrey. January 13

From Mr Roger Ordish
Sir, There is said to have been a low-cost production of *Snow White and the Seven Dwarfs*, for which the budget could run to only one Dwarf.

At his first entrance, coming to the aid of Snow White, he would turn to the wings and declaim: "You six stay there; I'll deal with this."
Yours faithfully,
ROGER ORDISH,
Lewes, East Sussex. January 12

From Mrs Joanna Miller
Sir, Mr Peter Semlyen would have had no cause for complaint had he attended the production of *Peter Pan* at Plymouth's Theatre Royal. Here we had a plethora of Indian warriors, an amazingly large and amusing crocodile and Peter Pan in full flight. Oh yes, we did!

Three cheers for provincial theatre.
Yours faithfully,
JOANNA MILLER,
Plymouth. January 2

Computer novices

From Mr Ken Broad

Sir, A few weeks ago I thought it time I got round to honouring my 2002 new year's resolution and enrolled on a computer course, only to stumble at the first hurdle when my "module" (bit like a book, really) asked me to "power up and access the operating environment". It transpired that all I was required to do was turn the damn thing on.

I've already made my resolution for 2003. It does not concern computers.

Yours sincerely,
KEN BROAD,
Church Aston, Newport, Shropshire.
December 28

From Mr Stephen P. Morse

Sir, I have great sympathy for Mr Ken Broad in his first encounter with the computer. I inherited my computer from my son, who had upgraded himself. This has a number of advantages.

I was introduced to it by a person rather than by a booklet or a salesman.

Though he lives 150 miles away I have a free "help-desk". He can immediately pinpoint the problem since the set-up was designed by himself.

Stupid mistakes are often forgiven – though I sometimes sense a slight edge in the remark, when asking for assistance: "What have you actually done?"

I cannot recommend this arrangement too highly.

Yours faithfully,
STEPHEN MORSE,
Cambridge. January 3

From Mrs Joan Woolard

Sir, After much coaxing, a pensioner school-friend has finally become computerised.

Her first e-mail message proclaiming the fact arrived by the morning post.

Yours etc,
JOAN WOOLARD,
Fleet Hargate, Lincolnshire. January 7

From Mr John Nichols

Sir, I am, as are Mr Ken Broad and Mr Stephen P. Morse, a technophobe. I am made to feel particularly inadequate when my not yet four-year-old grandson gets on the web and downloads programs.

My face is only partially saved by the fact that his small fingers cannot turn on the switch on the wall. I power up the system; after that I go to lie down in a darkened room.

Yours faithfully,
J. W. L. NICHOLS,
Holton, Suffolk. January 11

Happy retirement

From Mr Keith Hanlon

Sir, I gave up my seat in chambers in 2001, at the age of 72, only to be inundated ever since by requests, largely of a pro bono nature, for legal advice from friends, old clients, and their contacts.

Such is the problem that I am thinking seriously of giving up this retirement thing before the ever-growing list of jobs affects disastrously the domestic scene.

Yours faithfully
KEITH HANLON,
Pangbourne, Berkshire. January 1

From Mr David Harding

Sir, If in order to have a happy retirement I must play golf three times a week, play tennis, trek for 15 miles on Dartmoor, go to the horse races and have an allotment, the sooner they raise the retirement age the better.

Yours faithfully,
D. A. HARDING,
Barnt Green, Birmingham. January 4

Street hazards

From Mrs A. Sherwood De Ortiz

Sir, Electric wheelchair users may be required by law to pass a driving test and hold third-party insurance (report, January 2).

May I suggest similar requirements be

made of users of the ankle-biting, three-wheeled "off-road" pushchairs?
Yours faithfully,
A. J. ORTIZ,
Linton, Cambridgeshire. January 1

Garden calendar

From Mrs Kate Price
Sir, One of my neighbours is mowing his lawn, but I don't know if it is the end of this year's grass-cutting season or the beginning of next.

I wasn't even intending to get my own mower serviced for at least another month.
Yours faithfully,
KATE PRICE,
Salisbury. January 1

Grateful thanks

From Mrs Sarah Richards
Sir, Andrew Billen writes of "the whole embarrassing fag" of Christmas thank you letters (T2, January 2).

Until a week ago I shared his view. Since then my 13 and 11-year-olds have completed all of their letters at their own behest (after years of cajoling), and today the elder received a thank-you letter from her music teacher for a mere packet of paper serviettes. This produced one of the broadest smiles of an already happy Christmas, and was proof that this painful task is eventually worthwhile, and that giving (especially handwritten and personal thanks) is infinitely more rewarding than receiving.
Yours faithfully,
SARAH RICHARDS,
Poole, Dorset. January 2

From Mrs Marion Davies
Sir, When my children were small, an aunt and uncle of mine always sent them a gift token at Christmas, even though we rarely saw each other. When the children grew up, I gently suggested to my aunt and uncle, whose only income was their state pension, that perhaps the time had come when they need no longer send a present at Christmas.

My aunt agreed. "But," she said plaintively, "we won't get a thank-you letter. We always look forward to that."
Yours faithfully,
MARION DAVIES,
Godalming, Surrey. January 6

Shredded wits

From Mr N. J. Inkley
Sir, Whilst I know that advertisers use mellifluous phraseology I was still surprised to see, in a mail-order catalogue, a hand-operated paper shredder described as "battery-free".

The potential usage is enormous – and yes, this is written with a battery-free implement.
Yours,
NEIL INKLEY,
Preston, Lancashire. January 3

From Mr Frank Bilton
Sir, Mr N. J. Inkley's battery-free paper shredder sounds relatively friendly. The one I bought recently was menacingly called a "hand shredder". Fortunately it has not lived up to its name yet.
Yours faithfully,
FRANK BILTON,
Earl Soham, Suffolk. January 6

From Mr Thomas Tugendhat
Sir, I always thought a battery-free paper shredder was called a pair of scissors. It can even become a remote-controlled paper shredder with the addition of a two-year-old.
Yours sincerely,
THOMAS TUGENDHAT,
London SW1. January 8

From Mr Terence W. Wiseman
Sir, The paper shredder at a colleague's office has printed on top, complete with explanatory pictograms: "No Pins, No Staples, No Hands, No Neckties."
Yours faithfully,
TERENCE W. WISEMAN,
Market Rasen, Lincolnshire. January 8

Games for all ages

From Mr John Constable

Sir, Classification of computer games as suitable for ages 3, 7, 12 and 16 (report, December 30) is welcome. Personally I should appreciate labelling for residual abilities at the other end of the age scale, say 80-plus.

Yours obediently,
JOHN CONSTABLE,
Pershore. January 4

Late notice

From Dr Edward Young

Sir, A month after my mother's death at 94, my sister, who had lived with her, opened a letter from the local authority addressed to "Mrs Winifred Young, deceased". It read: "Dear Mrs Young, We write to inform you that your Council Tax benefit has now ceased, owing to the change in your circumstances."

Who says the art of letter writing is lost?

Yours sincerely,
EDWARD YOUNG,
Reading, Berkshire. January 6

From Dr Chris Hartley

Sir, When my father died in August last year, we duly forwarded a copy of the death certificate to the NatWest bank, requesting that his name be removed from the joint account held with his wife. The deceased eventually received a letter requesting his signature as authority for the bank to comply.

Is there anybody there?

With kind regards,
CHRIS HARTLEY,
Hayley Green. January 7

From Mrs Shirley Creighton

Sir, My husband died in May last year. In August a letter arrived from his medical insurance company, addressed to "The Late Mr J. S. Creighton". This began: "Dear Mr Creighton, Welcome to the reassurance of another year of healthcare protection".

My tears were tempered with laughter.

Yours faithfully,

SHIRLEY CREIGHTON,
Mill Hill, London NW7. January 7

From Mrs Imogen Mottram

Sir, We recently received in the post a letter and voucher addressed to my late father, who died two years ago. The £2 voucher was sent because apparently he has spent over £40 in the past year on items at a particular pharmacy in Central London.

Is there anybody there?

Yours faithfully,
IMOGEN MOTTRAM,
Benington, Hertfordshire. January 13

From Mrs Sabrina Duncan

Sir, After my father's death I went into my local branch of Lloyds TSB Bank and asked to open an executor's account for the administration of his estate.

I was duly informed that I would have to make an appointment with the manager to do so and, having fixed a date and time, was then asked: "And will your father be attending with you?"

Yours faithfully,
SABRINA DUNCAN,
Lymm, Cheshire. January 15

Signs of age

From Mr Kevin Lowe

Sir, At a country funeral last week in Co Down many of the mourners – in their mid-fifties – were of a similar age to the deceased.

A local cattle dealer was prompted to remark: "I see they're starting to take them from our pen now."

Yours faithfully,
KEVIN LOWE,
Portadown. January 1

Roy Jenkins

From Mr John Szemerey

Sir, When Roy Jenkins came to Brussels on his appointment as first British President of the European Commission, some of his francophone colleagues wondered how to pronounce his surname. "Jen", it was explained, sounded similar to "Jean", and "kins" was like "quinze", French for 15.

From then on he was known to friends and colleagues as Le Roi Jean XV. Mrs Jenkins was known simply as La Reine.

I do not know if he was ever called that to his face, but if he knew about the nickname – which is highly likely as he had his ear close to the ground – he would have greeted the information with a regal chuckle.

Yours faithfully,
JOHN SZEMEREY,
Overijse, Belgium. January 6

Entering the lists

From Mr T. E. Sharratt

Sir, The greatest change wrought by mobile phones (Matthew Parris's Comment, January 4) is that no one writes shopping lists any more.

Yours sincerely,
TOM SHARRATT,
Hoghton. January 4

From Mrs J. West

Sir, Mr T. E. Sharratt is mistaken in his assumption that no one writes shopping lists since the advent of mobile phones. I do.

I enjoy the mental and physical dexterity required to compile a long list – which is left behind when I go out. I am then engaged in trying to recall what was on the list, only to get home and find that the most essential items have been forgotten, but some attractive extra items have been acquired.

All this activity provides the illusion of independence in a life increasingly dominated by machines which talk to me.

Yours faithfully,
JUNE WEST,
Twickenham. January 8

From Mr David Dunsmore

Sir, I must contradict Tom Sharratt. I found my wife Jane's list by our computer. She does a list prior to shopping on the internet.

Yours faithfully,

DAVID R. DUNSMORE,
Botley, Oxford. January 9

From Mr Chris Priestley

Sir, In this household we too have shopping lists. A paper for such a list is left out for the family to add any items for supermarket shopping. I duly go shopping, get all the items and then return home. As we put the goods away a new list is immediately commenced of those items that were so obvious that they were not put on the first list.

The best lists are those that you write after completing a number of tasks and then have the satisfaction of ticking them all off.

Yours faithfully,
CHRIS PRIESTLEY,
Letchworth, Hertfordshire. January 14

From Mr N. H. Parmee

Sir, If, when out shopping, the truly list-afflicted person buys something that was not on his list but should have been, he will quickly and furtively write it in and immediately cross it off.

Yours faithfully,
NICHOLAS PARMEE,
London SW11. January 19

From Mr Ian Landau

Sir, Even with a list some people seem unable to complete their shopping without resort to the mobile phone.

Yours sincerely,
IAN LANDAU,
London N2. January 21

From Mrs Josephine Treadwell

Sir, Having been invited to dinner we were warmly greeted by our hostess who, as she led us into the sitting room, briefly marked a piece of paper on the hall table.

As I passed I saw a comprehensive list of her pre-dinner party chores. All the points had been crossed off, including the last: "Greet guests".

Yours faithfully,
JOSEPHINE TREADWELL,
Brightwell-cum-Sotwell, Oxfordshire.
January 22

From Mr Peter Stamford

Sir, A gentleman shopping, list in hand, mobile phone to ear, is surely exercising discretion over valour and seeking divine guidance from the list author.

Who would want to arrive home with the wrong kind of beans?

Yours sincerely,
PETER STAMFORD,
Port Elgin, Ontario. January 22

From Mr Brian Sharman

Sir, I was sent off to the supermarket by my dear wife for emergency supplies, following the birth of our daughter several years ago. I lost her list and so returned with what I considered the basic necessities of life, namely some wine and a copy of your newspaper.

I am pleased to report that I have never been sent shopping again.

Yours faithfully,
BRIAN SHARMAN,
Ibberton, Dorset. January 25

From Mrs Julia Scholfield

Sir, Before going to bed at night, my sister-in-law writes a list of things to do.

First on the list is "Get up".

Yours faithfully,
JULIA SCHOLFIELD,
Haslemere, Surrey. January 25

From Mr Peter Keer

Sir, I apologise for the lateness of this contribution to the current debate.

It was at the bottom of my list.

Yours faithfully,
PETER KEER,
Uckfield, East Sussex. January 29

Recipe for disaster

From Mr Michael O'Hare

Sir, Yesterday I searched the internet for a recipe for cherry clafoutis, today for ricin (reports, January 8).

I found them both with equal ease.

Yours faithfully,
MICHAEL O'HARE,
Bramhall, Cheshire. January 8

Building the future

From Mrs Monica Rushton

Sir, It is unfortunate that your informative report (T2, January 2) on vocational courses bore the headline "Bob the Builder class" – lower class, presumably.

How is the country ever going to produce competent, qualified tradespeople when they are equated with a children's cartoon character?

Yours faithfully,
M. A. RUSHTON,
Oakham, Rutland. January 2

From Mrs Fran Clemmow

Sir, I have a word of encouragement for Mrs Monica Rushton, who complained about undervalued tradespeople.

My niece, with an Oxford degree in French, plus two other languages gained from working and living abroad for six months, as well as three years' IT training and experience in an accountancy firm, is taking evening classes in plumbing with a view to a career change.

Her sister told me that her entire Christmas wish list came from the plumber's professional equipment catalogue.

Yours sincerely,
FRAN CLEMMOW,
Sandy, Bedfordshire. January 10

From Dr Chris Maddock

Sir, Over the years I have been able to tackle various plumbing jobs at home, albeit more slowly than a professional. But then, early in my research student days I was advised that a PhD in chemical engineering was no more or less than the Plumbers' Highest Diploma.

Yours faithfully,
CHRIS MADDOCK,
Teddington. January 13

Doers and thinkers

From Professor Sir Frederick Holliday

Sir, As a former vice-chancellor of two British universities and now the chairman of Northumbrian Water I assure you that the same aptitudes are required of me in both jobs.

More seriously, society has always required a variety of skills. Adam Smith pointed out years ago that the market will resolve such matters if it is not distorted. The academic market these days is confused, confusing and distorted; therein lies much of the problem that afflicts graduates and plumbers.

Yours sincerely,
FRED HOLLIDAY,
Northumbrian Water Limited, Durham.
January 16

The fairer sex

From Mr Chris Hookway
Sir, I read with fascination Mary Ann Sieghart's reference (Comment, January 3) to "useful female traits such as teamwork and people skills".

I intend to repeat these words to my wife and teenage daughter when I am next compelled to disengage them from mortal combat.

Yours faithfully,
CHRIS HOOKWAY,
St Peter Port, Guernsey. January 5

Snowed under

From Mr David Whiter
Sir, It is reassuring to see the Household Cavalry get through (front page picture, January 9) despite "the heaviest snow in recent memory" which closed down parts of Britain and amounted to more than two inches in some places.

Welcome back, White Terror.
Yours faithfully,
DAVID WHITER,
Swavesey, Cambridge. January 9

Marital scrapes

From Mrs Joy Plowman
Sir, My husband and I play a highly competitive two-handed version of Scrabble

(T2, January 2) where, contrary to the rulebook, if the word challenged is correct the challenging player forfeits a turn.

This gives a frisson to the game, especially as my husband insists that bluffing is honourable, and gamesmanship features largely in play. He is now banned from prefacing dodgy words with "This is a very old Scots/Cornish/Irish word", and I am banned from complaining of the abnormal number of vowels in my hand.

Our 54-year marriage will probably survive these encounters.
Yours faithfully,
JOY PLOWMAN,
Bromley, January 6

Peace formula

From Mr Leon Pollock
Sir, The mathematical formula for happiness (report, January 6) puts me in mind of the old equation for industrial peace which I came across in the mid-1970s at GKN: $P = A/2 + SS2$.

Peace (P) occurs when the unions ask for

an amount (A), the company pays half and squares the shop steward.
Yours faithfully,
LEON POLLOCK,
Sutton Coldfield, West Midlands. January 7

Nitty-gritty

From Mr Martin Turner
Sir, After the recent snowfall, I noticed that my road had not been gritted.
Upon inquiring of my local council, I was told that its grit stocks had "gone off". Past their "grit by" date?
I remain, Sir, your obedient servant,
MARTIN TURNER,
Northfleet. January 10

For a rainy day

From Mr David Ealey
Sir, It seems British business is active in supporting new ideas as we start 2003. The Southend branch of a high street store has for sale a range of "water repellent umbrellas".
Yours faithfully,
DAVID EALEY,
Leigh-on-Sea, Essex. January 13

From Professor Roger Dyson
Sir, David Ealey is wrong to say that water-repellent umbrellas are a new idea. They are what we carry about all day to prevent it from raining.
Yours faithfully,
ROGER DYSON,
Fryerning, Essex. January 14

Schoolboy sailor

From Mr L. Fraser-Mitchell
Sir, It is difficult to find the words to describe the pleasure it gave an "old sea dog" like myself to read of the remarkable achievement of the 15-year-old Sebastian Clover, the youngest person to sail the Atlantic single-handed (report, January 13).
Like Ellen MacArthur before him, he has added another small but memorable chap-ter to the endless saga of the achievements of this great seafaring nation.
All the fine traditions of courage, seamanship and adventure are safe in the hands of young people like these.
I have the honour to be, Sir,
Yours sincerely,
LESLIE FRASER-MITCHELL,
Necton, Norfolk. January 13

Honest ambition

From Mr Geoff Roper
Sir, Readers may be pleased to know that young people keep an eye on career development.
After asking my class recently to complete a form as to their future intentions, one lad had written beside "life goals" – "plumbing or burglary".
Yours faithfully,
GEOFF ROPER,
Winterton, Great Yarmouth. January 17

Olympic bids

From Mr Michael Bright
Sir, I would be happy for London to enter and win a bid to host the 2012 Olympics (Richard Morrison, Comment, January 16) but I could not survive nine years of the media moaning that nothing was going to be ready in time and politicians blaming each other.
Yours faithfully,
MICHAEL BRIGHT,
Oxford. January 17

From Mr Nicholas Wibberley
Sir, The Royal Household has consummate command of organisation, spectacle and detail, as the world has so recently been reminded. Were Her Majesty to look graciously on a request to take the nation's Olympic bid in hand, not only would the funds flow but the results would be unsurpassable.
Yours faithfully,
NICHOLAS WIBBERLEY,
Barnstaple. January 18

Class mobility

From Mr Dick Bidgood

Sir, Whilst thumbing through my 2003 pocket diary I noticed that the publishers had added a small fact or anniversary relevant to each day.

On the 3rd of June it states: "British Rail abolished 3rd class travel – 1956."

However, on scanning the rest of the pages I could not find any reference to the anniversary of its reintroduction.

Yours, a stoic traveller,
DICK BIDGOOD,
Potters Bar, Hertfordshire. January 18

Too early bird

From Mr Derrick Watson

Sir, This morning my milkman delivered a brochure entitled "Christmas hampers 2003".

Yours faithfully,
DERRICK WATSON,
Greetham, Rutland. January 16

From Mrs Mary Mellor

Sir, To some people January 2003 may seem early to order a hamper for Christmas 2003, but to the poor it is rarely too early.

Yours sincerely,
MARY MELLOR,
Brailsford, Derbyshire. January 22

Bridge in odd straits

From Mr Stephen V. Straker

Sir, Your report on the proposed bridge over the Strait of Messina makes interesting reading. However, the accompanying diagram comparing the bridge with existing structures is somewhat bizarre. We have the Empire State Building, Canary Wharf and Nelson's column (bastions of imperial measurements) all recorded in metres, and the tower height of the Italian bridge shown in feet. Curiouser and curiouser.

Yours faithfully,
S. V. STRAKER,
Reigate, Surrey. January 15

From Mr Max Hampson

Sir, Until I saw your illustration of the proposed new bridge I had not fully realised the extent of Britain's influence on EU policy. Your picture clearly shows all traffic driving on the left, indicating there may soon be a directive coming from Brussels that will at last bring the Continent in line with the UK. In addition, you show a London taxi crossing the bridge, demonstrating that in the new Europe cabs will go south of the Strait of Messina.

Yours faithfully,
MAX HAMPSON,
London N12. January 15

Student quotas

From Lieutenant-Colonel D. P. Earlam

Sir, Now that there is a proposal for a regulator to ensure that certain categories of student are admitted to universities (report, January 18), is it not time to appoint someone to make local councils employ a suitable quota of dukes as dustmen?

I have the honour to be, Sir,
Your obedient servant,
DAVID EARLAM,
Canterbury, Kent. January 20

Language difficulty

From Mrs Sue Cain

Sir, I have gone on-line to try to buy some software. I have been offered the following language choices: Universal English, World Wide English, European English, US English, International English – but not English. I am at a loss to which of these is the closest to English as I know it.

Yours faithfully,
SUE CAIN,
Kingston-on-Thames, Surrey. January 20

From Mrs Simone Landau

Sir, Mrs Sue Cain wonders what type of English is spoken in the UK. Until my recent trip to Switzerland, I would have thought that it might be labelled European. But I watched an undubbed episode of *East-*

Enders on BBC Prime in Basle with sub-
titles – in English.
Yours faithfully,
SIMONE LANDAU,
London NW4. January 22

Homework blues

From Mr Neville D. Lewis

Sir, When I suggested to the son of a friend
that I would abolish compulsory homework if I could, he replied with feeling that
I would be "the best headmaster in the
world".

I suppose standards might fall a little, but
at least our children would be more happy
without the overtime every night. Or do we
regard them solely as numbers on a chart,
where all that counts is the final score?
Yours faithfully,
N. D. LEWIS,
Bury St Edmunds, Suffolk. January 20

From Mrs Theresa Bennett

Sir, Children at our local primary school
who fail to complete their homework may
find themselves being kept in at lunch or
playtimes. Surely this is a little drastic?
Perhaps they are, after all, just numbers on
a chart.
Yours faithfully,
THERESA BENNETT,
Welwyn Garden City. January 23

From Mr David Robinson

Sir, I once asked the head teacher of a state
secondary school (in Torbay) why he was
so insistent that his pupils were set homework.

His reason was quite simple: "Because if I
wasn't, parents would send their children
elsewhere."
Yours faithfully,
DAVID ROBINSON,
Marldon, Devon. January 22

From Mr A. Belfrage

Sir, Parents would also be much happier if
school homework was abolished. Regularly
coercing and forcing reluctant children to
do homework strains family relationships.

Happier children and their parents may
even raise standards.
Yours faithfully,
A. BELFRAGE (IT teacher),
London W13. January 27

From Mr Giles Whiting

Sir, In our household it is the regular coercing and bullying of reluctant parents to
do homework that strains family relationships.
Yours etc,
GILES WHITING,
Taunton, Somerset. January 28

From Mr N. V. Bevan

Sir, At 7.15 last night what might loosely be
described as my extended family quietly
and contentedly settled down to their
homework. Calm prevailed for an hour and
a half before younger members prepared
for bed while others watched television
and relaxed with friends.

Teachers were on hand to help with any
problems. The pattern is repeated daily with
no "coercing or forcing". A boarding education must be the answer to the distressed
parent's prayer.
Yours faithfully,
NICK BEVAN (Headmaster),
Shiplake College, Henley-on-Thames.
January 29

From Mrs Adele Thorpe

Sir, Mr Giles Whiting is lucky. Our family
relationship became strained when my
daughter gained a D for my sewing up of a
cushion shortly before she (and I) gave up
domestic science.
Yours faithfully,
ADELE THORPE,
Jordans, Beaconsfield. February 1

From Mrs Patricia Launchbury

Sir, Message from school: "The answer is
correct, but tell your mother we don't use
this method any more."
Yours faithfully,
P. LAUNCHBURY,
Chatham, Kent. February 4

From Mr C. J. Brown
Sir, Perhaps the teacher who admonished a mother with "we don't use this method any more" should have asked how it was that Mrs Patricia Launchbury could remember how to solve the problem after a number of years, while her child could not do so a matter of hours after being taught.
Yours faithfully,
C. J. BROWN,
Wokingham, Berkshire. February 5

From Mr Neville Denson
Sir, I think it's disgraceful for mothers to do children's homework. Have the children no friends? In my day there was mutual help.
    I remember getting my algebra homework back with a line through it and the cryptic comment: "See Goodall."
Yours faithfully,
NEVILLE DENSON,
St Bees, Cumbria. February 5

From Mrs Sarah Manning
Sir, As a six-year-old I eagerly awaited the day when I would be given homework and could join my father (a barrister) in the dining room where he worked at night.
    Parents who read or study at home in front of their children are the best source of inspiration.
Yours,
SARAH MANNING,
Scalford, Leicestershire. February 6

From Mr Andrew Hicks
Sir, Imagine my embarrassment a few years ago, as a head teacher, when my assistance with my daughter's second attempt at isometric drawings caused her grade to drop from C-minus to D.
Yours faithfully,
ANDREW HICKS,
Streatham, London SW16. February 6

From Mr D. B. B. Owen
Sir, When confronted with an obvious piece of plagiarism, my maths master would come out with this slightly modified version of Genesis, xxvii, 22: "The voice is Jacob's voice, but the hand is the hand of Esau."
Yours faithfully,
DENIS OWEN,
Stafford. February 7

From the Vicar and Area Dean of Kirkham
Sir, Sarah Manning's father may have inspired her to do her homework. One day my two daughters, in their early teens, threw my pyjamas into the study and shouted: "You spend so much time in there you might as well sleep there."
Yours faithfully,
GODFREY HIRST,
Lytham St Annes. February 7

From Mr Andrew Wolfin
Sir, Homework for me was always a misnomer. Mine was almost exclusively done during breaktime, in the toilets, or on the coach to school.
Yours, etc,
ANDREW WOLFIN,
London NW4. February 8

From Mr David Green
Sir, My younger brother received a school report which included the entry: "He has the brains of his brother for Latin Prose translation."
    Even our parents couldn't work out which, if either of us, was being insulted, and in what respect.
Yours faithfully,
DAVID GREEN,
Castle Morris, Nr Haverfordwest. February 9

From Mrs R. E. Bruton
Sir, Some years ago my grandson and I were awarded an A-minus for his project on "Little Welsh trains".
    Today he is building me a superfast computer and instructs me on the use of the internet.
    What goes around, comes around.
Yours truly,
ROSA BRUTON,
Southgate, Swansea. February 7

From Mrs Mary Cottrill

Sir, When we were anxious that our teen-age daughter was not being given enough homework, it was suggested by a teacher that perhaps she was doing it in the library during her lunch break.

Any reassurance was short-lived, however, since she replied to our query regarding this possibility with the words: "Library? What library?"

Yours faithfully,
MARY V. COTTRILL,
Lymm, Cheshire. February 11

From Mrs S. J. Watchorn

Sir, When my son was struggling with long division, two sets of homework came back with the cryptic comment "WDM".

Inquiry at school revealed that it meant: "Well done, Mum."

Yours faithfully,
S. J. WATCHORN,
Earls Barton, Northamptonshire. February 10

From Mr Christopher Balkwill

Sir, Your correspondents whose children allow them to do their homework must have discovered a secret which has eluded me. Neither of my sons takes any notice of me. The younger (now 13) would rather refer to the internet.

Yours,
CHRIS BALKWILL,
Abingdon. February 13

From Mr Paul Silver-Myer, FCCA

Sir, I complained bitterly in school that I would never need to use algebra in the real world and, anyway, it was way beyond my capabilities.

Sadly, my daughter's request for help with her maths homework has proved me wrong in the first case and right in the second.

Yours faithfully,
PAUL SILVER-MYER,
London W1. February 13

From Mr Forbes Abercrombie

Sir, I got a B for my wife's first Open University essay. When I stopped helping her she got As.

Yours faithfully,
FORBES ABERCROMBIE,
Rogate, Petersfield. February 14

From Mr R. G. Osmond

Sir, I recall a schoolfriend appealing against the award of a detention on the ground of *force majeure* – ie, that his father had in some way been responsible for the offence. The headmaster, a liberal man for his times (he retired 40 years ago), decreed that the father had the option of serving the detention instead of his son, but served it must be. My friend was further told to advise his father that he had only narrowly avoided a caning.

I am, Sir, your obedient servant,
RICHARD OSMOND,
London SW1. February 17

From Mr John Rashley

Sir, For ten years of my life I completed the wretched stuff unwillingly and for another 31 I was forced to set it, and then mark the often unending results of pupils and parents alike. Now, in retirement, I look forward each day to my favourite corner of your newspaper and what do I find?

Homework!

Yours, etc,
JOHN RASHLEY,
Huxham, Exeter. February 19

In praise of Delia

From Mrs Penelope Freeston

Sir, I was sorry to read that Delia Smith has finally hung up her whisk.

I was an early disciple; her books are splattered with memories of good things; her book of cake recipes is falling apart. Like so many, I trusted her recipes to work and generations have enjoyed the fruits of our labours.

Although food fashions change, nobody did it better. As *The Times* once said: "Blessed be Saint Delia."

Yours faithfully,
PENELOPE FREESTON,
South Woodford, London E18. January 21

Odd antecedents

From Rabbi Lionel Broder

Sir, Scientists solemnly inform us (report, January 21) that Man is descended from the aardvark. Last week (report, January 17) they claimed that dinosaurs developed wings by racing up hillside slopes.

I'll stick to Genesis.

Yours sincerely,

L. BRODER,

London NW4. January 21

From Mr James Wilde

Sir, First, the bad news – the monophagous aardvark is an early ancestor of Man.

Secondly, the good news – the omnivorous Delia Smith is to give up her television and book career.

Yours faithfully,

JAMES WILDE,

Castle Cary, Somerset. January 21

From Mr R. Bruton

Sir, It could be worse – after all, aardvark never hurt anybody.

Yours faithfully,

RICHARD BRUTON,

Ewell, Surrey. January 21

All clear

From Mr Peter Wright

Sir, I should like to thank *The Times* Offers Direct (Sport, January 18) for informing me that the Mega-zoom binoculars with a "staggering 150 times magnification" are "particularly suitable for very long-distance use".

My education is now complete.

Yours faithfully,

PETER WRIGHT,

Portencross, Ayrshire. January 20

From Mr Oliver Chastney

Sir, After thanking *The Times* Offers Direct for informing him that Mega-zoom binoculars are "particularly suitable for long-distance use", Peter Wright maintains his education is now complete.

He may wish to reconsider his position when he learns that "if your bra is uncomfortable, you are wearing the wrong size" (T2, January 24).

Yours faithfully,

OLIVER CHASTNEY,

Cringleford, Norwich. January 24

Too quiet

From Mr Mark Crivelli

Sir, I know IDS is not having much of an impact on the electorate, but was it really necessary to put at the end of his Comment article today: "The author is Leader of the Opposition"?

Yours faithfully,

MARK CRIVELLI,

Worcester. January 22

Wrong notes

From Dr Sarah B. Perkins

Sir, If Jonathan Meades (Comment, January 18) objects to Pete Townshend, Joe Strummer *et al* being described as musicians on the basis that he has a low opinion of their music, then he will understand if, by the same token, I decline to refer to him as a columnist.

Yours faithfully,

S. B. PERKINS,

Didsbury, Manchester. January 19

Fighting talk?

From Mr Gert Imig

Sir, What a great headline on your front page today:

"Germany blocks the road to war."

Nothing wrong with that.

Yours sincerely,

GERT IMIG,

Claygate, Surrey. January 23

Asylum-seekers

From Mr Tom Jacobs

Sir, I was an asylum-seeker. Since finding asylum here, I have served in the British Army, taught British children, raised a

British family, helped to create wealth in British industry and now, at 74, teach my fellow citizens plumbing and electrics.

We should welcome asylum-seekers. They can help to enrich the nation's wellbeing.
Yours faithfully,
TOM JACOBS,
Twickenham. January 21

King-size life

From Mr Brian Campbell
Sir, Sir Duncan Oppenheim, past chairman of British American Tobacco, died aged 98 (obituary, January 22). What was his smoking record?
Yours faithfully,
BRIAN CAMPBELL,
Solihull. January 22

Esteem irony

From Dr David McA. McKirdy
Sir, "Evidence appears to be emerging in the US that high self-esteem can be destructive as it makes people respond aggressively when their inflated self image is threatened by criticism or perceived insult" (report, January 24).

I wonder if Professor Frank Furedi has any current world leaders in mind.
Yours truly,
DAVID McA. McKIRDY,
Rochdale. January 24

Happy disorder

From Mr Philip Lee
Sir, My sadness at the death of the caricaturist Al Hirschfeld (obituary, January 22) was tempered by his photograph, looking contented and surrounded with papers (many of them on the floor).

Here was a man who did not have an obsession with everything being filed away, but wished to be encompassed with his papers and matters dealing with his craft.

I have pinned his photograph on the door of a bedroom which I choose to call my study, as a rebuke to all those who exclaim,

when entering my room: "How on earth can you be happy working in such confusion?"
I am, Sir, your most obedient servant,
PHILIP LEE,
Radyr, Cardiff. January 23

Seeds of doubt

From Mr R. F. Sharp
Sir, I have received the latest *Times* Plants Direct catalogue addressed to me correctly by name, but with the accompanying letter starting off "Dear Mrs Sample". I am rather confused.
Yours faithfully,
R. F. SHARP,
Gillingham, Dorset. January 27

From Mr Michael Bird
Sir, Marketing men will be eager to know whether the computer which dubbed a male customer "Mrs Sample" has also given him a first name.

"Random" and "Free" rather charmingly come to mind.
Yours faithfully,
MICHAEL BIRD,
London SW13. January 28

Home deliveries

From Lady Huxtable
Sir, I have recently received from Sainsbury's a letter beginning: "Dear Lady Huxtable, Having a baby is a wonderful new life for both of you." It continues with offers of help and advice, money-off offers and the chance to join Sainsbury's "little-ones".

As it is some years since I qualified for a Senior Railcard this has come as a surprise. I am now watching the post in case, in this brave new world, this is the way that babies are to be delivered rather than the methods we used 40 years ago.

I am quite excited.
Yours faithfully,
MARY HUXTABLE,
Leyburn, North Yorkshire. January 28

Sleeping partner

From Mr Colin Burwell

Sir, My wife, although over the retirement age for women, continues to work for our county social services department.

She has just received her monthly salary notification slip, on which her location code is now shown as ZZZZ ZZZZ. Are they trying to tell her something?

Yours faithfully,

COLIN BURWELL,

Leigh-on-Sea, Essex. January 28

Mad, mad world

From Mr Allan Naylor

Sir, Reports today on the prospect of war with Iraq; war on global terrorism; firefighters' strikes; abysmal child protection agencies; and toys for pigs.

Have we gone completely mad?

Yours sincerely,

ALLAN NAYLOR,

Arlesey, Bedfordshire. January 29

University entrance

From Mrs Suzanne Houchin

Sir, I received yesterday a communication from the Open University. On the back of the envelope in large, clear type were the instructions: "To view contents, lift flap."

I am encouraged to believe I may be worthy of a first after all.

Yours,

SUZANNE HOUCHIN,

Stewkley, Buckinghamshire. January 28

A regular Guy

From Mr Harvey Rubens

Sir, You state that had the name Guy Trundle been known in 1936, King Edward VIII might never have abdicated.

Surely Mr Trundle deserves a posthumous award for services to the nation.

Yours faithfully,

HARVEY RUBENS,

London N12. January 30

From Mr Colin P. Boyce

Sir, Who needs Special Branch? Suede shoes with a suit – sure sign of a cad.

Yours faithfully,

COLIN P. BOYCE,

Blackboys, East Sussex. January 30

In the white stuff

From Mrs Ariella Lister

Sir, Go to war? We cannot even go home! ("Drivers face night in cold as snow brings roads to a halt", later editions, January 31.) If the councils won't send out staff to grit the roads or clear the snow with snowploughs, let's put our troops to work there.

Yours sincerely,

ARIELLA LISTER,

Mill Hill, London NW7. January 31

From Mr B. P. J. White

Sir, By coincidence, the Annual Report and Accounts 2001–02 of the Highways Agency were published on January 30, 2003, the day when I spent eight hours trapped on the M1.

I see that the chief executive's salary was £124,000, to which a performance bonus of £10,000 was added. I trust that he will receive no such bonus in 2003.

Yours faithfully,

B. P. J. WHITE,

Ashford, Middlesex. February 1

From Mr P. M. Demetriadi

Sir, It snowed in Switzerland on Tuesday.

After all the criticism in Britain after recent snowfalls, I was interested in an item in yesterday's *Tribune de Genève* which read (translated by me): "Snow causes shambles on the roads. Bad weather disrupts traffic, leading to several accidents. North Vaudois without electricity".

Yours faithfully,

PETER DEMETRIADI,

Wingfield, Norfolk. February 6

From Mr Jonathan Nicholas

Sir, It did indeed snow in Switzerland last week.

However, when newspapers here report

snow they mean 3ft rather than 3in, and disruption to traffic means that it takes ten minutes longer to get to your destination and not ten hours.
Yours,
JONATHAN NICHOLAS,
Geneva. February 10

Sticky fingers

From Mr Alan Ward

Sir, Quaglino's is declaring an amnesty to diners who have treated themselves to its iconic ashtrays (report, January 28).

I recommend the approach of a small restaurant I visited some 50 years ago, whose crested teaspoons were a similar temptation. A discreet sign read: "Our teaspoons are not medicinal, please do not take them after meals."
Yours faithfully,
ALAN WARD,
Wollaton, Nottingham. January 28

From Mr David Fouracre

Sir, If someone would steal all the ashtrays in every restaurant I might eat out more often.
Yours faithfully,
DAVID FOURACRE,
Moseley, Birmingham. February 3

House wine

From Mr David Politi

Sir, The Government's stock of wines, spirits and liqueurs is worth £1.5 million and contains 37,000 bottles of wine for hospitality (In brief, February 4).

How do I get an invitation?
Yours,
D. POLITI,
London SW7. February 4

House of Lords reform

From Mr Simon Ambrose

Sir, A wholly appointed House of Lords? Isn't that what we had before (with nobs on)?
Yours faithfully,

S. G. G. AMBROSE,
Bodmin, Cornwall. February 4

Family formulae

From Mr Douglas Goodman

Sir, Is there a mathematical formula that proves that whichever point in the UK my daughter departs from to return home in her car, the petrol tank will always be empty?
Yours faithfully,
DOUG GOODMAN,
Twickenham, Middlesex. February 5

From Dr P. Glaister

Sir, Mr Douglas Goodman's mathematical formula to prove that his daughter's petrol tank will always be empty when she returns home is commonly known as the law of diminishing returns.
Yours faithfully,
P. GLAISTER,
Earley, Reading. February 7

From Mrs Maureen Nyazai

Sir, The mathematical formula is the same which explains why, when visiting our daughters at university, the food cupboards are always empty.
Yours faithfully,
MAUREEN NYAZAI,
Godalming, Surrey. February 7

From Mr David Fillery

Sir, Mr Douglas Goodman's daughter is probably thinking about the same question, but from the opposite direction: "Why is it that whenever I leave the fuel tank empty, by some modern miracle of modern life, it is always full when I return to it?"

However, she probably realises it is not worth pushing her luck by publicising the phenomenon.
Yours faithfully,
D. E. FILLERY,
Leybourne, West Malling. February 8

From Mr Tony Bagnall Smith

Sir, What formula decrees that two potatoes, selected as exactly sufficient for my wife and myself, provide enough for a third helping when scraped, boiled and mashed? Surely it can't be the salt, pepper and blob of butter.

Yours faithfully,
TONY BAGNALL SMITH,
Bletchingdon. February 8

From Dr Simon Hayhoe

Sir, My grandfather, a retired mathematics teacher living alone at the age of 90, used to complain that there was a 100 per cent increase in the washing-up when I came to visit, but only a 50 per cent reduction when I left.

I beg to remain, Sir, your obedient servant,
SIMON HAYHOE,
Colchester. February 11

From Mr A. J. Colbert

Sir, Is there a parent-friendly formula for calculating the exact moment at which all student clothing needs washing urgently?

Yours faithfully,
A. J. COLBERT,
Walsall. February 8

Railway sandwich

From Mr Stuart King

Sir, During a week in which I and my fellow passengers have endured near cattle-truck conditions on the morning commute into Liverpool Street, I suggest the next time West Anglia Great Northern trains conducts an advertising campaign they consider the slogan: "WAGN – Bringing People Closer Together."

Sincerely,
STUART KING,
London EC2. February 6

Black thoughts

From Mrs Norma Bagshaw

Sir, I was relieved to read in *The Times* (report, February 6) that NPL Super Black is not destined to be used in newspapers.

The prospect of even blacker marks being deposited from your paper on my hands, clothes and furniture is too much to contemplate.

Yours,
NORMA BAGSHAW,
Stockport. February 6

Mixed messages

From Mrs M. Shaw

Sir, I received two letters from a mail order company. One told me that because I am "such a valued customer a special gift is reserved for you". The other informed me that, as I had not ordered recently, I would not be sent the latest catalogue.

Am I therefore prized, or not worth the paper they print upon?

Yours faithfully,
M. J. SHAW,
Birmingham. February 9

Roots of recession

From Mr David Bailey

Sir, This morning, I received my first chain letter for ten years.

We are definitely in a recession.

Yours faithfully,
DAVID BAILEY,
London W11. February 7

Machine manners

From Mr Michael Goodman

Sir, In the days when common civility seems to be at a premium I was absolutely amazed today to hear the words "thank you" – even if it was only from my inkjet printer when I gave it a new ink cartridge.

Regards,
MICHAEL GOODMAN,
Linton, Cambridge. February 9

From Mr Christopher Y. Nutt

Sir, Our dog, on hearing our computer say "Goodbye" of an evening, immediately gets up from under it and goes to her bed. Sadly she is more responsive to the silicon-chip spokeswoman than she is to any direct commands from me.

Yours faithfully,
CHRISTOPHER Y. NUTT,
Abington, Cambridge. February 10

Stubble and strife

From Mrs M. Murgatroyd

Sir, My husband, who is obviously suscep-
tible to a stroke (report, "Close shaves beat
death by whisker", February 6), remarked
that stubbly men do not die of heart attacks – they are nagged to death.
Yours faithfully,
M. MURGATROYD,
Loughborough, Leicestershire. February 10

Darwin Day

From Mr Richard Falconer

Sir, I note the British Humanist Association, in a letter today, calls for the creation
of a Darwin Day on February 12. This requires no legislation: the day should be left
to evolve through natural selection.
Yours faithfully,
RICHARD FALCONER,
Painswick, Gloucestershire. February 12

From the Reverend Philip McMullen

Sir, A Bank Holiday in respect of Charles
Darwin would be lovely, especially if, in the
light of recent scientific developments, it
could be called Aardvark Day.
Yours faithfully,
PHILIP McMULLEN,
Blackwood, Gwent. February 12

From Mr Stephen Richards

Sir, For those of us who believe that God
celebrated his creation by resting on the
seventh day, the only proper response to a
Darwin Day holiday would be to go to
work.
Yours faithfully,
STEPHEN RICHARDS,
Ballymena, Co Antrim. February 13

From Mr Jeremy Catto

Sir, Darwin, one of the most fair-minded of
thinkers, was distressed to be made a totem
of Victorian anti-religion; he would, I believe, equally dislike his posthumous misuse by the modern ayatollahs of atheism as
a transparent cover for proclaiming an
"anti-God day".

Yours, etc,
JEREMY CATTO,
Oriel College, Oxford. February 12

From Dr John D. Williamson

Sir, An extra bank holiday? Great! In Feb-
ruary? Yuk!
Yours sincerely,
JOHN D. WILLIAMSON,
Hove, East Sussex. February 12

From Lady Butterfield

Sir, The excellent suggestion for an annual
holiday named after Charles Darwin is
surely overdue. May I extend the idea to
holidays commemorating the names of
Chaucer, Newton, Faraday and Churchill?
It seems a pity that such glories of our na-
tional history are forgotten in our practice
of calling all our public holidays just "Bank
Holidays".
Yours faithfully,
I. BUTTERFIELD,
Cambridge. February 17

All in it together

From Mr Andrew N. Graham

Sir, The Reverend Dr Michael Lloyd pon-
ders the collective noun for politicians.
    Based on the huge amount of evidence be-
fore us, what else can it be but an ignorance?
Yours faithfully,
ANDREW GRAHAM,
Graham & Co (Accountants), Wombleton,
North Yorkshire. February 7

From Mrs R. Young

Sir, A prattle?
Yours faithfully,
ROSAMUND YOUNG,
Chipping Campden, Gloucestershire.
February 7

From Mr Mike Norris

Sir, Surely the collective noun for politi-
cians must be a tornado – a spinning mass
of hot air.
Yours faithfully,
MIKE NORRIS,
Amesbury, Wiltshire. February 14

From Mr Gerry Orme
Sir, A thicket?
Yours, etc,
GERRY ORME,
Boundary, Derbyshire. February 14

From Ms Nan Miller
Sir, A collective noun for politicians? Since the Pope declared Saint Thomas More to be their patron two years ago, perhaps it should be a Utopia.
Yours faithfully,
NAN MILLER,
Rochester, Kent. February 19

From Mr Adam Ogilvie-Smith
Sir, I suggest the collective noun for politicians is a forest. Consider the richness of the metaphor: dense; wooden; parts may die yet remain in place for years; and rising to the top prevents you seeing what is happening on the ground.
Yours faithfully,
ADAM OGILVIE-SMITH,
Longworth, Oxfordshire. February 26

From Mr Peter Beere
Sir, Not so much a thicket as a spinney.
Yours sincerely,
PETER BEERE,
Plymouth, Devon. February 25

From Dr Simon Honeyball
Sir, A political asylum?
Yours,
SIMON HONEYBALL,
Cheriton Fitzpaine, Devon. February 25

From Mr Alan Mercado
Sir, A dissemblance.
Yours sincerely,
ALAN MERCADO,
Hornchurch, Essex. February 25

From Mr Cecil H. Robinson
Sir, The book *An Exaltation of Larks* (Viking Penguin, 1991) contains an excellent collective noun for politicians: an odium.
Yours sincerely,
C. H. ROBINSON,
Winchester, Virginia. March 1

Australia rules
From Professor Chris Easingwood
Sir, Australia has taught the French how to make wine and the English how to play football.
   What remains?
Yours faithfully,
CHRIS EASINGWOOD,
Wilmslow. February 14

Timing is all
From Mr Frank Anstis
Sir, I read today that the Bank of England urges me not to panic. I won't.
   However, I am aware that if I had panicked when first advised not to do so three years ago, I would now be a much wealthier man.
   When should I panic?
Yours faithfully,
FRANK ANSTIS,
Truro. February 13

Wrong all round
From Mr B. H. Parker
Sir, I received through the post an envelope with a corrupted address. The first two lines were for some other person and the last five those for my house. Inside was an invoice for a four-figure sum from a company I do not know for a product I have not received. The addressee was a third party whose details bore no resemblance to anything on the envelope.
   The product? Professional addressing software.
Yours sincerely,
BRIAN PARKER,
Dartmouth, Devon. February 17

Essential supplies
From Mrs Joan Judd
Sir, Americans have received instructions on packing a home survival kit (report, February 13; T2, February 14).
   When in 1939 war was imminent, the first

thing I did was to fill a large biscuit tin with cosmetics and bury it in my garden.
Yours sincerely,
JOAN JUDD,
Tytherington, Gloucestershire. February 18

Royal consort

From Mr David Goodenday

Sir, Of our last six sovereigns, two have been women. Their husbands have been princes. Surely the time has come when the only person to have the title King or Queen should be the Sovereign and the wife of a King should have the same status as the husband of a Queen Sovereign.

This would deprive future generations of having a Queen Mum but it would also solve the ridiculous ongoing saga of Camilla Parker Bowles's title should she marry our future King. Above all, it is logical.
Yours faithfully,
DAVID GOODENDAY,
London N2. February 17

From Mr David Gifford

Sir, Mr David Goodenday suggests that the wife of a King should have the title of Princess. But whether she is styled Queen, Princess or just plain Mrs King, she is still the same person who has absolutely no authority (except the power to influence her husband). So why does it matter what she is called?
Yours sincerely,
DAVID GIFFORD,
Dorking, Surrey. February 19

From Mr Stuart Symons

Sir, So while Britain prepares for war, the Prince of Wales mulls a wedding with Camilla Parker Bowles.

Has the Palace sought and perhaps found a good time to bury bad news?
Yours faithfully,
STUART SYMONS,
Blonay, Switzerland. February 18

From Mr Keith Kyle

Sir, Surely the solution to the problem of Camilla Parker Bowles's status when she marries the Prince of Wales is that she should acquire one of the Prince's lesser titles.

She would therefore be known as Duchess of Cornwall or Duchess of Rothesay or, if the Wessex precedent of downsizing royal titles is to be pursued, Countess of Carrick. In each case the legitimacy of the marriage would be underlined but the sensitivities of the nation would be taken into account.

She should retain her title on her husband's accession, since what is the use of having a Parliament with sovereign powers if it is unable to make such a provision?
Yours faithfully,
KEITH KYLE,
London NW3. February 19

From Dr L. Butler

Sir, A suitable title for a royal consort already exists (and is vacant) for a divorcee who wishes to marry the Prince of Wales: Duchess of Windsor.
Yours faithfully,
L. BUTLER,
Swaffham Bulbeck, Cambridge. February 19

From the Archdeacon Emeritus of York

Sir, There is one clear precedent: the Duke of Edinburgh. In these politically correct days, should not the practice of not naming the Queen's husband "King" be followed when the monarch's spouse is female – for the sake of equality if nothing else?
Yours,
GEORGE AUSTIN,
Wheldrake, York. February 21

From Mr Robert Clark

Sir, If there is to be parity in the style assumed by the male and female consorts of reigning monarchs, there are other precedents than that identified by George Austin. When Queen Mary I married Philip II of Spain in 1554, he took the title of King of England, and the Earl of Darnley was proclaimed King of Scots upon his marriage to Mary Stuart in 1565.

There is no practical or constitutional reason why the husband of a future British Queen should not be named King Consort.

Yours, etc,
ROBERT CLARK,
London SW19. February 25

United's injury time

From Professor Lord Desai

Sir, Let's be fair to Sir Alex (reports, February 18). He was aiming at Arsene Wenger; Beckham was just in the way. And if the manager can't hit straight who can blame Giggsy?
Yours sincerely,
MEGHNAD DESAI,
House of Lords. February 18

Head count

From Mr Ed Welch

Sir, Your report that "the Kingdom (of Saudi Arabia) has one of the highest per capita execution rates in the world" could not be topped.
Sincerely,
ED WELCH,
Stokenham, Devon. February 19

Bad news and worse

From Mr Jim Cowley

Sir, The threat of war with Iraq. The threat of a terrorist attack in Britain.

Global warming. The split within Nato. Plunging stock market values and poor pension returns. Just when you think that things couldn't possibly get any worse – I hear that the Spice Girls may get together again.

Beam me up, Scotty.
Yours faithfully,
JIM COWLEY,
Bloxwich, Walsall. February 17

French way of action

From Mr David H. Walton

Sir, Peter Tatchell was surprised that he was arrested by the French police for a peaceful protest (report, February 21).

On past evidence the way to protest in France and not be arrested is to barricade the street with an overturned British lorry and a pyre of British sheep slaughtered at the roadside.
Yours truly,
DAVID WALTON,
Crowland, Peterborough. February 21

Certificate of merit

From Mrs Stella Kenrick

Sir, I was recently required to provide evidence of my 87-year-old mother's identity.

As she is resident in a nursing home she has no utility bills, no driving licence and no current passport. I was told that a birth certificate was not acceptable but that a firearms certificate would be. I was not sure whether to laugh or cry.
Yours,
STELLA KENRICK,
Worcester. February 21

Knotty concept

From Mr Peter Fullerton

Sir, It was thoughtful of *The Times* to provide today a clearly captioned photograph of a collar and tie, for those of your readers who might have been confused by the concept.
Yours faithfully,
PETER FULLERTON,
London SW1. February 24

From Mr Derek Dainton

Sir, Readers will have appreciated the accurately captioned picture of a collar and tie to illustrate the dressing-down story.

Could we now have a picture of an open-necked shirt to maintain editorial balance?
Yours faithfully,
DEREK DAINTON,
Findon, West Sussex. February 25

Personal touch

From Mr Lionel Phillips

Sir, When I wrote to my internet service provider recently I received the reply: "Your email did not reach a humanoid. It only reached Replicant Level 1."

I wonder if the same process explains my failure to have a letter published in *The Times*.
Yours hopefully,
LIONEL PHILLIPS,
South Croydon, Surrey. February 24

Just a thought

From Professor Emeritus Peter Forrester
Sir, The Iraqis, and indeed all of us, desperately need a decent, sensible chap to run Iraq. The Conservative Party, on the other hand, needs a proper stinker to keep it in order and form an effective Opposition.
Some joined-up lateral thinking is required.
Yours faithfully,
PETER FORRESTER,
Northam, East Sussex. February 25

Home from home

From Mr Geoff Watson
Sir, It is possible for the dedicated viewer to enjoy all of the following programmes on terrestrial TV this week: *A Place in France, Dream Holiday Home, I Want That House* (five times), *Escape to the Country, Living the Dream, Relocation, Relocation* and *A Place in the Sun.*
Does this tell us more about the British public's obsession with property, or programme-makers' obsession with cloning a successful idea *ad nauseam*?
Yours faithfully,
GEOFF WATSON,
Downend, Bristol. February 26

Out of this world

From Dr Kenneth Mullan
Sir, The *Pioneer 10* space probe runs out of fuel after 7.6 billion miles and 31 years of travel (report, February 27). Which fuel, and why does my car not run on it?
Yours faithfully,
K. MULLAN,
Belfast. February 27

Spending time

From Mr Keith Barnes
Sir, I was gratified recently to discover that Lloyds TSB, unlike many other public-facing organisations, has managed to retain a sense of decent service.
I called one of its oxymoronically named "helplines" with a travel insurance query and found myself held in a queue for over an hour. Having complained in writing at the waste of my time and having rendered an invoice for my usual charge-out rate of £150 per hour, I was delighted when the insurance division of the bank promptly paid the exact sum on my invoice into my account "as a gesture of goodwill".
Yours faithfully,
KEITH BARNES,
Nottingham. March 1

From Mr Frank Miles
Sir, I congratulate Mr Keith Barnes on getting Lloyds TSB to pay him for wasting his time by keeping him waiting for an hour to get an answer on the telephone.
When, exactly three years ago, I moved home, I was annoyed to have the London Electricity Board and British Gas expect me to read their meters both on leaving one premises and on arriving at the other. I told them I had more than enough other things to do on the day, but they said they had no meter-readers to spare.
So I billed each of them £20 for "employing" me to do their work (£10 a meter), and both paid up without argument.
Yours faithfully,
FRANK MILES,
Beckenham, Kent. March 4

From Mrs Frances Allison
Sir, I hope that as well as telling *The Times* that he had earned £40 from reading his gas and electricity meters, Mr Frank Miles also informed the Inland Revenue.
The taxman wants his share of the £5.10 my husband and I receive annually from the electricity distribution company that has a pole in our garden.

Yours sincerely,
FRANCES M. ALLISON,
Dittisham, Devon. March 10

From Mr Jeremy Wagener
Sir, The successful experiences of Keith Barnes and Mr Miles in persuading organisations to compensate them for time wasted may say more about bill payment procedures than a ready acceptance of the merits of either case.

It might be instructive (although not very ethical) randomly to test at what monetary level an apparently bona fide invoice for services rendered is questioned or rejected by a few large suppliers of goods or services.
Yours sincerely,
JEREMY WAGENER,
Stansted Mountfitchet, Essex. March 10

Cure-all

From Mr Robert Venables
Sir, Referring to a business acquisition, Mr Andrew Rosenfeld, the chief executive of Minerva, says (report, Business, February 26): "That is a vehicle we can build on and grow organically . . ."

It would appear that he has just resolved the nation's housing, transport and agriculture problems at a stroke.
Yours faithfully,
ROBERT VENABLES,
Petersfield, Hampshire. February 26

Local intelligence

From Mr Richard Hierons
Sir, On telephoning the Foreign and Commonwealth Office's travel unit for advice on visiting Riyadh, I was asked if Riyadh was the capital of the United Arab Emirates.
Yours faithfully,
RICHARD HIERONS,
London EC2. March 3

Parky pitches

From the Reverend Michael Windridge
Sir, My seven-year-old son has been so en-

thused by the superb satellite television coverage of the cricket World Cup that I am now a reluctant participant in the premature opening of the new cricket season here in our back garden in south Norfolk.

Although my son is right to insist that the late afternoons are indeed becoming lighter, I have yet to convince him that both the state of our wicket and the climatic conditions in East Anglia do not yet match conditions enjoyed by his cricketing heroes presently competing in Southern Africa.

Writing this on Shrove Tuesday I can assure your readers that, in my experience, the physical and sacrificial discomfiture of bowling with frozen fingers far exceeds those discomforts brought about by the most exacting of Lenten deprivations.
Yours sincerely,
MICHAEL WINDRIDGE,
Fritton Common, Norfolk. March 4

From Mr Philip Rogers
Sir, The Reverend Michael Windridge bowls with frozen fingers in Norfolk on Shrove Tuesday. We find this not unusual in The Parks at Whitsuntide.
Yours faithfully,
PHILIP ROGERS,
Oxford. March 5

From Mr Adam Isaacs
Sir, Living in Sweden in 1988 we had fixed the date for our first outdoor net for March 17. Unfortunately, on the day there was still 4ft of snow on the ground. The wicket was flat, but the ball didn't bounce much. Instead it rolled, leaving the seam covered all round with an inch of snow. We carried on for about 20 minutes, much to the bemusement of local residents.
Yours, etc,
ADAM ISAACS,
Everberg, Belgium. March 5

To the point

From Mr John Hinde
Sir, I have a contract note which tells me that on a recent modest purchase of shares in a bond fund the price per share to be

paid by me was £0.912899900936667. Here was I thinking that the frequent shaving of one tenth of one penny off the pump price of a litre of petrol was a tad overspecific.
Yours faithfully,
JOHN HINDE,
Esher, Surrey. March 4

Artless

From Mr M. Spensley
Sir, As a conceptual artist will not allow her work to be seen (report, March 3), perhaps the judges of the competition should award a conceptual cheque that cannot be seen.
Yours faithfully,
M. SPENSLEY,
Bushey, Hertfordshire. March 3

From Mr Stephen W. Allen
Sir, I suggest that the judges enter into the spirit of the exhibit and award the £20,000 prize, but simply not tell her where it is.
Yours, etc,
STEVE ALLEN,
Sedgley, Dudley. March 4

From Mr Nick Elsley
Sir, If conceptual modern art results in un-made beds, piles of rubbish and playing about with light switches, any threats by its creators to keep it hidden should be en-couraged.
Yours, etc,
NICK ELSLEY,
London N20. March 7

Accident-prone lorries

From Mr Harry Keane
Sir, You report (March 5) that "The Gov-ernment is to analyse thousands of crashes involving heavy lorries to discover why they are involved in so many crashes on Britain's motorway network."

Why bother? Any motorway user can tell the Government that they are driven sui-cidally close to the vehicle in front.
Yours faithfully,
HARRY KEANE,
Gillingham, Kent. March 5

From Mr Barry Severn
Sir, Lorries do not drive suicidally close to the vehicle in front, they do so murderously.
Yours faithfully,
B. SEVERN,
Southwell, Nottinghamshire. March 7

From Mr George Garside
Sir, Your correspondents are right to con-demn heavy goods vehicles being driven dangerously close to the vehicle in front, particularly on motorways.

HGVs take much longer to stop than cars, have abysmal acceleration and have the dy-namic qualities of a drunken hippopotamus.

The problem is the incompatibility of 40-tonne behemoths and cars weighing 40 times less. The solution is segregation. HGVs should be restricted to the inside lane during the hours of, say, 7am to 7pm.

This would not only reduce accidents but would also significantly ease congestion by encouraging lorries to use motorways dur-ing the night, when they are relatively empty.

Making better use of road resources would also have economic benefit in more predict-able journey times for both cars and com-mercial vehicles.
Yours sincerely,
GEORGE GARSIDE,
Formby, Merseyside. March 10

Which way up?

From Mrs Angela Bostock
Sir, Having three undergraduate sons, I know my way around most branches of Ikea pretty well. My husband and I shopped for and furnished an entire stu-dent house for five in South London one summer evening after work.

I am therefore more than familiar with most assembly instructions, but was quite surprised by those with a recent purchase: "Mirror Kolja 60cm round – can be hung horizontally or vertically."
Yours faithfully,
ANGELA BOSTOCK,
Stockport, Cheshire. March 6

From Mr Michael Ball
Sir, Mrs Angela Bostock has one more choice of hanging her circular Ikea mirror than the horizontal or vertical suggested in the instructions; presumably as it is a Swedish mirror, it can be hung on a ceiling as well as a wall.
Yours faithfully,
MICHAEL BALL,
Carshalton, Surrey. March 7

From Mr Oliver Chastney
Sir, On a recent visit to my son's student accommodation, I noticed that he had devised an imaginative horizontal mode for his circular Ikea mirror, atop a milk-crate. As such, an ideal coffee table.
   On reflection, empties tray might be a better description.
Yours faithfully,
OLIVER CHASTNEY,
Cringleford, Norwich. March 10

From the Reverend Michael Peet
Sir, Baffling instructions on a decorative candle: "Never place a candle underneath an overhanging horizontal surface – eg, a shelf or a ceiling."
Yours sincerely,
MICHAEL PEET,
London E3. March 8

Russian and English

From Mr Alan Sanders
Sir, Philip Howard (Comment, March 7) is wrong to say that Sir Edward Heath is known in Russia as "Mr Git". In keeping with the Soviet transliteration system Hitler was indeed Gitler and Hull was Gull, but Heath has always been Khit (lately "Ser Khit").
   Words like rouble, vodka or the gulag are not really loanwords. Like their Russian counterparts funt, viski and Nato, they have essentially retained the meanings associated with their country of origin. Better Russian examples would be steppe, taiga, pogrom and sputnik, which entered more general use. Meanwhile, Russian has created words like neboskryob (skyscraper), minomyot (mortar) and vertolyot (helicopter).
Yours sincerely,
ALAN SANDERS
(Student, Joint Services School for Linguists, 1956–58; BBC Russian monitor, 1961–90), Reading. March 7

Too early by half

From Mr Ray Hockaday
Sir, Today I withdrew money from a Sainsbury's bank cash machine.
   Half of my advice slip was taken up with a multicoloured panel wishing me a Merry Christmas.
Yours faithfully,
RAY HOCKADAY,
Chichester, West Sussex. March 4

From Mr Hugo McCracken
Sir, Sainsbury's extended Christmas season applies not only to cash withdrawals. "Christmas" also appears on the wrapper of the hot cross buns purchased in its Forestside store in Belfast today.
Yours faithfully,
HUGO McCRACKEN,
Belfast. March 11

Congestion charging

From Mr Alan Tunkel
Sir, This morning, King's Cross Underground station was closed because of overcrowding. The congestion charge would appear to be working.
Yours,
ALAN TUNKEL,
London WC2. March 11

Bluebells of Sussex

From Mrs Camay Chapman-Cameron
Sir, Whilst I am not surprised that so many counties voted for the bluebell as their county flower (report and leading article, March 10), to accuse the residents of Sussex of vote-fixing is a little harsh.
   These flowers are abundant in our road-

side verges, hedges and woodlands – we even have a local railway named after them.

When the chief executive of Plantlife suspiciously "detected clusters of voting in Sussex", I suspect it was simply because the voters were anticipating glorious clusters of bluebells.

Sincerely,
CAMAY CHAPMAN-CAMERON,
Hove, East Sussex. March 10

Down in the mouth?

From Mr Carlton Roberts-James

Sir, St James's Palace is to spend up to £50,000 a year improving storage for the 800 or so gifts received annually by the Prince of Wales (report, March 14).

Is this wise? There might not be so many from now on.

Yours faithfully,
C. ROBERTS-JAMES,
Walton Park, Milton Keynes. March 14

Fast learners

From Mr Derek Voysey

Sir, The Department for Education and Skills kindly informs your readers in an advertisement ("Simple mistaks undermine everything", March 7) that "One in five British employees have poor literacy and numeracy skills" and offers its assistance in rectifying this lamentable situation.

I see from today's edition that grammar has triumphed and that, in an otherwise identical ad, "have" has yielded to "has".

Might we be permitted the smallest of wry smiles?

Yours faithfully,
DEREK VOYSEY,
Hazlemere, Buckinghamshire. March 10

Young ambition

From Mr Francis Harvey

Sir, What a shame that the singer Charlotte Church was included in your "Pretentious? Moi?" column (T2, March 11) for saying:

I might do a trilogy. I'd love to be a writer. I love writing and reading. And I love psychology and philosophy and ancient history. So anything to do with all those things.

Such cultural enthusiasm should be encouraged in a 17-year-old and is refreshing compared with the somewhat lower ambitions of many of her peers.

Yours faithfully,
F. HARVEY,
Exeter, Devon. March 11

Junk mail

From Mr A. J. F. Weller

Sir, Nine items through the door today.

I have nothing but praise for those philanthropic institutions who spend millions of pounds annually just to acquaint me of two things. Yes, the postman has called, and no, my Premium Bond has still not won me a million pounds.

Yours,
A. J. F. WELLER,
Totton, Hampshire. March 13

From Mr John O'Byrne

Sir, The inserts in magazines and newspapers are there for a purpose. They remind us we would be paying much more for our papers without them.

Yours truly,
JOHN O'BYRNE,
Dublin. March 14

Support for war, pleas for peace

From Mr Paul Harris

Sir, I remind conservatives who threaten the freedom of speech of anti-war protesters of this gem from President Teddy Roosevelt:

To announce that there must be no criticism of the President, or that we are to stand by the President, right or wrong, is not only unpatriotic and servile, but is morally treasonable to the American public.

Yours faithfully,
PAUL HARRIS,
San Diego, California. March 18

From Mr Graham Evans

Sir, Given that international law "is not 'law' in any conventional sense", the diplomats' rule of thumb should always be: when the law is against you argue the facts, when the facts are against you argue the law. Of course, this reads much better in French.

Yours sincerely,
GRAHAM EVANS
(Author, *Penguin Dictionary of International Relations*, 1998), University of Wales, Swansea. March 18

Tricks of the trade

From Mr Chris Whitby

Sir, I was surprised to see in a trade mail order catalogue mailed to me this morning that I can buy a tool pack entitled Cabinet Maker, which comprises a 16oz rubber mallet and a 7lb sledgehammer.

Then I remembered flat-pack furniture.
Yours faithfully,
CHRIS WHITBY,
Peckleton, Leicestershire. March 17

From Mrs Sue Roffe

Sir, Forget the flat-pack furniture. Any tool pack labelled Cabinet Maker and comprising a 16oz rubber mallet and a 7lb sledgehammer is a must for any prime minister.
Yours faithfully,
SUE ROFFE,
Stratford-upon-Avon, Warwickshire. March 19

Ban the bun

From Mrs Jenifer Grigg

Sir, Hot cross buns (report and Comment, March 17) were traditionally served on Good Friday, which, for the benefit of your non-Christian readers, was the day our Lord was crucified.

Unfortunately, increased commercialism, combined with a decline in Christian observance, has meant that hot cross buns (and Easter eggs) are being sold since just after Christmas.

If everybody ate hot cross buns only on Good Friday, when schools are on holiday, then everybody would be happy – except perhaps the bakers.
Yours faithfully,
JENIFER GRIGG,
Byton, Presteigne. March 17

From Mr John Muir

Sir, The banning of hot cross buns as a symbol likely to offend non-Christians raises an interesting scenario. During the siege of Vienna by the Ottoman Turks in the 17th century, a Viennese baker prepared bread in the shape of the Islamic religious symbol, the crescent.

Are Christians in danger of being offended by croissants?
Yours faithfully,
JOHN MUIR,
Great Shelford, Cambridge. March 19

Our curious world

From Professor James S. Harrison

Sir, I see that what was thought to be a new discovery about Hitler's health was already noted about 50 years ago. This is an example of perpetual rediscovery, along with such topics as the presence of arsenic in samples of Napoleon's hair, Salieri's role in the death of Mozart and the knotty problem of the direction of circulation of water going down the plughole.

Researchers note that the period of recurrence of questions being asked about these topics is upwards of 20 years but are divided as to whether this frequency corresponds to the generation gap of 25 years or to 22 years, which is two sunspot cycles.

Further work is evidently required, supported by a large grant from a major research institution.
Yours sincerely,
JAMES HARRISON,
Cheltenham. March 14

From Mr Dean Bullen

Sir, Professor James Harrison argues for research to be carried out into "perpetual rediscovery".

Has such research not already been un-
dertaken?
Yours truly,
DEAN BULLEN,
West Hampstead, London NW6. March 19

Judges' background

From Mrs Wendy Outhwaite
Sir, Surely it is unsurprising that judges are
"overwhelmingly male, white and public
school and Oxbridge educated" (report,
March 17). This reflects the profile of the
legal profession when today's judges were
just starting out. Nowadays, it's different.

Let's just select the best candidate on
merit, whether they are male, female, her-
maphrodite, black, white, green, Oxbridge
or Uxbridge.
Yours faithfully,
WENDY OUTHWAITE,
London SW6. March 17

Global policeman

From Mr Geyve Walker
Sir, In defence of the US, William Rees-
Mogg writes (Comment, March 17): "If
there is only one policeman in the village,
it is no good for the parish council to expect to tell him what to do."

But if the policeman has appointed himself to the job, on the basis that he is the
richest person in the village and the only
one who possesses a big stick, and he's inclined to turn a blind eye when his pals mis-
behave or where the misbehaviour poses no
threat to his own immediate family, then
should not all the villagers be feeling just a
bit nervous?

In my village that sort of arrangement
went out with the feudal system.
Yours faithfully,
GEYVE WALKER,
Tirril, Cumbria. March 17

A good walk spoilt

From Mr Forbes Abercrombie
Sir, Your headline, "Golfers not only vic-

tims of dystonia", above Eileen Gascoigne's
letter (March 18) is, of course, correct.

Golfers are also victims of bad luck, ca-
pricious winds, inexplicable bounces and,
according to P. G. Wodehouse, "the uproar
of the butterflies in the adjoining meadows".
Yours sincerely,
FORBES ABERCROMBIE,
Rogate, Petersfield. March 18

Fighting flyposting

From Mr Neil Barrass
Sir, Might not Westminster City Council
be more effective in its fight against fly-
posting if it left the posters in place and
added its own over the top, saying "Cancelled"?
Yours sincerely,
NEIL BARRASS,
Singapore. March 20

What you see . . .

From Mr Huw James
Sir, My supermarket salmon loin, "farmed
in the tidal waters around the Orkney Isles
to gain a firm and succulent texture with a
full flavour when cooked", bears the allergy
warning "contains fish".
Yours,
HUW JAMES,
Llanishen, Cardiff. March 21

From Mr Ernie Todd
Sir, After reading of Huw James's surprise
at the warning on his salmon, I checked
the label of the "Co-op Mild & Creamy
French Brie (Flavour strength 2)" from my
village store.

Sure enough, the allergy warning is im-
parted: "Contains cow's milk."
Yours,
ERNIE TODD,
Long Hanborough, Oxfordshire. March 24

From Mrs Lucy Lermer
Sir, I sympathise with Mr James. My Asda
cucumber purchased yesterday has the reassuring message: "Suitable for vegetar-
ians."

Yours sincerely,
LUCY LERMER,
London N14. March 22

From Mr Paul Britland

Sir, Mr Huw James's concerns regarding his salmon loin bearing an allergy warning "contains fish" may not be the full story.

It sounds as though even before it left the labelling plant it had already been contaminated by nuts.

Yours sincerely,
PAUL BRITLAND,
Torquay. March 25

From Mr Mike Davis

Sir, Recently I purchased an ordinary and apparently harmless 60m measuring tape. On the packaging there is the exhortation: "Wear safety goggles."

Yours faithfully,
M. C. J. DAVIS,
Great Missenden, Hertfordshire. March 31

From Mrs Lynne Potter

Sir, On Mothering Sunday I was the happy recipient of a card from my 22-year old daughter.

On the reverse was the following warning: "Not suitable for small children under 36 months."

Yours,
LYNNE POTTER,
Hexham, Northumberland. March 31

From Mr David Drew

Sir, A just-opened packet of Nimble "Amazing Grain" sliced bread bears the advice: "Remove wrapper before eating this."

Yours faithfully,
D. G. DREW,
Ludgvan, Penzance. March 29

From Mrs Paddie Breeze

Sir, Seventeen "important safeguards" apply to my new electric kettle, all of which I appreciate except for the instruction: "Do not use near any source of water."

Yours faithfully,
PADDIE BREEZE,
Hawksworth, Leeds. March 31

From Mr Charlie Flindt

Sir, Mr Mike Davis's "apparently harmless" measuring tape probably poses the same safety threat as my wicketkeeping glove liners, which, having been put through a thorough testing and certification system, proudly bear their European CE mark.

Yours faithfully,
CHARLIE FLINDT,
Hinton Ampner, Hampshire. April 1

From Mrs A. D. Blanchard

Sir, My son's work uniform trousers contain a small label with the European CE safety mark and the legend "Minimal Risk".

As they have waist adjusters, belt loops and buttons for braces, I can see that there is little danger of their falling down, but I still think the trailing drawstrings in the hems are a trip hazard.

Yours faithfully,
ALICE BLANCHARD,
Ipswich. April 3

From Mrs Sally Lewers

Sir, Unlike Mr Mike Davis's tape my recently purchased 60m measuring tape does need the advice to "wear safety goggles". It is used for dangerous games with our young and effervescent ginger cat.

Yours faithfully,
SALLY LEWERS,
Marshwood, Dorset. April 2

From Mrs Stephanie Jenkins

Sir, Clementines from Somerfield bear a label stating "Remove the skin and break into segments", but neglect to advise the consumer what to do after that.

Yours faithfully,
STEPHANIE JENKINS,
Headington, Oxford. April 8

From Mrs Jo Morrison

Sir, The complimentary packet of peanuts I was offered on a flight to the States bore the instruction: "Open the packet. Eat nuts."

Yours faithfully,
JO MORRISON,
Great Cransley, Northamptonshire. April 8

From Mr Ian Bland

Sir, Recent correspondence mentioned labels offering unnecessary advice, but *The Times* cannot be accused of incomplete assistance. In the Gardening section, "Ten ways to save your spine" (April 12), we are told: "Always kneel with at least one knee on the ground, use alternate knees or kneel on both knees."

Other variants would seem unworthy of a mention.

Yours faithfully,

IAN BLAND,

East Dulwich, London SE22. April 16

From Mr Duncan Heenan

Sir, A recently purchased box of firelighters warns me that they are "Highly Flammable". I would be disappointed if they were not.

Yours faithfully,

DUNCAN HEENAN,

Niton, Isle of Wight. April 23

From Mr Julian Hall

Sir, Your recent consumer correspondents seem to be beset with unnecessary instructions or ridiculous exclusions. Not so here in Oxford, where last week our delicatessen had on sale, labelled without any qualification, "Welsh Dragon paté".

Yours sincerely,

JULIAN HALL,

Oxford. April 28

From Mr C. J. Spurrier

Sir, Found on the underside of a box of sweets: "Do not read whilst carton is open".

It wasn't.

Yours faithfully,

CHRIS SPURRIER,

Eversley Cross, Hampshire. May 6

From Mrs Debbie Beasley

Sir, I realised why I had been struggling with my new digital telephone when I read the following instruction in the user's manual: "When the other person answers, speak."

Yours,

DEBBIE BEASLEY,

Langdon Hills, Essex. May 10

From Mr Patrick Hickey

Sir, When a headlamp failed on my not-old car, I went to the manual to check the bulb specification.

A search under B for bulb produced nothing. A reference to L for lights drew a blank. Nothing doing at E for electrics, I for illumination, or H for headlamps.

Ditto P for parking lights.

A toothcomb search found the answer under C for changing a bulb.

What a wonderful idea. File everything under M for mending the car. Or H for help.

Yours faithfully,

PATRICK HICKEY,

Caerphilly. May 15

From Mr Martin G. Sexton

Sir, My granddaughter in America has a new scooter. On the handlebars a precautionary note reads: "Caution, this product moves when used."

Yours faithfully,

MARTIN G. SEXTON,

Norwich. May 16

From Mr Ron Lyon

Sir, Mr Patrick Hickey is not the only one to have been baffled by a reference system designed to bamboozle.

The Highland News at Inverness some years ago had a news editor who set up and ran a filing system according to his own highly individualistic agenda. A reporter seeking cuttings on the Loch Ness monster tried the files under L, N and M without success and asked in some exasperation where the monster was filed. "Under P," he was told, "for Phenomenon."

Yours faithfully,

RON LYON,

Inverness. May 18

From Mr Paul McClure

Sir, I recently bought a glass paperweight on which there was a label stating that the product was "easy to use".

This I can confirm to be true.

Yours faithfully,

PAUL McCLURE,

Exeter. June 1

From Mr Norman Braidwood

Sir, The label on "Tesco Pudding Rice" helpfully adds "ideal for rice puddings".

Yours faithfully,

NORMAN BRAIDWOOD,

Edinburgh. June 5

Vices and virtues

From Canon Julian Sullivan

Sir, You report (Faith News, March 15) that Unilever has been accused of blasphemy over its new range of Magnum ice-cream with the theme of the seven deadly sins. A spokesman said in defence: "There are a number of different words and phrases in many different languages which mean different things to different people."

May I respectfully point out that lust, sloth, greed, gluttony, envy, revenge and vanity are universal vices which have a destructive effect on human society regardless of age, language, faith or culture.

Unilever should repent immediately by renaming its ices with the seven contrary virtues according to the Catholic catechism, namely chastity, diligence, liberality, temperance, charity, meekness and humility. These are universal qualities which make life better for everyone, against which there is no law.

Yours faithfully,

JULIAN SULLIVAN,

Sheffield. March 16

Revival of Bath's spas

From Mr David Hyatt

Sir, Your claim that "Grateful Ancient Celts" bathed in the hot springs of Bath 10,000 years ago (leading article, March 17) is rather wide of the mark.

The first Celts arrived in these islands from Central Europe between 2,500 and 2,700 years ago. As for the people living here 10,000 (or even 3,000) years ago, whatever name they gave themselves is unknown.

Yours faithfully,

DAVID HYATT,

London E5. March 17

From Mr Merrick Baker-Bates

Sir, The spokesman who claimed that the Japanese "would not like" nudity in the reviving waters of Bath (report, March 17) had clearly not experienced one of their onsen resorts. Having wallowed happily in a score or more of such hot springs, I can attest to the fact that the Japanese, certainly in their own country, have no qualms about nudity.

When I took the members of our Commercial Department to a hot spring for a bonding weekend in 1981, both sexes plunged in, showing a naked display of Anglo-Japanese solidarity. The only Japanese faint heart was my secretary, a lady brought up in strait-laced America.

Yours, etc,

MERRICK BAKER-BATES

(Commercial Counsellor, British Embassy, Tokyo, 1979–82), Creaton, Northamptonshire. March 17

From Mr John Priestley

Sir, In the article about the hot springs in Bath (T2, March 17), we are told that one of the treatments available is "watsu (a form of shiatsu carried out in water)".

I am none the wiser.

Yours faithfully,

JOHN PRIESTLEY,

Halifax. March 18

Council tax rises

From Mr Edward Coales

Sir, I have just received my council tax demand for 2003–04, which this year has increased by 18 per cent and means that I must now find an extra £251 from my diminishing pension.

In four years my council tax has risen by 52 per cent. The proportion of spending allocated to the Suffolk Police Authority has, however, increased in that time by 95 per cent. I am beginning to understand why the police are generally referred to as the Bill.

Yours faithfully,

EDWARD COALES,

Wortham, Suffolk. March 22

Equal in death?

From Sir Michael Moore

Sir, I wonder if the general public is aware that if a serviceman dies in action his next of kin will get twice his salary as a death-in-service payment, whereas an MP's will get four times if he expires merely by tripping over in the House or at home.

Yours faithfully,
MICHAEL MOORE,
Porchester, Hampshire. March 25

From Dr Joseph Swan

Sir, As Sir Michael Moore knows, servicemen and women, unlike MPs, do not vote for their own pay, pensions, or death-in-service payments.

The fact that those of the politicians are so high is surely a reflection of their ethics – and they wonder why so many people do not bother to exercise their vote.

Yours faithfully,
JOSEPH SWAN,
Onchan, Isle of Man. March 28

From Mr Peter Boggon

Sir, Arguably, MPs should receive pension and death benefits in line with the least generous in the public service sector. This might concentrate their minds on achieving fair provision for all.

Yours faithfully,
PETER BOGGON,
Welwyn, Hertfordshire. March 26

Open and transparent

From Mr Christopher J. Bowden

Sir, The notes received with my council tax bill prominently display the "Crystal Mark – Clarity approved by Plain English Campaign" logo on the cover.

The last four pages of the booklet each has the heading: "Plain English Campaign's Crystal Mark does not apply to this page as the wording has been set by the Government."

Yours faithfully,
CHRISTOPHER J. BOWDEN,
Little Waldingfield, Suffolk. March 24

Royal milkmen

From Mrs Elizabeth Charles

Sir, In today's obituaries you mention Dr Thomas Ashton of Express Dairies and that one of his duties was that when the Royal Family made overseas visits, he supervised the processing and supply of milk from their own farms for their use.

This was a great simplification to previous procedure, for when King George V and Queen Mary went to India on the Medina for the royal durbar in 1911, they took their own three cows and the milkman.

Yours faithfully,
ELIZABETH CHARLES,
Saffron Walden. March 25

Ups and downs

From Mr Richard Baker

Sir, Two headlines in your Business section: "Standard Life mourns end of double-digit returns" and "Ex-Standard Life chief paid £844,000 bonus".

Is this an example of a twin-track economy or a life of double standards?

Yours faithfully,
RICHARD BAKER,
Winchester, Hampshire. March 25

Origin of muggles

From Mr David Wasley

Sir, Muggle is an English word used in the West Country, mostly Somerset, and long predates J. K. Rowling (report, March 24). Whilst its usage today is uncommon, I have heard the word used to mean "soft-headed".

It was used by the Somerset author the Reverend S. H. A. Hervey in the opening sentence of his remarkable *The Wedmore Chronicles*, in the late 19th century. With characteristic humour he calls himself muggled to have dedicated himself to a journal of contemporary village life and reflections on all the fascinating stories, recollections and characters of Wedmore. Somerset words – field names, family names, archaeology and his own station as vicar are examined in the finest detail.

I hope the word can now be attributed to Hervey in *The Oxford English Dictionary*.

Yours,
DAVID WASLEY,
Chesham, Buckinghamshire. March 26

From Mr Bill Oxley
Sir, The word "muggle" was not invented by J. K. Rowling, although she may have invented a new meaning.

When I was a youth on Tyneside in the Fifties "muggle" was used in the plural to mean marbles. I dare say it still is.

Yours faithfully,
BILL OXLEY,
Warrington. March 26

From Mr Nigel Halsby
Sir, No less an author than John Steinbeck, in *Sweet Thursday* published in 1954, mentions muggles as slang for marijuana.

Perhaps J. K. Rowling had pot luck in trying to create a new word?

Yours faithfully,
N. HALSBY,
Northwood HA6. March 26

From Dr Alister McFarquhar
Sir, Your correspondents suggest that muggle means soft-headed and, in the plural, marbles.

This gives a new pertinence to the phrase "lost his marbles".

Yours,
ALISTER McFARQUHAR,
Downing College, Cambridge. March 28

Doubtful identity

From Mr Anthony Wilmot
Sir, Stephen Dalton in his notes about *Double Indemnity* (Films, T2, March 27) describes Raymond Chandler as a "pulp crime novelist". This would have been justified had he been referring to James Hadley Chase or Hank Janson; but to say this of Chandler is rather like saying P. D. James is a writer of "bodice ripper whodunnits".

Indeed, Chandler can be forgiven if he is now reaching for a .38 revolver rather than simply turning in his grave.

Yours criminously,
A. WILMOT,
London SW20. March 27

Media views on conflict

From Mr Richard Stanley
Sir, "Heroic defiance last night . . . courageous . . . they will stride forward with renewed belief . . . heroes everywhere . . . the captain was immense."

All of this was in the first two paragraphs of a report (March 26). The battle for Basra? Or Baghdad? Or Umm Qasr? No, it was Arsenal defeating Chelsea in a football match.

Yours,
RICHARD STANLEY,
Halifax. March 27

From Mr Robert Blake
Sir, While I was in the Army I worked briefly as a reporter on the four-page *Iraq Times* run by the military public relations unit in Baghdad in 1943.

Three pages were in English, the fourth in local Arabic. As none of us could read Arabic the back page was produced by an Iraqi sub-editor.

Production was stopped one day by a man from the British Embassy who pointed out to our editor that the headline over the back-page football report read, "Death to Churchill – British go home".

Yours faithfully,
ROBERT BLAKE,
Stockport. March 30

Seeing stars

From Dr D. A. Earnshaw
Sir, Anthony Browne (Thunderer, March 28) complains about the "blight" of "light pollution". But I recall, as a teenager, the terror of finding myself totally lost in the middle of a bed of rhododendrons, trying to find my way home out of People's Park

from the public library in Halifax, during the wartime blackout.

Public lighting helps people to avoid dangers; unlit sections of motorways are much more hazardous than those that are well illuminated. This is more important than being able to see the stars.

Yours faithfully,
D. A. EARNSHAW,
Earl Shilton, Leicester. March 28

From Mrs Patricia Anderson
Sir, Well done Anthony Browne for saying what I have been thinking for years about the problem of light pollution.

The last time I saw a starlit night was in northern Greece, staying at the ecotourism centre near the village of Dadia, which had two or three dim street lights only. Scops owls sat about on telegraph wires, hooting gently. The walk back was entirely unlit and the starlit nights magical.

Yours faithfully,
PATRICIA ANDERSON,
Holt, Norfolk. April 1

From Mr Andrew H. Hooper
Sir, Those of us who bemoan the light pollution in our towns and cities are not seeking the absence of public lighting, but that it be used efficiently. This would actually increase the lighting available to help people to avoid the dangers that your correspondent Dr D. A. Earnshaw is so concerned about.

Current lighting designs waste significant proportions of the light skyward or sideways, thereby denying the public both the safety they seek and the stars they currently cannot see.

Yours faithfully,
ANDREW H. HOOPER,
Derby. April 1

From Mrs Caroline Charles-Jones
Sir, Appreciation of the night sky is one of the things guests at our holiday cottage seem to appreciate. But we have also had, over the years, children who ask what are the "dots" in the sky; adults who complain of the depth of the darkness; and also a

visitor who, during a nocturnal thunderstorm, declared that she wished she had taken a cottage at the bottom of the hill as it "would have been farther away from the storm".

Yours faithfully,
CAROLINE CHARLES-JONES,
Newport, Pembrokeshire. April 4

Bombing campaigns

From Dr Stanley Glover
Sir, It may be that, for elaborate political reasons, it becomes necessary to bomb people for their own good.

I am not qualified to comment on such sophisticated arguments but, from my own experience as a child in Britain during the early part of the Second World War, it is unlikely that those performing this function will be regarded as nice guys.

Yours faithfully,
STANLEY GLOVER,
South Normanton, Derbyshire. March 28

Early learning

From Mr Paddy McEvoy
Sir, As a long-term critic of the mania for assessment that rampages through the education service from top to bottom, I feel your headline "Tiny babies do worse in exams" really does take the rusk.

Yours,
PADDY McEVOY,
Holywood, Co Down. March 25

Peak of achievement

From Mr Roger Bowmer
Sir, As one born in Rochdale I was fascinated to learn of the prescience of our townspeople in 1804 in nicknaming t'cut "the Everest of Canals" (report, March 29), 60 or so years before the peak was named in honour of Sir George Everest, the chief surveyor of India.

Yours faithfully,
ROGER BOWMER,
Littleborough, Lancashire. March 29

Frontline strains

From Mr Mike Allen

Sir, I have experienced one, albeit very personal, benefit from the current world situation.

Two months ago I looked approximately 20 years older than Tony Blair, but now . . .
Yours faithfully,
MIKE ALLEN,
Shoeburyness, Essex. April 1

From Mrs Aileen Warren

Sir, Would now be a good time for all those who didn't sing it the first time to join in a couple of choruses of *Things Can Only Get Better*?
Yours faithfully,
AILEEN WARREN,
Walcote, Leicestershire. April 1

From Mr Paul Pritchard

Sir, Mrs Aileen Warren's suggestion of a couple of choruses of *Things Can Only Get Better* is quite apt. However, perhaps *The Long and Winding Road* would be more appropriate.
Yours faithfully,
PAUL PRITCHARD,
Swyre, Dorchester. April 3

Each-way bet

From Mr Geoffrey Trimm

Sir, "High class: the Babylonian terracotta relief is thought to depict a prostitute and to have hung outside a brothel, or it may be the figure of a goddess" (caption, April 2).

A perfect example of the definite maybe.
Yours faithfully,
GEOFFREY TRIMM,
Ashcott, Somerset. April 2

London's turning

From Ms Frankie de Freitas

Sir, In Oxford Street today I was handed a handsome "Walking Map" of London produced by Transport for London. A note says: "This map has been produced with SOUTH at the top to make it easier to ori-entate when walking into Central London."

How does it help anyone to have an up-side-down map? How do they know which direction I'm coming from, anyway?
Yours faithfully,
FRANKIE de FREITAS,
London NW3. April 2

Perils ahead in Iraq

From Mr Gareth Williams

Sir, Having apparently discovered that Saddam's favourite wine is Mateus Rosé (report, March 31), do we have proof at last that Iraq possesses chemical weapons?
Yours faithfully,
GARETH WILLIAMS,
Blackheath, London SE3. April 1

Mortgage lending

From Mr Andy Crowe

Sir, There is a simple solution to the irresponsible and inflationary proposals of the Halifax to lend up to six times the income of its borrowers (report, April 3).

It is to make reckless lending a defence to any possession action that is sought.

This should reduce homelessness and negative equity at a stroke.
Yours,
ANDY CROWE,
Bishops Waltham, Hampshire. April 3

Never too old

From Mr Graham Roberts

Sir, This time last year, on my 59th birthday, I was at 18,000ft in the Himalayas.

Today, as a joke present, my wife has applied for my bus pass.

The age of 60 should not become an automatic tollgate through which we pass into a land of lost content.

We should not be inveigled into believing that we are old. Forget the bus pass, live a little.
Yours faithfully,
GRAHAM ROBERTS,
Rhos-on-Sea, Colwyn Bay. April 3

From His Honour Patrick Halnan

Sir, I enjoy using my half-price bus pass but do not understand why I have to renew it every year. I get older, not younger.

Yours truly,
PATRICK HALNAN,
Cambridge. April 10

From Mrs P. N. Carr

Sir, I have just closed the front door on an opinion poll representative, whose first words were: "I'm looking for people under 60."

Sorry, I said, my husband and I are over 70. As she turned away, I asked out of interest what the poll was about.

"Oh," she said, "views on politics, local government, developing countries . . . "

I take it that the views of those over 60 are of no consequence.

Yours faithfully,
P. N. CARR,
Rochford, Essex. April 2

Clued up

From Mr Noel Fryer

Sir, I congratulate your crossword compiler. I have read your newspaper for the last 45 years but only today has he achieved the same level of intelligence as me. I have completed his crossword for the first time.

I look forward to tomorrow with interest to see whether he has got the answers right.

Yours etc,
NOEL FRYER,
Oakhanger, Crewe. April 3

The Big Read

From Mr S. Fryer

Sir, It might be interesting to determine how many of the votes for the nation's favourite book (Jeanette Winterson's Thunderer, April 5) will have been cast by people who had read it, how many by people who had merely seen the BBC dramatisation, and how many by those who weren't sure whether they were voting off "the one with the spotty face" or were ringing for a pizza delivery.

Yours sincerely,
S. FRYER,
Birmingham. April 5

From Mr John O'Byrne

Sir, Despite Jeanette Winterson's objections I felt enriched by BBC Two's *The Big Read.*

To make her feel better, I've just voted for her *Oranges Are Not The Only Fruit.*

Yours truly,
JOHN O'BYRNE,
Dublin. April 6

Blowing in the wind

From Mr Peter Allen

Sir, Paul Simons (Weather Eye, April 5) reports on the phenomenon whereby fine sand is sucked up from the Great Western Desert in Algeria, and the Sahara, and deposited on this country. Does this natural occurrence not make a nonsense of the claim by some agriculturalists that seed from genetically modified plants cannot possibly contaminate crops growing in a neighbouring field, provided they are separated by a barren "safety zone" of but a few metres' width?

Yours sincerely,
PETER ALLEN,
Worthing, West Sussex. April 5

All that glisters

From Mr C. W. D. McLean

Sir, Before a small army of journalists, on dictator watch, visits my bathroom may I just point out for the record that my taps are not gold (report, April 8). They are brass.

Yours faithfully,
COLIN McLEAN,
Six Mile Bottom, Suffolk. April 8

All strung up

From Professor Emeritus R. E. Asher

Sir, If binding a statue with a mile of string

constitutes an artistic statement, could not the same be said of cutting through the string with a pair of scissors (report, April 7)?

Perhaps the perpetrator would have been commended rather than arrested if he had labelled his action "The Kiss, freed from bondage".

Yours, etc,
R. E. ASHER,
Edinburgh. April 7

Iraq's spin-doctor

From Dr Ann Williams

Sir, I do hope Alastair Campbell has spotted the potential of Muhammad Said al-Sahhaf, the Iraqi Minister of Information (report, April 8), and will be offering a job to this genial and charming man.

I have never seen anyone tell such bare-faced lies with so much cheerful relish; one feels that even if American tanks were demolishing the studio around his ears, he would still be happily describing how they were fleeing towards the Kuwaiti border with the Republican Guard in hot pursuit. What a credit he would be to the British spin-doctor industry.

Yours sincerely,
ANN WILLIAMS,
London E11. April 8

From Mr Leslie McLoughlin

Sir, As your Foreign Staff points out, the Iraqi Information Minister is unique in his denial of plain facts and in his use of terms of abuse in Arabic.

He should be given full marks for coolness, as I saw on Iraqi television by satellite recently when he continued to speak to the cameras from the War Room while the wall maps shook and the curtains blew in from bomb blasts. But in the final analysis he should be marked down for overacting and playing to the audience. Like another political figure performing for the last time to a world audience, he could almost be heard saying: "I am enjoying this!"

One must be fair, though. In using the rare word *uluj*, the minister was not alleging that the allied invaders lacked religious faith. The word implies "uncouth, barbarian".

Yours faithfully,
LESLIE McLOUGHLIN,
Institute of Arab & Islamic Studies, University of Exeter, Exeter. April 8

Reactions to the fall of Baghdad

From Mr Alan Humphreys

Sir, George Galloway, the BBC, Tam Dalyell, Tony Benn, *The Independent*, Piers Morgan, Robin Cook, *The Guardian*, Vanessa Redgrave, Ms Dynamite, Chris Smith.

Their views took one hell of a beating.
Rejoice! Rejoice!

Yours faithfully,
A. HUMPHREYS,
London SW12. April 9

From Mr Trevor Trotman

Sir, The fact that a war is brought to a quick conclusion does not prove that it was right to go to war.

Yours faithfully,
TREVOR TROTMAN,
Croydon. April 9

From Mr Neil Cooper

Sir, How do we know that the giant statue of Saddam destroyed on Wednesday wasn't of one of his doubles?

Yours faithfully,
NEIL COOPER,
Birmingham. April 9

Nature calls

From Mrs Peter FitzGerald

Sir, I have heard a radio report from Baghdad that dogs start howling ten minutes before a bomb lands. Here in Somerset, pheasants start cackling ten minutes before Concorde passes overhead; this is followed by the windows rattling as the plane passes over the Bristol Channel.

Yours faithfully,
SARAH FitzGERALD,
Penselwood, Somerset. April 8

From Mr James Williams

Sir, How fortunate the inhabitants of the West Country are (Mrs Peter FitzGerald's letter). When they hear cackling pheasants they can expect, ten minutes later, Concorde to rattle their windows – though not for much longer (report, April 11).

Pity the poor Baghdadis when they hear dogs barking; they must wonder if, in ten minutes, they will have any windows left.

Yours faithfully,
JAMES WILLIAMS,
Aston Rowant, Oxfordshire. April 11

From Mr Roger Smith

Sir, Seemingly, the dogs in Baghdad gave early warning of impending onslaughts.

I was a child in London during the Blitz and remember our dog settling under the stairs before we were in for a particularly bad raid. Normally my mother would disregard the air-raid sirens, but if the dog moved, we were brought down from bed and joined him under the stairs in the safest place.

The dog was invariably right about the scale of the bombing.

Yours faithfully,
ROGER SMITH,
Itchenor, West Sussex. April 14

From Mr Harold Palmer

Sir, Dogs bark or hide before bombing and pheasants call before Concorde passes over. Here, in my house, five minutes before the evening meal is served, the smoke alarm goes off.

Yours faithfully,
HAROLD PALMER,
Ellesmere, Shropshire. April 16

Midlife crisis

From Sir John Curtiss

Sir, A word of comfort for those suffering from the angst of reaching 40 (T2, April 8). By the time you are 80 you will have forgotten all about it.

Yours sincerely,
JOHN CURTISS,
Milford-on-Sea, Hampshire. April 10

Glowing report

From Mr Robert Longley

Sir, You report the loss of glow-worm colonies. Some thirty-five years ago I wrote to you in response to a similar report. Now, as then, our colony is still going strong, with regular appearances from females.

Our grassland is not exposed to strong lighting and the continued presence of our insect friends is reassuring.

Yours faithfully,
ROBERT LONGLEY,
Cranbrook, Kent. April 9

Flights of fancy?

From Mr Jerome Phillips

Sir, It is my impression that we no longer have airports in the UK. They have all been converted to shopping centres with runways attached.

Yours faithfully,
JEROME PHILLIPS,
Isfield, East Sussex. April 11

Full house

From Mrs Meg Gale

Sir, Two weeks ago letters from British Gas to four different gentlemen, all unknown to me, arrived correctly addressed to my home.

Two days later another four letters arrived, correctly addressed, for a further four gentlemen.

Concerned for my reputation as churchwarden lest it appear that I am living with eight different gentlemen, I contacted British Gas. I was reassured that the problem in its database had been identified and corrected. The conversation concluded amicably with the suggestion from them that all that remained was for the parish to pray for its errant churchwarden.

Last Saturday, letters arrived for another 12 gentlemen.

Yours faithfully,
MEG GALE,
Caversham, Berkshire. April 11

Winning the peace

From Mr Richard Bruton

Sir, As so often, W. C. Sellar and R. J. Yeatman get it right. In the Great War section of the incomparable *1066 and All That* they write: "Though there were several battles in the War, none were so terrible or costly as the Peace . . ."
Yours faithfully,
RICHARD BRUTON,
Ewell, Surrey. April 12

Plus ça change?

From His Honour Judge Anthony Rumbelow, QC

Sir, I have received the latest judicial I.T. newsletter. It advises that: "The Judicial Liaison team have been given new e-mail addresses. Please note that the old addresses will remain live indefinitely."
Yours,
A. RUMBELOW,
Manchester. April 12

Equal opportunities

From Mrs Penelope A. Walker

Sir, Now that we have male pacemakers in women's marathon races (report, Sport, April 12), why not male servers in women's tennis?
Yours faithfully,
PENELOPE WALKER,
Pissouri, Cyprus. April 13

From Mr Erik Eriksen

Sir, Why not women servers in men's tennis – and make a game of it?
Yours faithfully,
ERIK ERIKSEN,
Worthing. April 14

Lost for words

From Mr P. F. V. Waters

Sir, Fox's "Limited Edition" of Strawberries & Cream Crunch Creams states on the wrapper that the biscuits are filled with "cream-flavoured cream". There must

surely be a fine distinction between this and plain cream.
Yours faithfully,
PETER WATERS,
Rickmansworth, Hertfordshire. April 10

Belated thanks

From Mrs Patricia Young

Sir, I gave up teaching in June 1990. Last week I received a letter from Charles Clarke, Secretary of State for Education and Skills, thanking me for my contribution to education and wishing me a long and happy retirement.
Yours faithfully,
PAT YOUNG,
London SW14. April 15

Double or quits?

From Mr Neil Thomas

Sir, Of Saddam himself, I can understand, but why have there been no sightings of any of his umpteen doubles?
Yours faithfully,
NEIL THOMAS,
Bury St Edmunds, Suffolk. April 16

Cup cheers

From Mr Philip Warner

Sir, Dr Thomas Stuttaford could tell you why French men had fewer heart attacks the day they won the World Cup.
  They celebrated with red wine.
Yours faithfully,
PHILIP WARNER,
Cadnam, Southampton. April 15

Question of flesh tints

From Mr Thomas Harding

Sir, Your photograph today of Spencer Tunick's naked installation at Tuesday's opening of The Saatchi Gallery suggests that all but one of the reported 200 participants were coloured a pallid northern European pink. Is this an artistic choice (a pink period?) or should the Government appoint an "access tsar" to ensure that a

suitably diverse ethnic representation is chosen next time?
Yours faithfully,
THOMAS HARDING,
London W1. April 16

Food for thought

From Group Captain A. R. Gordon-Cumming, RAF (retd)

Sir, Yesterday I bought for my garden two nice aquilegias. The gaudy label attached to them carried the following advice in four languages: "Do not consume".

If only rabbits could read.
I remain, Sir, a frustrated gardener,
SANDY GORDON-CUMMING,
Chichester. April 14

Bird's eye view

From the Vicar of St Gabriel's, North Acton

Sir, What a relief! Life must be getting back to normal when today the BBC 6pm radio news found time to publicise the nesting problems of endangered hen harriers (In brief, later editions, April 15) instead of the dangers facing RAF Harriers and their crews.

It would be good to think that the people of Iraq were able to share such concerns.
Yours faithfully,
KEITH ROBUS,
North Acton, London W3. April 14

Inspirational life

From Dr Susan Baker

Sir, I found myself curiously drawn to read the obituary of Timothy Preston today, described as "one who spent a lifetime avoiding work and study in the pursuit of pleasure". What an uplifting start to the day it proved to be.

Through this piece I am sure Mr Preston touched as many people in death as he had done in life.
Yours faithfully,
SUSAN BAKER,

Cranfield School of Management, Cranfield, Bedfordshire. April 16

Self-restraint

From Mr Alan Millard

Sir, After reading that trauma victims might be better off forgetting their bad experiences, I have decided not to send you a letter telling you all about my operation.
Yours sincerely,
ALAN MILLARD,
Lee-on-the-Solent. April 16

Foreign exchange

From Mr Michael Banister

Sir, Your report on the likelihood of dual euro-pound pricing is being pre-empted in at least one quarter. Today I collected my regular prescription from the local pharmacy and was alarmed to note that the pills were in a carton carrying instructions printed entirely in Italian.

Even more worrying was the price (*prezzo*) clearly shown as Euro 14.16. Is the NHS ahead of events for once?
Yours faithfully,
MICHAEL BANISTER,
Solihull, West Midlands. April 16

Eric the impenetrable

From Mr Benjamin John Sheriff

Sir, Eric Cantona's famous quotation that explained the actions of the media by pointing out that "when the seagulls follow the trawler, it is because they think sardines will be thrown into the sea" is neither "French philosophy" nor "pretentious gibberish" (report, April 15).

It is, rather, a good old-fashioned metaphor – the birds follow trawlers expecting food, and the media follow footballers expecting titbits of information.

Perhaps it is time to lay to rest the myth of Mr Cantona's impenetrable remarks.
I remain, Sir, your obedient servant,
BENJAMIN JOHN SHERIFF,
West Norwood, London SE27. April 15

A mad, mad world

From Mrs D. J. Knight

Sir, I love Tony (Michael Gove), Blair is mad (Matthew Parris), America is a wannabe tyrant (Simon Jenkins), Rummy (Rumsfeld) is yummy (Stephen Pollard).

I don't know about other readers, but my head is spinning.

Yours sincerely,
DIANA KNIGHT,
Barton Mills, Suffolk. April 16

Making a meal of it

From Mr Russell Hewitson

Sir, Whilst staying in a London hotel recently, I was served at breakfast by a waiter whose badge described him as a "breakfast operative".

Yours faithfully,
RUSSELL HEWITSON,
School of Law, Northumbria University,
Newcastle upon Tyne. April 19

That'll do nicely

From Mr Timothy W. G. Bacon

Sir, I am privileged, I am assured, to receive an unsolicited personal invitation to apply for the American Express Platinum Card.

With my invitation it seems Amex has a new way to pre-screen applicants: not putting a stamp on the envelope. Anyone who can afford to collect these letters from the Post Office can surely afford the annual fees for the Platinum Card. I will admit, though, that even with my "platinum lifestyle" £1.13 seems a bit steep.

Yours faithfully,
TIMOTHY W. G. BACON,
Catsfield, Kent. April 20

Tame creatures

From Mr Peter Morrogh

Sir, My daughter, aged 21, decided that the answer to the crossword clue "Domesticated, docile" (four letters, last letter "e")

was "wife". A female colleague in my office said that unquestionably it must be "male".
Yours faithfully,
PETER MORROGH,
Sandymount, Dublin. April 20

Mixed signals

From Mr Barry Ferguson

Sir, Our bottle of handwash declares, in silver letters, that it is ORIGINAL.

Above, in bolder red letters, it proclaims that it is NEW. How can this be?
Yours perplexedly,
BARRY FERGUSON,
Shaftesbury, Dorset. April 19

Thinking man's sauce

From Mr Charles Hennessy

Sir, In his article "Sex and the single cook" (T2, April 18), Richard Owen lists as an ingredient for pasta "chopped spring opinions". In this household, that item flourishes all year round.
Yours faithfully,
CHARLES HENNESSY,
London SW7. April 19

Costs of smoking

From Miss P. C. Bradfield

Sir, As a 67-year-old maiden auntie I am perturbed but not dissuaded by the health police proclamation that "Smoking can damage the sperm and decreases fertility". A more effective warning in my case might be: "Smoking seriously damages the pocket."
Yours faithfully,
PAMELA BRADFIELD,
Bournemouth, Dorset. April 21

From Mr Stuart Sexton

Sir, On my latest packet of pipe tobacco is the warning, in large letters, "Smoking when pregnant harms your baby". As a grandad, I really must be careful.
Yours faithfully,
STUART SEXTON,
Sanderstead, Surrey. April 22

Too hot to handle

From Mr K. W. Crawford

Sir, I was recently sent a spare part for my new gas cooker; the delivery note had the stern warning: "This product must be fitted by a properly qualified engineer."

The item? An extra oven shelf.

Yours, etc,

KEN CRAWFORD,

Caterham, Surrey. April 21

From Mr Ray Smith, CEng

Sir, Mr K. W. Crawford may be comforted to learn that appliance manufacturers are equally aware of the risks arising from cold as from heat.

I was warned (in bold type) that "in the interests of consumer safety this part should only be fitted by a suitably qualified person with the machine disconnected from the mains supply". Being a chartered engineer I thought I might reasonably take the risk of placing the new ice tray in the freezer.

Yours carefully,

RAY SMITH,

Yarlington, Wincanton. April 22

Hamlet's on hold

From Mr R. W. Broadhead

Sir, I have received a greetings card showing Shakespeare on his mobile phone, hearing: "If you want 'to be', press 1; if you want 'not to be', press 2."

Perhaps "dumbing down" (report, April 17) is simply moving with the times.

Yours sincerely,

BOB BROADHEAD,

Petersfield. April 21

Toys for our times

From Ms Tig Thomas

Sir, I am used to toy manfacturers trying to reflect the spirit of the age, and was delighted when Barbie moved on from doing her hair to a useful career as a vet. But I think the makers of Playmobil small plastic figures have gone one step too far with their latest.

Alongside the Classroom Assistant and Firefighter (gender carefully non specific) they are now offering an Arms Trader. He comes with an anonymous-looking case holding various weaponry.

Yours sincerely,

TIG THOMAS,

Melton, Suffolk. April 22

From Mrs Susan Lyle

Sir, Not only are there toy Arms Traders in our house Playmobil has gone a step further. A few weeks ago my six-year-old picked up the Firefighter wearing breathing apparatus and exclaimed: "Look, here is a weapons inspector."

Yours faithfully,

SUSAN LYLE,

Worth, West Sussex. April 24

Fortune calls

From Dr John H. Greensmith

Sir, A friend has a new mobile phone which has, as a free feature, daily horoscopes.

I suspect that all the forecasts will be favourable, or subscribers might return the phone. Or perhaps they will predict something like: "Someone – from very far away – is expecting a call from you"?

Yours sincerely,

JOHN GREENSMITH,

Downend, Bristol. April 21

Watching this space

From Professor Sir William Asscher

Sir, With failing vision due to macular degeneration I have to prioritise my reading First choice goes to your last letter. Always relevant, often witty and short enough to be read with a magnifying glass.

Yours faithfully,

WILLIAM ASSCHER,

Llangan, Vale of Glamorgan. April 22

From Mr Graham Breeze

Sir, Correspondents who seek publication at the top of this page wish to inform lesser mortals, whilst those who aspire to be at the bottom merely seek to amuse.

The consequences of reversing this order are too delicious even to contemplate.

Yours faithfully,
GRAHAM BREEZE,
Hawksworth, Leeds. April 23

Cambridge spies

From Mr N. V. Henfrey

Sir, Thank you for carrying on St George's Day the news that the BBC is to screen an "heroic" portrayal of the Cambridge spies, together with the magnificent tributes to them by the actors who are to play them and the observation by Jane Tranter, BBC head of drama, that "It would be very bland drama which just said these men were heinous traitors . . ."

At one creative swoop St George has been rendered horseless. Last seen: badly winded and making for the long grass.

Yours sincerely,
NORMAN HENFREY,
East Horrington, Somerset. April 23

The search for WMD

From Mr Ronald Eyres

Sir, By sponsoring a wider search for weapons of mass destruction in Iraq (report, April 18), apparently without any deadline, America has adopted what France and Germany were proposing (under UN auspices) before war could be justified.

The US, however, preferred Alice in Wonderland justice: sentence first, verdict afterwards.

Yours faithfully,
RONALD EYRES,
London NW5. April 23

Is anybody there?

From Mrs Johnne Abrams

Sir, After attending an uplifting and songful Eucharist on Easter Day I returned home to open up Saturday's Faith page and was vastly amused to read that an American atheist has won the right to pray at a city council meeting for deliverance from "weak and stupid politicians" (The Register, April 19).

Well, amen to that – but to whom or what does an atheist pray?

Yours faithfully,
JOHNNE ABRAMS,
Basingstoke. April 22

From Mr Ormond Uren

Sir, Mrs Johnne Abrams asks "to whom or to what does an atheist pray?"

What I have been trying to understand for most of my life is to whom or to what does a non-atheist pray?

Yours sincerely,
ORMOND UREN,
London NW5. April 24

From Mr J. W. Simson

Sir, In the absence of any alternative you pray to yourself.

The function of prayer at the practical level is to clear and calm the mind and to enable one to concentrate deeply and clearly upon particular issues or individuals. Some people find it helpful to believe they have God on the other end of the line.

The idea of God can be contemplated at two levels. The first is as the culmination of human ideals and aspirations. In that sense He is a human construct but none the less real or useful for that. At the other level He may exist in the interstices of space and time in a state likely to be forever beyond human comprehension. The response to that can only lie between faith and agnosticism: atheism is not an option.

Yours, etc,
JOHN W. SIMSON,
Shorwell, Isle of Wight. April 26

From Mr William Sant

Sir, Mr J. W. Simson seems to be telling me, an atheist, that atheism is not an option.

I don't believe a word of it.

Yours,
WILLIAM SANT,
Southend-on-Sea. May 2

Spelling it out

From Miss Catherine Negus

Sir, My suspicion that the Government and exam boards believe most sixth formers to be half-wits was confirmed last week when I received the Instructions and Guidance for Students booklet for my AS-level history course essay. On the front the Assessment and Qualifications Alliance had deemed it necessary to print:

Instructions You must read these instructions carefully.

You must then carry out the tasks in accordance with these instructions.

Yours faithfully,
CATHERINE NEGUS,
Solihull. April 23

From Mrs Kate Fehler

Sir, Sixth-form history students should be grateful that their exam boards do not consider it necessary to print more disturbing instructions.

On my exam admission advice received last week from the Chartered Institute of Management Accountants I was dismayed to read the following, among Special Instructions: "Take life or stairs to second floor."

Yours faithfully,
KATE FEHLER,
Sheffield. April 24

From Mr Michael Banister

Sir, I have just received from a building society a booklet entitled Be Better Off With a Clear Explanation.

Under the heading Reclaiming Tax it says: "If you already receive a repayment claim form each year, your tax office will continue to send your form automatically. All you have to do when you receive the form is fill it in and send it back."

Why didn't I think of that?

Yours faithfully,
MICHAEL BANISTER,
Solihull, West Midlands. April 28

From Mr David P. Charters

Sir, Today appears an advertisement for summer jackets. Their main advantage is that they have pockets "for wallet, passport, keys, etc".

Eureka! I have spent the 55 years of my life wondering what those big square patches were on my clothing.

Thank you.

Yours faithfully,
DAVID P. CHARTERS,
Bluntisham, Huntingdon. May 6

Open book

From Mr A. J. Duckworth

Sir, An information slip from Oxted Library:

Easter opening times 2003
Good Friday 18 April 2003 Closed
Saturday 19 April 2003 Closed
Easter Sunday 20 April 2003 Closed
Monday 21 April 2003 Closed.

Yours faithfully,
TONY DUCKWORTH,
Oxted, Surrey. April 22

St George's day(s)

From Mrs Christine Matthews

Sir, James Delingpole (Thunderer, April 23) was more accurate than he realised when he wrote "it's only St George's Day . . . a day like any other".

This year it truly was like any other, for, as April 23 fell in Easter Week, St George's Day has been moved in the church calendar to next Monday, April 28.

Still time, then, to get out the flags.

Yours faithfully,
CHRISTINE MATTHEWS,
Wilton, Wiltshire. April 23

From Mrs Mary Stastny

Sir, Since he shares the name of the famous dragon-slayer, my husband is an enthusiastic supporter of St George's Day. A woman in a Dales village recently, spotting an English flag sticker on the back of my husband's car, stopped to ask him if he was Swiss.

Since he is Anglo-Czech and it was her flag which was in question, words failed him.
Yours sincerely,
MARY STASTNY,
Whorlton, Co Durham. April 24

Rainmaker

From Dr Edward Young
Sir, I have just read Paul Simon's excellent Weather Eye article (April 23) warning that our current spring drought is now the worst for over 300 years. It is pelting with rain.

What else can he do?
Yours sincerely,
EDWARD YOUNG,
Reading, Berkshire. April 24

Contradiction in terms

From Mr Peter Jaeger
Sir, My wife's and my new Visa cards arrived by registered mail yesterday with a leaflet describing the sophisticated technology the bank is using to combat credit-card fraud.

With them was a second pair of cards, for a Mr and Mrs Robinson, whom we have never met but who we can guess are even less impressed.
Sincerely yours,
PETER JAEGER,
London SE21. April 20

Really necessary?

From Mr Bill Moore
Sir, You report (April 24) that because of the Sars epidemic, Lloyds TSB, NatWest, and the Royal Bank of Scotland have all banned non-essential travel to the affected regions.

But doesn't efficiency suggest that non-essential travel should not take place at any time? What is the nature of this non-essential travel to the other side of the world?
Yours faithfully,

BILL MOORE,
Youlgrave, Derbyshire. April 24

From Mr Robert Levy
Sir, Can we expect the Government shortly to be announcing the appointment of a Sars Tsar?
Yours faithfully,
ROBERT LEVY,
Hale, Cheshire. April 24

Spud-bashing

From Mr David Finlay
Sir, Your obituary of *Times* journalist John Young (April 23) recalled that, for failing to report the square potato for making better chips, he was reprimanded crisply. Were we supposed to take this with a pinch of salt?
Yours sincerely,
DAVID FINLAY,
London NW11. April 24

Local elections

From Mrs Christine Jeffreys
Sir, Returning home after a morning's leaflet drop for the forthcoming local elec-

tions, I was pleased to learn from a small boy that his granny had already voted for me.

He said: "Gran didn't know which three to vote for, so she used a pin to pick the names and one of them was yours."

Yours faithfully,
CHRISTINE E. M. JEFFREYS,
Cotgrave, Nottinghamshire. April 25

From Mr Lyn Thomas
Sir, I was standing in the hallway this afternoon when a leaflet dropped through the letterbox. I immediately picked it up. It read: "Unfortunately there was no reply when Edwina Hart, the Labour candidate for Gower, called today. We hope we can count on your support in the Assembly Election on Thursday, 1st May."

Sincerely,
LYN THOMAS,
Pontarddulais, Swansea. April 24

Taking the strain

From Mr Mike Lawlor
Sir, I have a permanent health insurance policy from Friends Provident, to which I cannot contribute after the age of 55.

When I telephoned my insurance broker to ask why this was, I was told that it was because of my occupation. "You are a teacher, you see, and you can't get more of a stressful job than that."

Perhaps, then, after reaching my 55th birthday I should follow the advice of Thomas Carlyle: "It were better to perish than to continue schoolmastering."

Yours sincerely,
MIKE LAWLOR,
Teddington, Middlesex. April 25

Yesterday's man

From Mr Max Robinson
Sir, Your front page today has a picture of the former Deputy Prime Minister of Iraq in the uniform of the old regime.

Is that Tariq Aziz or Tariq Azwaz?

Yours faithfully,

MAX ROBINSON,
Ightham, Kent. April 25

Waugh war jaw

From Mr Winston Fletcher
Sir, Lord Copper, proprietor of *The Beast*, briefed ingenu war correspondent William Boot as follows (Evelyn Waugh, *Scoop*, 1938):

I never hamper my correspondents in any way . . . Remember that the Patriots are in the right and are going to win. *The Beast* stands by them foursquare. But they must win quickly. The British public has no interest in a war which drags on indecisively. A few sharp victories some conspicuous acts of personal bravery on the Patriot side and a colourful entry into the capital. That is *The Beast* Policy for the war.

Yours faithfully,
WINSTON FLETCHER,
London SW7. April 27

Win-win enterprise

From Mr Andrew Radclyffe
Sir, If I were an entrepreneur involved in reconstructing Iraq I would seriously consider opening a flag-making factory. I suspect there will be considerable demand in the next year or two for the Stars and Stripes, either for waving or burning.

Yours faithfully,
ANDREW RADCLYFFE,
Honiara, Solomon Islands. April 27

Archers' angst

From Mrs Janet Whitehill
Sir, There may be "nowt so queer" as country folk (leading article, April 21), but in my view there is nowt so annoying as arts reporters letting the cat out of the bag too early.

I refer, of course, to Adam, the apparently gay son of Jennifer Aldridge from *The Archers*, whose sexual propensity has, it seems, been hinted at already (though not picked up by this reader).

I realise that some big new storyline in *The*

Archers is overdue, following Brian's dramatic confession, but I (and probably 4.5 million other fans) do not want to be told what it is in advance.

Shame on you!

Yours sincerely,

JANET WHITEHILL,

Pinner, Middlesex. April 22

Canon fodder

From Mr Mark Startin

Sir, Recent correspondents on the relative sizes of tank engagements included Field Marshal Sir John Stanier, but also Dom Alberic Stacpoole, OSB (April 18).

Today you carry a letter from Canon Michael Saward on the same subject.

Is it that tank battles have some special appeal to members of the clergy? Or do they simply have a greater chance of having their letters printed?

Yours faithfully,

MARK STARTIN,

East Morton, Keighley. April 23.

From Canon John Wheatley Price

Sir, I can assure Mr Mark Startin that there is no pro clerical bias from the Editor. He has always rejected my canonical salvos.

Yours faithfully,

J. WHEATLEY PRICE,

Knowle, Solihull. April 28

Making do

From Mr F. Irish

Sir, Your report on the use of a condom in DNA research reminded me of when I was a laboratory assistant in 1950 at the British Non-ferrous Metals Research Association.

In those days it was frequently necessary to improvise when building apparatus. We wanted to make something like a large bicycle tyre valve and needed an elastic, thin tubular membrane.

The elderly head of department went to a chemist shop in Euston for a packet of Durex and, when asked if he wanted them "with or without teat", replied that it didn't matter, as he was going to cut the end off anyway.

Yours faithfully,

F. IRISH,

London W5. April 24

Exploring instinct

From Dr Charles Cockell

Sir, Your leading article, "Life on Mars" (April 26), put the argument that robots are safer and cheaper at exploring the solar system than human beings. To my mind the crucial point has nothing to do with economics or safety.

Would Scott have abandoned his expedition to the South Pole if a robot had landed there in 1911? Would Hillary and Tenzing have thrown in the towel and gone home if a robot had been dropped on the summit of Everest in 1952?

The reason that humans will explore space is because we need to. We are an exploring species.

Your comment that mankind "may be better off staying at home" fills me with sadness. The day that mankind decides that it is better to let robots go exploring for us will be a day when our purpose is lost.

Yours faithfully,

CHARLES COCKELL,

Cambridge. April 26

Goodbye?

From Mr Chris Duckling

Sir, I note that Anne Robinson was told by her accountant that she was wealthy enough never to have to work again.

Was there ever a better case for the client accepting the professional's advice?

Sincerely,

CHRIS DUCKLING,

Bexhill-on-Sea. April 29

Cup that reassures

From Mr R. Arch

Sir, Facing the prospect of an imbibing *faux pas*, imagine my delight to be in-

formed by the packaging on my Tesco Premium teabags that they were "Suitable for everyday use. Throughout the day."
Yours dutifully,
RICHARD ARCH,
London NW10. April 29

Art of the message

From Mr Royston Deitch

Sir, You report today that New York is being eclipsed by London as the world capital of modern art. No one should believe, however, that London artists have only the power to shock. They also have a grasp of world affairs, as shown by the graffito I saw this morning on a wall where Dalston's Kingsland Road runs into trendy Shoreditch: "War is so last century."
Yours faithfully,
ROYSTON DEITCH,
London N5. April 30

Protecting artefacts from looters

From Mr Michael Cole

Sir, The conference on the looting of the Iraqi National Museum (report, April 26) took place amid the splendours of the Mesopotamian collection at the British Museum. I hope no one was so rude as to ask how in earlier centuries these treasures made their way to London.
Yours faithfully,
MICHAEL COLE,
South Kensington, London SW7. April 30

From Mr Dale Scarboro

Sir, The looting of Baghdad's Iraq Museum under the careless eyes of the US Army brings to mind the following passage from John Aubrey's *Brief Lives*:

Thomas, Lord Fairfax of Cameron, Lord General of the Parliament Army: when Oxford was surrendered (June, 24, 1646) the first thing General Fairfax did was to set a good guard of soldiers to preserve the Bodleian Library . . . He was a lover of learning, and had he not taken this special care, that noble library had been utterly destroyed.

Yours faithfully,
DALE SCARBORO,
Cheltenham, Gloucestershire. May 1

Laws of nature

From Mr Jeremy Zeid

Sir, Scientists are spending £3.1 million looking for a particle, the invisible Wimp (weakly interacting massive particle) that may not exist, but that is the point of science and research: to learn. At least they admit the possibility. One such theoretical particle being the speedy Tachyon that travels faster than light and is believed to get heavier the slower it goes.

Meanwhile the wimps in government pour billions into the unreformed and inefficient public sector for services that barely exist and then claw it all back in higher taxes and then fail to learn. In the case of the NHS and education, the more Taxyons poured in, the heavier it gets and the slower it goes.

Wimps may be theoretical, but I know a black hole when I see it.
Yours faithfully,
JEREMY ZEID,
Kenton, Middlesex. April 30

Teller's cheer

From Mr Paul Moynagh

Sir, On returning home this morning to a late breakfast and *The Times* after two solitary and rather boring hours "telling" for the local elections, my gloomy mood was greatly lightened by Pugh's chuckle-making front-page polling station cartoon today ("I just come here for the peace and quiet").

With so few voters and no other tellers there to keep me company, I had plenty of time to ponder whether it was for the imposition of this experience that we felt it worth sacrificing so many lives in Iraq.

Let us hope the Iraqis have their own Pughs.
Yours sincerely,
PAUL MOYNAGH,
Kingswear, Devon. May 1

Professionals foul

From Mr John Mellin

Sir, In the article on money-laundering mention is made of "professionals such as lawyers, accountants, estate agents and casino operators".

Professionals? Lawyers? Yes, in the main. Accountants? I suppose so. Casino operators?

Well, times change. But estate agents? Now you are being silly.

Yours faithfully,
JOHN MELLIN,
Salterforth BB18. April 30

Knight after knight

From Mrs Audrey Wilson

Sir, You report that the father and son knighthoods of Amar and Ravinder Maini are thought by the Imperial Society of Knights Bachelor to be unique in recent times.

As secretary to Sir Christopher Cockerell for the last 26 years of his life, I well remember his pride in having achieved a knighthood for services to engineering (including the invention of the hovercraft) in 1969. His father, Sir Sydney Cockerell, was made a knight in 1934 for services to the arts.

Yours sincerely,
AUDREY WILSON,
Dibden Purlieu, Hampshire. April 30

From Mr R. J. Gluckstein

Sir, Sir Isidore Salmon (1876–1941), the chairman and managing director of Lyons & Co, Ltd, was knighted in 1933 and had two sons: Sam (1900–80), also chairman of Lyons, and Julian (1903–78), both of whom were knighted, in 1960 and 1969 respectively.

Yours faithfully,
R. J. GLUCKSTEIN,
London NW7. April 30

From Mr Shivaji Ghosh

Sir, The Mainis are not the first pair of British Asians to be knighted in successive generations. In the first half of the 20th century, under the British Raj, Rajendra Nath Mukherji – also spelt Mookerjee – (1854–1936) and later his son, Biren, were both knighted for services to industry.

Yours sincerely,
SHIVAJI GHOSH,
London NW4. May 8

From Major R. J. K. Cassels

Sir, My grandfather and father were both doubly dubbed.

My grandfather, General Sir Robert Cassels, was appointed GCB in 1933 and GCSI in 1940 whilst my father, Field Marshal Sir James Cassels, was appointed KBE in 1952 and GCB in 1961.

The GCB collar is returnable on death and my father was honoured to be presented with the same collar as my grandfather.

I remain, Sir, your very humble servant,
R. J. K. CASSELS,
Errol, Perthshire. May 16

From Mrs Margaret Ziegler

Sir, My father was knighted as Sir Archer Cust in 1959, his father as Sir Lionel in 1927 and his grandfather as Sir Reginald (date forgotten), or does it spoil it that Sir Lionel was KCVO and not a Knight Bachelor?

Yours sincerely,
MARGARET ZIEGLER,
Ringwood, Hampshire. May 7

From Lieutenant-Commander F. L. Phillips, RNR (retd)

Sir, Spare a thought for those doubly dubbed. Vice-Admiral Sir James Somerville, Flag Officer Force H at Gibraltar in the Second World, was already a KCB when, on Trafalgar Day 1941, he was appointed KBE. As quick as a flash, Andrew Cunningham, Commander-in-Chief Mediterranean Fleet, signalled: "What, twice a knight at your age?"

I have the honour to be, Sir, your obedient servant,
LAWRENCE PHILLIPS,
Northwood, Middlesex. May 7

A bigger box

From Mr John Greenhalgh

Sir, With an ever-increasing percentage of the population now overweight or obese, has widescreen television been invented to accommodate the expanded girth of our television presenters?

Yours faithfully,
JOHN GREENHALGH,
Nailsea, Bristol. May 3

Legal wangles

From Dr Alan Gibson

Sir, You publish (Law, April 29) the complaint of a reader who had purchased ineffectual legal advice on the signing of a will and who wondered if, like the purchaser of faulty goods, he or she might expect redress. I was gobsmacked by the response from the College of Law that the expectation was unfair "as solicitors, unlike retailers, give no guarantees of quality".

Yours faithfully,
ALAN GIBSON,
Cholsey, Oxfordshire. April 29

Hidden riches

From Mr Reg Fort

Sir, Your television reviewer (T2, May 1) jokingly suggests that what distinguishes aristocrats from hoi polloi is that they have multiple names but prefer to use none of them.

On the same day your obituary of a frighteningly upper-class lady (The Register) reports that her only daughter, Marie-Anna Berta Felicie Johanna Ghislaine Theodora Huberta Georgina Helene Genoveva, is generally known as "Bunny".

Yours sincerely,
REG FORT,
Tewkesbury, Gloucestershire. May 2

Dunfleecing

From Mr Peter Golden

Sir, On occasion I have noticed letters to *The Times* from: "The Old Post Office", "The Old School House", "The Old Bank", and even, "The Old Police Station".

How is it, therefore, that I have never seen one from "The Old VAT Office" or "The Old Inland Revenue Building"?

Yours,
PETER GOLDEN,
Harrow. May 1

Match of the day

From Mrs Gill Marshall

Sir, If the proposed merger between Bath and Bristol rugby union clubs takes place (Sport, May 5), will the resulting team be called Barstool?

Yours faithfully,
GILL MARSHALL,
Taunton. May 5

From Dr J. David Abell

Sir, Mrs Gill Marshall may be unduly nostalgic in suggesting "Barstool" as a title for the proposed Bath and Bristol RUFCs merger. With the ferocity of modern rugby, perhaps "Borstal" might be more appropriate.

Yours faithfully,
J. DAVID ABELL,
West Bridgford, Nottingham. May 6

Remedy not so drastic

From Ms Catherine Henderson

Sir, On the pack of a recent purchase from a garden centre was the claim that it would "kill ants for up to five weeks".

Yours faithfully,
CATHERINE HENDERSON,
Lancaster. May 2

I'm only here . . .

From Mr Tony Johnson

Sir, Since Budget Day, I have been carrying out a survey of pubs in the South East to discover one where the price has increased in accordance with the "penny a pint" announced by Gordon Brown (report, April 10).

Although I have yet to meet with success,

as an act of public spiritedness I feel that I should continue this research.
Sincerely,
TONY JOHNSON,
Rottingdean, Brighton. May 5

Coughing on cue

From Mr Will Holland
Sir, During the snooker final at the Crucible there was sustained coughing in between shots.

The organisers should check as to who was informing Mark Williams which shot to make.
Yours sincerely,
WILL HOLLAND,
London SW11. May 6

Beliefs and convictions

From Mr Jack Harrison
Sir, Peter Stothard (T2, May 6) says of Blair and Bush: "Both are religious men," as if that is a positive attribute.

Michael Gove (Comment, same day) writes: "The Christian faith that Bush and Blair share, and which is also held by Iain Duncan Smith, enriches these men as politicians and extends their sympathies."

Well, that is news to the atheist. Many find strong religious belief rather scary.
Yours faithfully,
JACK HARRISON,
Royston, Hertfordshire. May 6

From the Reverend Monsignor John T. Dunne
Sir, Commenting on religious belief Mr Jack Harrison, speaking perhaps as an atheist, says: "Many find strong religious belief rather scary."

But the atheist tells us that we arrive out of obscurity and mainly by chance; that we live in a Universe without any intelligent purpose or direction; and that we finally disappear into total annihilation.

Now that I find really scary.
Yours sincerely,
JOHN T. DUNNE,
Bishop Thornton, Harrogate. May 7

New balls

From Mr Tim Woolford
Sir, Whilst being interviewed by BBC TV at the World Snooker Final in Sheffield the Minister for Sport, Richard Caborn, confidently informed us that "Wembley is, of course, synonymous with tennis".

Little wonder, then, that the planning for the new stadium has been rather lacking in direction.
I remain, Sir, yours truly,
TIM WOOLFORD,
London SW1. May 6

Final settlement

From Mr Francis Abberley
Sir, "Mortgages are bad for your health, say doctors" (report, May 7). This should come as no surprise: the word mortgage does literally mean "dead pledge".
Yours faithfully,
FRANCIS ABBERLEY,
London SW1. May 7

None so deaf . . .

From the Reverend John Fairweather-Tall.
Sir, Commenting on his partial deafness, the Archbishop of Canterbury, Dr Rowan Williams, says: "I have one ear that is purely decorative" (Weekend, May 3).

Surely every sensible husband has that.
Yours faithfully,
JOHN FAIRWEATHER-TALL,
Elburton, Plymouth. May 4

Colourful clergy

From Mr John Carney
Sir, The Bishop of Willesden, the Right Reverend Peter Broadbent, "has dyed his hair purple in an effort to make people see that church leaders are human" (The Register, May 3). "People think," he says, "there's an oddness about them."

Perish the thought.
Yours faithfully,
JOHN J. CARNEY,
Tankerton, Kent. May 5

Game-show politics

From Mr Michael Ball

Sir, Rosie Kane, a new MSP, says she hopes that the Scottish Parliament is going to become on television a bit like the programme *Big Brother* (report, May 8).

Now there's an idea to banish voter apathy and it could be extended to Westminster – give us a chance to vote them off one at a time.

Yours faithfully,
MICHAEL BALL,
Carshalton, Surrey. May 8

Mind-bending

From Mr Bevis Hillier

Sir, Reading that "Japanese scientists have coaxed embryonic stem cells to form sperm . . . ", I could not help thinking what a challenging entry that would have made on the extinct television quiz show, *What's My Line?* It really puts the saggar-maker's bottom-knocker in the shade.

I wonder if the late Gilbert Harding and the late Lady Isobel Barnett would have got "warm".

Yours sincerely,
BEVIS HILLIER,
London WC2. May 9

From Mr Nick R. Thomas

Sir, Mr Bevis Hillier wonders how much of a challenge the occupation of "coaxing embryonic stem cells to form sperm" would have posed for the panellists on the television quiz show *What's My Line?*

Surely much would have depended upon the accuracy of the contestant's mime?

Yours faithfully,
NICK R. THOMAS
(*What's My Line?* contestant, Meridian TV, 1995), Bournemouth, Dorset. May 12

Agony uncle

From Mr Bernard Selwyn

Sir, There is nothing more infuriating than Philip Howard's advice to his correspond-

ents (Modern Times, Weekend, May 10, etc) not to allow themselves to become infuriated about conduct which is unquestionably infuriating.

Yours sincerely,
BERNARD SELWYN,
London SW5. May 10

From Dr Henry Campbell

Sir, Mr Bernard Selwyn criticises Philip Howard's advice column.

In response to such "infuriating conduct", if I have read PH correctly, by all means become infuriated – but don't show it.

I remain, Sir, your obedient servant,
HENRY CAMPBELL,
Birchington, Kent. May 13

From Mrs Jeanne Carlton

Sir, I have always thought how civilised Philip Howard's advice is, and wonder if he is able to follow it himself.

Yours faithfully,
JEANNE CARLTON,
Ashford, Kent. May 13

Tory transport policy

From Mr John Horam, MP for Orpington (Conservative)

Sir, You reported me today as arriving at the Conservative MPs' weekend in a "silver Mercedes soft-top".

If only. Actually it was my faithful 12-year-old Ford Sierra, survivor of three general elections.

Yours sincerely,
JOHN HORAM,
House of Commons. May 10

Wigs and gowns

From Mr Malcolm Bowden

Sir, A comparison of the first photograph on your front page today with that of a former archbishop on page 3 admirably underlines the common historical origin of barristers' and Anglican clergymen's formal dress (letter, May 8), with the archbishop arguably having the edge in the field of 17th-century chic.

Will the judges' modernisation cause the Church of England to review its fancy dress code? I would like to think so, but somehow I doubt it.

Yours sincerely,
MALCOLM BOWDEN,
Hartford, Cheshire. May 9

From Mr Mark Smith

Sir, No sooner have I bought my young son the replica judge's outfit he so craved than the Lord Chancellor announces the "new" judicial kit.

Yours,
MARK SMITH (Barrister),
Manchester. May 12

Voting on the euro

From Mr Bryan Cassidy

Sir, I note that a number of the opponents of the euro (report, later editions, May 12) are senior figures in the retail world from companies such as Dixons Group plc, Next plc, WHSmith Group plc, etc.

It is natural that the retail trade is opposed to anything which would enable us to compare UK prices with the generally lower prices for the same goods elsewhere in the eurozone.

Yours faithfully,
BRYAN CASSIDY,
Cassidy & Associates International, London W8. May 13.

Plum's pearls

From Professor Emeritus D. F. Brewer

Sir, P. G. Wodehouse's letter to *The Times* about his difficulties with crossword puzzles was not, as stated in your third leader today, his only one.

On November 30, 1937, he wrote, in response to a previous correspondent's remarks about Bertie Wooster's receding chin:

On the other hand, everything is relative. Compared with Sir Roderick Glossop, Tuppy Glossop, old Pop Stoker, Mr. Blumenfeld, and even Jeeves, Bertie is undoubtedly opisthogna-

thous. But go to the Drones and observe him in the company of Freddie Widgeon, Catsmeat Potter-Pirbright, and – particularly – of Augustus Fink-Nottle, and his chin will seem to stick out like the ram of a battleship.

Yours faithfully,
DOUGLAS BREWER,
Lewes, East Sussex. May 10

Why are we all here?

From Professor Colin Howson

Sir, A life-supporting Universe may well require extreme fine-tuning of the constants of nature, but from that and the fact of our existence it certainly does not follow that "it does look as if we were meant to be here".

To compute the most likely explanation of our existence requires consideration of all the data, which must include the fact of widespread and apparently random suffering, and of all the logically possible ways it might occur and their antecedent probabilities.

Anything like exact computation is impossible without much more information, but in the light of what we have it seems no less reasonable to believe that the Christian explanation fares rather poorly even against the hypothesis of chance occurrence, let alone against the composite "agency unknown or nonexistent", than vice versa.

Yours faithfully,
COLIN HOWSON (Professor of Logic),
London School of Economics and Political Science, London WC2. May 10

From Mr Steve Kershaw

Sir, Professor Colin Howson asserts that "To compute the most likely explanation of our existence requires consideration of all the data," and that "Anything like exact computation is impossible without much more information".

Perhaps, though, as Professor of Logic he may be able to compute the likelihood of someone several centuries BC correctly guessing that the Earth is round, that the

WHY ARE WE ALL HERE?

Universe is expanding and that energy can be converted to matter (see Isaiah xl, 22 and 26).

One correct guess could be considered lucky, two an amazing coincidence, but three almost impossible without his being tipped the wink by the original designer and creator.

Yours sincerely,
STEVE KERSHAW,
Swindon. May 15

From Mr William Sant

Sir, Whilst platoons of academics batter each other gladiatorially with logic, there will be armies of untutored clear-thinkers to whom it will be blindingly obvious that we are all here by accident.

Yours,
WILLIAM SANT,
Southend-on-Sea. May 15

From Mr Neville N. Bradpiece

Sir, We are here because this planet is neither hot enough nor cold enough to be completely antiseptic.

Yours, etc,
NEVILLE N. BRADPIECE,
Manchester. May 15

From Mr Jonathan Porter

Sir, Mr Steve Kershaw could have added to his list of predictions in Isaiah xl that at verse 31 he appears to predict the invention of the aeroplane.

Amazing.

Yours faithfully,
JONATHAN PORTER,
Market Drayton. May 21

From Dr Frank S. Rickards

Sir, Sir Fred Hoyle, the astronomer and developer of the steady-state theory of the Universe, put it neatly:

The idea that life was put together by a random shuffling of constituent molecules can be shown as ridiculous and improbable as the proposition that a tornado blowing through a junk-yard might assemble a Boeing 747 from the materials therein.

My own conviction is that this extraordi-

nary dance of life we all enjoy calls out for a choreographer.

Yours truly,
FRANK S. RICKARDS,
Oswaldkirk, North Yorkshire. May 28

From Mr Jocelyn Walker

Sir, If indeed we are here as a result of an accident which began with the collision of gases in an otherwise void, then surely, if there is such a thing as a law of probability, eventually the exact same accident will replicate itself?

I therefore look forward to the same random (or otherwise) displacement of particles which has led to me writing this letter to *The Times* today occurring again within, say, the next trillion, trillion years. How unfortunate that under the same law of probability, it is no more likely to be published then than it is now.

Yours faithfully,
JOCELYN WALKER,
London SW1. May 29

From Mr William Garrett

Sir, The idea that the creation of life from random shuffling of molecules is as improbable as the assembly of a 747 by a tornado in a junkyard seems to me a very misleading analogy.

The biological equivalent would be the emergence of a human being from a stirred tank of chemicals. Given a planet covered with chemical compounds, lightning and a billion years, the first lucky little reproducing blob, with no competition, was driven upwards by evolution towards perfection. Er, that's us.

Yours sincerely,
WILLIAM GARRETT,
Harrow, Middlesex. June 2

From Mr David Kelsey

Sir, If life had been described before its creation, then its subsequent emergence might indeed be as unlikely to have resulted from chance as the creation of a Boeing 747 from a tornado in a junkyard.

In the absence of a prior specification, the proper comparison is with a tornado in a

junkyard producing an unusual and interesting arrangement of materials.
Yours faithfully,
DAVID KELSEY,
Middlesbrough. June 2

From Eur Ing Francis O. J. Otway
Sir, It cannot be entirely accidental that human beings are here today. Whatever being organised the Universe selected elements that made life possible. If there had been no carbon, there would have been no life. This being many of us call God.
Yours faithfully,
FRANCIS O. J. OTWAY,
Painswick, Gloucestershire. May 21

From Mr Norman Levine
Sir, Why are we here? To produce the next generation. And enough of us do this.
  The rest (if we are lucky) is just a pleasant way to pass the time.
Yours sincerely,
NORMAN LEVINE,
Barnard Castle, Co Durham. May 21

From Mr Alan Mercado
Sir, Quite simply, we're 'ere because we're 'ere.
Yours sincerely,
ALAN MERCADO,
Hornchurch, Essex. May 21

Promotion in the bag

From Mr Ian Wilkinson
Sir, Your article on women in the City recommends certain essentials in the handbag in order to make a good first impression.
  My lady colleague certainly achieved that whilst at her first engineering meeting with the Ministry of Defence. Shortly into the meeting, one leg of the table gave way and the entire table was only saved from collapse by the quick reactions of those who were still awake.
  Realising that a loose nut was the cause of the problem, she rifled through her handbag and produced a set of spanners with which she fixed the leg back herself.

I doubt that any of those present will ever forget her.
Yours faithfully,
IAN WILKINSON,
North Dunstable. May 12

Sporting chance

From Mr David Soskin
Sir, From the Government that brought you the Dome 2000 – the Olympic Games 2012 (report, later editions, May 15).
Yours faithfully,
DAVID SOSKIN,
London NW3. May 15

From Mr Tom Ruben
Sir, Olympic Games in London nine years from now? Barely time to get the necessary planning permissions.
Yours sincerely,
TOM RUBEN,
London W5. May 16

From Mr David Whitter
Sir, The Government makes a popular decision to support a bid for the Olympics and immediately the undermining criticisms begin. Is it any wonder that we are considered an underperforming country?
Yours sincerely,
DAVID WHITTER,
Enfield. May 17

Worth a punt

From Mr Nick Locock
Sir, Oliver Letwin, Shadow Home Secretary, suggests (report, May 15) that a Tory victory at the next election would be a miracle.
  Two weeks ago (May 3) you reported that Iain Duncan Smith had wagered £120 at 3 to 1 – with Coral – on the Tories winning the next general election. Was he being naive? The odds against "miracles" should be very much longer.
Yours sincerely,
NICK LOCOCK,
Whitsbury, Hampshire. May 15

Core concerns

From Mrs M. M. Robinson

Sir, You report today that Professor David Stevenson plans to investigate the Earth's core using a probe embedded in molten metal, propelled by a nuclear explosion in a "reverse volcano". The probe will transmit data by seismic waves, "the vibrations which cause earthquakes".

I do hope he's not intending to do this anywhere near Sevenoaks.

Yours faithfully,
J. A. ROBINSON,
Ightham, Sevenoaks, Kent. May 15

Keeping in touch

From Mr Paul Petrie

Sir, Caitlin Moran (Comment, May 14) uses the latest phone survey to suggest that men have discovered the joys of gossiping, thanks to their mobile phones.

This survey apparently reveals that men spend 3,000 minutes a month on their mobile phones. A cost of 30p per minute (also stated in the article) gives an annual bill of £10,800. Perhaps an extreme case of lies, damn lies and statistics?

Yours faithfully,
PAUL PETRIE,
London SE24. May 14

From Mr Bob Rodwell

Sir, Never condemn current youngsters' obsession with their mobiles and computers.

We are currently enjoying almost daily communication from a 22-year-old granddaughter making her way on an open-ended circuit of the globe with not much more than a rucksack and its contents. Today we have been in contact with her in backwoods Guatemala with ease.

It's a great improvement over the time, only ten years or so ago, when her uncle made a similar odyssey and was reliant upon erratic, tardy and expensive airmails to stay in touch.

Yours faithfully,

BOB RODWELL,
Gloucester. May 19

From Mr Richard Need

Sir, The recent report showing how much young people depend on their mobile phones to provide comfort and security seems to justify my name for them: ear dummies.

Yours faithfully,
RICHARD NEED,
Cheam, Surrey. May 14

Difficult journey

From Mr Nigel Griffiths

Sir, The Radio 4 news this morning referred to the Palestinian bombs threatening to "derail the road map to peace before it has got off the ground".

Looking on the bright side, it is at least unlikely to be torpedoed.

Yours faithfully,
NIGEL GRIFFITHS,
Burton, Wirral, Cheshire. May 19

Branches everywhere

From Mr Simon Cuffin-Munday

Sir, Many years ago I spent long happy hours climbing beech trees in a wood near my family home. Although I have some experience of oak, I would say that beech has the advantage. The bark is more comfortable and yet still easy to grip and is a great deal cleaner than the oak. Ask any parent responsible for cleaning up tree-climbing offspring.

Some of the enjoyment has been eroded by advances in safety – 40 years ago we had no ropes or helmets (report and photographs, May 14).

Yours faithfully,
SIMON CUFFIN-MUNDAY,
Kelsall, Cheshire. May 14

From Lord Cunliffe

Sir, It is well known that the world is divided into two sorts of people: those who climb trees, and those who don't. I am in my seventies, remain firmly in the first cat-

egory and am planting oaks for my great-grandchildren to climb.
Yours faithfully,
ROGER CUNLIFFE,
London N6. May 14

From Mr Roger W. H. West

Sir, Back in 1957, when I was a boy, the Lady Margaret Professor of Divinity at the University of Cambridge came to visit my parents. I decided to impress him by climbing to the top of a tall holm oak – one of a pair.

Having reached the top, I was surprised to find that I was being addressed by the eminent professor from the top of the adjacent oak.

Having seen him again recently and having found him both mentally and physically active at the age of 93 after a lifetime devoted to scholarship, I would not be surprised to hear that he still has a yearning to climb trees.
Yours faithfully,
ROGER W. H. WEST,
Wick, South Gloucestershire. May 22

From Mr Peter Grafton

Sir, Lord Cunliffe's apparent penchant for climbing trees in his seventies is, perhaps, further evidence of the DNA similarity between humans and chimpanzees. No offence intended!
Yours faithfully,
PETER GRAFTON,
Limpsfield, Surrey. May 21

Stretched economy

From Mr Chris Smith

Sir, I was overawed by the number of stretch limousines that passed me on the M4, heading away from Cardiff on Saturday evening following the FA Cup Final, as I drove from Swindon.

I counted 43. Is this an indication of the current wealth of the nation?
Yours,
CHRIS SMITH,
Chippenham, Wiltshire. May 19

From Mrs C. Stock

Sir, Mr Chris Smith wondered whether the number of stretch limousines apparently returning from the FA Cup Final last Saturday was an indication of the current wealth of the nation.

However, after being invited (by a very generous work colleague) to attend Ascot races in June, I have found that local overnight accommodation is unavailable and the cost of coach, rail or taxi far exceeds the cost of hiring a stretch limousine, which will accommodate six people, further reducing the individual costs.

No matter how embarrassing it is to arrive somewhat like an Elvis impersonator, these limousines are relatively cheap and you are ferried door to door and on time.
Yours faithfully,
C. STOCK,
Drayton, Norfolk. May 21

Home from home

From Mr Kenneth Cleveland

Sir, "A stable block, which became a pigsty in the 1950s, is now home to visiting academics . . . " (The Register, May 12).

How appropriate.
I am, Sir, your obedient servant,
KENNETH CLEVELAND,
Armathwaite, Cumbria. May 20

Trades and professions

From Mr Barrie Behenna

Sir, Many years ago, I was assisting the Commission for Higher Education in Sierra Leone, and I well recall the distinguished Sierra Leonian educationist Dr David Carney saying, in the context of the increasing shortage of trained engineers, technicians and craftsmen in the country, that if you teach all your plumbers to become philosophers, then neither your theories nor your pipes will hold water.
Yours sincerely,
BARRIE BEHENNA,
Teignmouth, Devon. May 20

Buzz ticket

From Mr Brian E. Saunders

Sir, It is with concern that I learnt of the plight of bumblebees as revealed by your Countryside Editor.

My wife and I wish to extend a welcome to *Bombus ruderatus* and any of his remaining cousins to fly in and visit our modest one-third acre in Cheshire, where we have 22 out of the 28 desirable plant varieties listed. No landing charges.

Yours faithfully,
BRIAN E. SAUNDERS,
Tarporley, Cheshire. May 16

Caramba!

From Mr Oliver Chastney

Sir, Tonsorial shortcomings deny me the ability to emulate David Beckham's latest hairstyle.

However, donning a sombrero made from a copy of *The Times* (instructions, Sport, May 21) seems an ideal alternative to anyone wishing to look like a complete prat.

Yours faithfully,
OLIVER CHASTNEY,
Cringleford, Norwich. May 21

Pet equality

From Canon R. N. W. Elbourne

Sir, If my fully inoculated and Toxocara-free dog "fouls" the verge outside my house without my removing the evidence (which I do), I am liable to a fine of £1,000. If I take precautions to discourage the neighbourhood cats from doing the same to my own garden (which they do), I might have to pay compensation to their owners (In Brief, later editions, May 22).

Does not this make the law a steaming heap of ass droppings?

Yours,
NIGEL ELBOURNE,
Congleton, Cheshire. May 22

From Mr Thomas Muirhead

Sir, Canon Nigel Elbourne is concerned that the law imposes on him as a dog owner a liability which does not apply to cat owners. However, this inequality of legal status extends beyond responsibility for their respective pets' toilet habits.

For instance, a neighbour running over the canon's dog would have to stop and give his relevant details, but if the neighbour's cat were to be run over by the canon no further action would be required.

This levelling of the playing field, so to speak, may, or may not, afford him some consolation.

Yours faithfully,
THOMAS MUIRHEAD,
Gloucester. May 23

Snow and frost in May

From Sir Edward Peck

Sir, In his always interesting column, Paul Simons (Weather Eye, May 19) recalls the legend of St Dunstan's unholy pact with the Devil to blight his competitors' apple trees with a frost at this time of year.

There are less scurrilous precedents for frosty weather in May: the German Eisheiligen ("Ice Saints") from May 11 to 13; and here in North-East Scotland we are well aware of the "Gab o' May", when snow showers are to be expected around May 8; nor should one forget that one of Alexander Buchan's "cold periods" falls between May 9 and 14.

I prefer to recall that St Dunstan was, as Simons points out, "one of the most enlightened men of his generation".

Yours faithfully,
EDWARD PECK,
Tomintoul, Banffshire. May 20

Stop the world

From Mr Chris Whitby

Sir, The Inland Revenue sells 600 properties to a company based in a tax haven for leaseback to provide "the best value for money for taxpayers" (report, Business, May 19); GSK's chief executive had a pension package that would "pretend that he is three years older than he actually is" for annuity rate calculation (report, Business, same day); the Financial Services Authority's managing director describes an unsatisfactory situation as "highly sub-optimal" (report, Business, same day).

I'm cancelling my subscription to *Private Eye* magazine as superfluous.
Yours faithfully,
CHRIS WHITBY,
Peckleton, Leicestershire. May 20

Truly, madly, deeply

From Ms Gillian Ewing

Sir, I would love to write a letter to *The Times*, but how to sign off? On this page on May 19 there were no fewer than six varieties of valediction.
Cheers!
GILLIAN EWING,
Malton, North Yorkshire. May 20

Be prepared

From Mr Christopher Y. Nutt

Sir, The Burning Bush, a plant supposedly growing from the biblical original (Exodus iii, 1–16) from which the Lord spoke to Moses through the flames, the bush not being consumed, is the centrepiece in St Catherine's Monastery in Sinai.

A postcard just received here clearly shows that the monks have installed a large fire extinguisher next to it.
Yours faithfully,
CHRISTOPHER Y. NUTT,
Little Abington, Cambridge. May 20

Hard drives

From Mrs Gentian Walls

Sir, I seem to meet so many people who announce with great pride that they don't know how to turn a computer on. They usually say it in a tone indicating a certain intellectual superiority, as some people in the Sixties used to announce that they had no intention of ever buying a television set.
Yours faithfully,
GENTIAN WALLS,
Midhurst, West Sussex. May 24

From Dr B. G. Trower-Greenwood

Sir, I congratulate all those who in the Sixties announced that they would never buy a television set and kept their word. They must have had infinitely more time than most of us to do useful things. And if they implied "intellectual superiority" then, they almost certainly have it now.
Yours faithfully,
BRIAN G. TROWER-GREENWOOD,
Leicester. May 31

Nul points for the UK

From Mr Huw Beynon

Sir, Why is it that an essentially musical people, a nation that generated an endless parade of instantly disposable yet hugely catchy number-one hits for the Spice Girls – perfect fodder for the Eurovision Song Contest, surely – regularly comes up with such dire, tuneless pap for this annual parade of the dropped jaw? We should be told.
Yours,
HUW BEYNON,
Llandeilo. May 25

From Mrs Joan Salter

Sir, Nul points. At last, some news to make us truly proud.
Yours sincerely,
JOAN SALTER,
London N10. May 25

From Mr Mack G. Hann

Sir, Noting the number of songs sung in English, I could not help wondering, a propos a federal Europe, are we supposed to be joining them, or might they perhaps wish to join us?
Yours faithfully,
MACK G. HANN,
London SW3. May 24

From Mr Simon Herbert

Sir, I urge Tony Blair to call a referendum on whether or not we should enter the Eurovision Song Contest next year.
Yours faithfully,
SIMON HERBERT,
Eastbourne, East Sussex. May 26

Multiple fractures

From Mrs Anne Hardwick

Sir, The stupidest word break I have ever seen appeared in your newspaper today (later editions): ". . . masterpieces such as Canaletto's *View of Horseg-uard's Parade".*
It even beats bat-hroom.
Yours sincerely,
ANNE HARDWICK,
Twickenham, Middlesex. May 21

From Mr Frank Woodgate

Sir, I am delighted to see in today's T2 that the wonderful bridge player, Zia Mahmood, is continuing his practice of betrotting the glo.
Yours faithfully,
FRANK WOODGATE,
Blackheath, London SE3. May 27

From Dr Sara Serpell

Sir, The word-break I remember best is "bed-raggled", because it so exactly describes what I see in the mirror first thing in the morning.
Yours faithfully,
SARA SERPELL,
Wellesbourne, Warwick. June 1

From Mrs Jane Cullinan

Sir, When occasionally I altered the name of my restaurant from "The Last Resort" to "La Stresort", the debate amongst the more pretentious linguists about the meaning of the word "stresort" was sometimes alarming in its ferocity. It did, however, provide splendid entertainment for the staff.
Yours faithfully,
JANE CULLINAN,
Padstow, Cornwall. June 2

Defective vision

From Mr Philip D. Badrock

Sir, Rapidly approaching my 79th birthday, I am suffering from a deepening complex over the number of unmissable films I have missed. Please, Sir, is there a missed pix fix for this malady?
Yours truly,

PHILIP D. BADROCK,
Chislehurst. May 26

From Mr Andrew Wolfin

Sir, To select which "unmissable" films to miss, Mrs Alison Wilcock should adopt the following: if it's a film of a book, read the book instead; if it's a musical, fast-forward to the songs; and, if the film title is suffixed with a number higher than two – avoid it.
Yours faithfully,
ANDREW WOLFIN,
London NW4. June 4

From Mr Chris Holman

Sir, If Andrew Wolfin follows his own advice – to avoid films with a title suffixed by a number higher than two – he will have missed some memorable movies, including *Henry V*, *Richard III* and *The Magnificent Seven.*
Yours faithfully,
CHRIS HOLMAN,
Rugby. June 6

Parliament's defences

From Mr Brian McCabe

Sir, Surely a fortune awaits someone who can produce aesthetically pleasing concrete blocks (report and photograph, May 24)?
Yours faithfully,
B. J. P. McCABE,
Liverpool. May 24

From Mr A. G. Richards

Sir, Mr Brian McCabe inquires how to make concrete blocks aesthetically pleasing.
Perhaps by painting the words "Turner Prize entry" onto them?
Yours faithfully,
A. G. RICHARDS,
Garsington, Oxfordshire. May 29

From Mr Martin Ornstein

Sir, Here in the US, such blocks are known as "Jersey barriers", due to their original and intended purpose as highway median dividers, first used on the New Jersey Turnpike. I commiserate with Mr McCabe, as Washington DC has also sprouted quite a crop of them, protecting our precious museums, monuments and government facilities.

As for making them aesthetically pleasing, however, I have my doubts. The last attempt to beautify a concrete barrier, I believe, was in Berlin.
Yours faithfully,
MARTIN ORNSTEIN,
Burke, Virginia. May 28

From Mr Mike Eggleton
Sir, Surely a simulated stone box filled with a foot of loam would present an attractive sight when kept full of political flowers. Red roses, yellow daffodils and, of course, bluebells.
Yours faithfully,
MIKE EGGLETON,
London W5. May 29

From Mr Peter Wright
Sir, Were the concrete blocks around Parliament to be placed in a complete ring and stacked, say, four high, the United Kingdom might be a much, much better place.
Yours aye,
PETER WRIGHT,
Portencross, Ayrshire. May 30

Uplifting coincidence
From the Rural Dean of Ipswich
Sir, How intriguing that the 50th anniversary of the conquest of Mount Everest on May 29, 1953, falls on Ascension Day.

A gift for preachers.
As ever,
PETER TOWNLEY,
Ipswich, Suffolk. May 25

Crime wave
From Dr Edward Young
Sir, I have just bought a device to protect my son's car against theft. It comes with a caution that reads: "When fitting Stoplock for the first time, make sure that it does not pinch your steering wheel.
Yours sincerely,
EDWARD YOUNG,
Reading, Berkshire. May 27

Cut-price dilemma
From Mr Roy A. Hughes
Sir, I find myself on the horns of a dilemma. My local barber charges "over 65s" less than others, and on my last visit he erroneously included me, in my 61st year, in that concession.

Now I find that although the concession remains, the price has been increased by over 14 per cent.

About which aspect should I complain?
Yours,
R. A. HUGHES,
Whitchurch, Hampshire. May 27

Relative slump
From Mr J. M. L. Stone
Sir, You publish today wills showing estates as follows: £28 million (two), £12 million (one), £5 million (one), £4 million (one), £3 million (one), £2 million (nine) and £1 million-plus (16).

Clearly there are some for whom the slump in the market has not been totally disastrous.
Yours, etc,
J. M. L. STONE,
London W1. May 27

Last word
From Mrs Jo Dean
Sir, At 90 my mother has taken out a funeral plan with the excellent Age Concern Enterprises Ltd. She has specified that she wants cremation.

The letter of confirmation from Age Concern offers her "a very warm welcome". My mother says she can't wait.
Yours faithfully,
JO DEAN,
Cheltenham. May 28

From Mr Raj Kothari
Sir, My grandfather, a lifelong socialist, wanted funerary matters to be in the hands of the Co-op. When the time came the undertaker worked out a price, and then ear-

nestly added: "But, of course, you don't get the stamps."
Yours, etc,
RAJ KOTHARI,
Marshwood, Dorset. May 29

Fine support

From Mr Jim Clarke
Sir, In the Boy Scouts there was a high-level award called the "Bushman's Thong" (report and Comment, May 28). Now I'm glad I left before I got one.
Dib dib dob.
Yours,
JIM CLARKE,
Gweek, Cornwall. May 28

Boardroom salaries

From Mr J. B. Millar
Sir, Mike Parton, chief executive of Marconi, is reported as having "staked his reputation on a prediction that sales would recover in the second half of this year" (Business, May 30).
Could he not give a lead to senior executives in other companies and stake his salary on his prediction?
Yours faithfully,
J. B. MILLAR,
Holywood, Co Down. May 31

Baby carriage

From Mr Neil Roland
Sir, As the proud owner of a 1959 Wilson pram in which I wheel my son Felix around Didsbury village, I can only agree with Richard Kelly (Weekend, May 24) about the glories of classic prams.
We discovered ours in an 11-room rambling shop in Ardwick, Manchester, where the very charming owner deals with stage and screen inquiries for her antique prams while her husband restores their huge collection, many of which are shipped abroad. It was our best baby investment, and proves that not everything aesthetic has to go when number three arrives.

Yours,
NEIL ROLAND,
Didsbury, Manchester. May 28

Poetry in motion

From Mrs Cynthia Milton
Sir, I enjoyed Philip Howard's musings on the poetry of the shipping forecast this morning.
He would appreciate a Betjemanesque road sign on the A34 south of Oxford: "Milton, Chilton, Didcot, Wantage".
Yours faithfully,
CYNTHIA MILTON,
Thatcham, Berkshire.
May 30

From Father Bob Rainbow
Sir, Further to Cynthia Milton's poetic road sign, pre Beeching porters at Kidderminster Junction used to drop a couple of aitches when announcing stations along the now-preserved Severn Valley line, thus ringing out: "'ighley, Arley, 'ampton train!"
Yours,
BOB RAINBOW,
Bristol. June 2

From Mr Christopher Godley
Sir, John Betjeman was not the only poet to inspire our road signs: just south of Reading, the melodic sign to "Beech Hill, Mortimer and Stratfield Saye" could have come straight from John Masefield's *Cargoes*.
Yours faithfully,
CHRISTOPHER GODLEY,
Haslemere, Surrey. June 6

Exam help

From Mrs Yvonne Edwards
Sir, Having been a *Times* reader since I was doing my O levels, I have always found your paper to be both informative and educational.
Now my son is sitting his GCSEs these findings are confirmed. Not only have you thrown considerable light on his English

Language pre-released material about an African traditional healer ("Medicine men, a curse or cure?", T2, May 28), but today you featured his geography case study as well (the Three Gorges Dam).

Any chance of some erudition on algebra by Wednesday please?
Yours faithfully,
YVONNE EDWARDS,
Leighton Buzzard, Bedfordshire. May 29

Ladies of a certain age

From Mrs Helen Simpson
Sir, I was born on June 1 of a year I prefer not to disclose, and my birth was duly recorded in *The Times*. It struck me, on reading the birth announcements in your Coronation souvenir, that if the lady whose birth is announced there is playing the same game as I, she is in dire trouble.
Yours faithfully,
HELEN SIMPSON,
Pinner, Middlesex. June 1

From Dr Judy R. M. Allen
Sir, It was with great surprise and pride that I found that your paper has done me the honour of marking my 50th birthday by reissuing *The Times* of June 3, 1953 – the edition that announced, on the front page, my arrival in this world.
Yours sincerely,
JUDY R. M. ALLEN
(Research Fellow in palaeoecology, School of Biological and Biomedical Sciences, University of Durham), Esh Winning, Co Durham. June 2

Weapons of mass destruction

From Mr Malcolm Bowden
Sir, When I was at school, "military Intelligence" was offered as an ironic example of an oxymoron.

Might "reliable Intelligence" now fulfil the same role?
Yours sincerely,
MALCOLM BOWDEN,
Hartford, Cheshire. June 3

Mission to Mars

From Mr Richard O'Hagan
Sir, I understand that *Beagle 2* is carrying music by the band Blur and a piece of art by Damien Hirst. Is this an attempt to convince the Martians that we on Earth have no culture worth invading us for?
Yours faithfully,
RICHARD O'HAGAN,
Rowberry Morris, Solicitors, Reading. June 2

Comparatively precise

From Mr H. M. Dixon
Sir, I once heard that during a scientific conference, one of the scientists remarked: "At least there is one thing which cannot be accurately measured, and that is the beauty of women" (Professor David Lowenthal's letter, May 27).

His colleague replied: "Oh, yes it can. The standard unit is the millihelen. This is defined as the amount of beauty which would cause the launch of exactly one ship."
Yours truly,
H. M. DIXON,
Oswestry, Shropshire. May 27

From Mr S. Rahman
Sir, May I propose that a microhelen be defined as the amount of feminine beauty that at least justifies pushing the boat out?
Yours faithfully,
S. RAHMAN,
Wembley Park, Middlesex. June 4

From Vice-Admiral Sir Ian McGeoch
Sir, Surely anyone with a grain of gallantry measures feminine pulchritude in troy weight?
Yours faithfully,
IAN McGEOCH,
Ixworth, Suffolk. June 11

From Mrs Rosemary Platt
Sir, Your correspondents debate the measurement of feminine beauty in milli- or microhelens, but my husband is dubious about the merits of such continental units of pulchritude.

He is, and always will be, an avid supporter of the British Standard Eyeful.
Yours faithfully,
ROSEMARY PLATT,
Sutton Coldfield. June 9

Gaelic versus English

From Mr Bob Mackinnon

Sir, Ben Macintyre asserts (Comment, May 31) that there is only one "pallid" word for rain in the English language, whereas there are five in Gaelic.

What about spit, drizzle, shower, downpour and cloudburst?
Yours faithfully,
R. MACKINNON,
Little Neston, Wirral. June 3

From Mr R. E. Pears

Sir, The very size of its vocabulary, together with its simplicity – no gender and no accents – makes English eminently suitable as a world language. Granted that spelling and pronunciation are a minefield; but this in itself is a reflection of the multiplicity of sources.

I am all for the preservation of Gaelic, if only because there are no more beautiful sounds than Welsh when it is sung and English spoken by a native Gaelic speaker.
Yours sincerely,
R. E. PEARS,
Penicuik, Edinburgh. June 4

From Mr Andrew McClintock

Sir, I am not so certain that ". . . modern English will never split off into distinct parallel forms, as the Romance languages evolved from Latin". In Outer Mongolia about five years ago I met a Swede who was teaching English to Mongolian teachers so that they could in turn instruct their pupils. What language were those pupils likely to end up with? Not English, I am sure.
Yours, etc,
ANDREW McCLINTOCK,
Sheffield. June 3

From Mr Michael Murphy

Sir, I am confident that if any Swede were to teach English to any foreigner, Mongolian or not, that pupil's English grammar would be more correct than that used by most in this country.
Yours faithfully,
MICHAEL MURPHY,
North Harrow, Middlesex. June 6

From Mr Matthew Dick

Sir, Whilst awaiting a morning flight to the US at Heathrow airport recently, I decided to treat myself to breakfast in one of the airport lounges. Upon my asking the waitress whether the establishment's orange juice was freshly squeezed, she replied: "It's freshly squeezed out of a carton."

English is indeed a wonderfully rich language.
I remain, Sir, etc,
MATTHEW DICK,
Henfield, West Sussex. June 7

Cashless society

From Mr R. Anthony Vigurs

Sir, A sign, prominently displayed above a van sales showroom just opened in Beckenham, proudly states: "All major credit cards excepted."

Is the tide turning at last?
Yours faithfully,
ANTHONY VIGURS,
Beckenham, Kent. June 7

Sign language

From Mr D. A. E. Hunt

Sir, It seems that John Prescott's V-sign (report, photographs and People, June 6), also made an appearance in the same day's crossword (clue 1 down): "Poetic gesture from beefcake, oddly."
Yours faithfully,
DAVID HUNT,
Ringmer, Lewes. June 7

Where's Harry?

From Mr David Vanderpump

Sir, I spotted the young man on your front

page today immediately as the artiste currently known as prince.
Yours faithfully,
DAVID VANDERPUMP,
Godalming, Surrey. June 9

Going overboard

From Mr Keith Jarvis

Sir, Stephen Pollard (Thunderer, June 9) says that "we cling to the monarchy as an anchor to the past" and that "because it is such an anchor . . . we need to throw it overboard and set ourselves free".

I am no sailor but I have always believed that throwing the anchor overboard was meant to impede progress rather than permit it.
Yours faithfully,
KEITH JARVIS,
Ledbury, Herefordshire. June 9

From Mr James Longrigg

Sir, Mr Keith Jarvis suggests that by seeking to throw overboard the "anchor" of the monarchy, Stephen Pollard would "impede progress rather than permit it".

But surely that all depends upon whether or not the anchor continues to be attached to a vessel. Stephen Pollard's analogy may be retained – if the anchor is not.
Yours sincerely,
JAMES LONGRIGG,
Rowlands Gill, Tyne and Wear. June 10

Political football

From Dr Noel Lawn

Sir, Perhaps as a pro-Europe gesture, we could give David Beckham to the Spanish in exchange for keeping Gibraltar.
Yours,
NOEL LAWN,
Woodbury, Devon. June 11

Medical note-taking

From Mr Ernest Simon

Sir, My late father liked to recall a report he read in *The Times* in which the abbreviation "W.I.L.P.", used by a casualty depart-

ment doctor to describe how a patient received cuts and bruising in the face, turned out to mean "walked into lamp-post".
Yours faithfully,
ERNEST H. SIMON,
Merstham, Surrey. June 9

From Mr Bernard Garston

Sir, When I was a medical student I was baffled by the abbreviation B.N.O.R. I walked the entire length of a hospital to discover from a nurse in the obstetric unit that the meaning was "bowels not opened regularly".
Yours faithfully,
BERNARD GARSTON,
Hale, Cheshire. June 12

From Mr Mike Godsal

Sir, As a retired vet I have also come across useful acronyms on medical notes.

Some years ago a colleague handed me notes with D.M.I.T.O. written on them.

It stands for "dog more intelligent than owner".
Yours faithfully,
MIKE GODSAL,
Stone, Buckinghamshire. June 12

From Mr W. H. Cousins

Sir, An amusing abbreviation, "VZBW", was occasionally used by the Americans when, during the Second World War, they joined us on the aircraft route across Africa between Accra and Cairo. On that route, the harmattan (sand storm) sometimes rose to over 10,000 feet.

VZBW stood for Visibility Zero, Birds Walking.
Sincerely,
W. H. COUSINS,
Upminster, Essex. June 16

From Mrs Harriet Coates

Sir, At my son's school, a well-loved master writes exasperatedly in the margin of boys' work "ATBQ": Answer The — Question!

It seems to work.
Yours faithfully,
HARRIET COATES,
Lower Heswall, Wirral. June 14

From Mr Kenneth Hulbert

Sir, Many years ago I accompanied my detective sergeant on inquiries into a serious matter, and called at a hospital to see medical notes to confirm dates of admission and discharge. Each day bore the abbreviation "LOS" and we asked what that represented.

Matron drew herself up to her full height, saying: "Loose Offensive Stools."

Outside we were helpless with laughter.

Over the years we exchange Christmas cards and they are unsigned but bear three letters: "LOS".

Sincerely,
KENNETH HULBERT,
Chippenham, Wiltshire. June 20

From Mr Edward Green

Sir, When I studied at the Army Staff College as a junior major in 1980, "BGO" was in vogue for red-ink corrections of our work. Yes – Blinding Glimpse of the Obvious.

Sadly, I received it several times.

Yours faithfully,
EDWARD GREEN (Major, retd),
Lichfield, Staffordshire. June 19

From the Very Reverend David Frayne

Sir, It was the Anglo-Catholic late Bishop of Southwark, Mervyn Stockwood, who often spoke off the record about his evangelical "NKC" – Not Keen on Communion – parishes.

Further, when their incumbents offered him only Horlicks as a nightcap when staying overnight, he would enter in his diary "NTSS" – Next Time Send the Suffragan.

Yours sincerely,
DAVID FRAYNE,
Gillingham, Dorset. June 18

From Mr R. W. Pullan

Sir, I was told by a doctor friend of mine that in Cairo, during the Second World War, should an officer contract a venereal disease the cause would be entered on their notes as "BBC" – Bitten By Camel.

Yours sincerely,
R. W. PULLAN,
Hampton, Middlesex. June 18

From Dr Noreen Hunt

Sir, The most nonchalant abbreviation I ever encountered was/is "HDQ".

Knowing many alumni of the English Roman Catholic seminary, Douai, died for their priesthood, I was scanning a list of English and Welsh martyrs solely for Douai references but became distracted by the frequent abbreviation "HDQ".

Like an intrusive wasp it interrupted my exercise. I checked the abbreviations key: "Hanged, Drawn and Quartered".

Yours faithfully,
NOREEN HUNT,
Lewes, East Sussex. June 23

From Professor Emeritus Brian G. Palmer

Sir, My wife and I were sharing impressions with one of our fellow cruise passengers who confessed to being in her late eighties. We thought the cruise thoroughly enjoyable and, though expensive, excellent value for money. It emerged that it was her 43rd. She quickly added that it was her "VIP". With a smile she explained: "Vanishing Inheritance Plan".

Yours faithfully,
BRIAN PALMER,
Rotherfield Peppard, Oxfordshire. June 22

From Ms Sue Dodson

Sir, I was surprised when a sloth-like friend said she was off to ski in Portugal (in the summer). Then she explained: "SKI: Spending the Kids' Inheritance".

Yours faithfully,
SUE DODSON,
Cambridge. June 24

From Mr Christopher Cone

Sir, As a new recruit to Sotheby's Victorian Picture Department in Belgravia in the late 1970s, I was instructed that the initials to be used for any pictures of insufficient value for auction were "NSV": "No Sale Value".

I was also informed, no doubt with a hint of mischief, that the equivalent initials at the supposedly more genteel Christie's were "NQOCOTD": "Not Quite Our Cup Of Tea Dear".

Yours faithfully,
CHRISTOPHER CONE,
London SW1. June 26

From Sir Robert Sanders
Sir, I was always delighted when a minute from my boss ended with "TINHAT".
 Not a warning to take cover but "There Is No Hurry About This".
Yours faithfully,
ROBERT SANDERS,
Crieff, Perthshire. June 27

Sum of knowledge

From Mrs O. Greenwood
Sir, Our education system has failed. I have just seen this calculation deemed necessary by a local shop: "Growbags two for £4. That's £2 each."
Yours faithfully,
O. GREENWOOD,
Ealing, London W5. June 15

From Mr Derek Faulkes
Sir, I cannot understand the contention of Mrs O. Greenwood that our education system has failed (growbags two for £4 = £2 each).
 I have checked the answer on my calculator and it is correct.
Yours faithfully,
DEREK FAULKES,
Eastbourne. June 16

From Mr Michael J. Hoy
Sir, Has the US educational system also failed?
 Last year a sign in the bedding department of a large store in Orlando read: "This is a duvet . . . pronounced doo-vay."
Yours faithfully,
MICHAEL J. HOY,
Fenay Bridge, Huddersfield. June 16

From Mr David Carter
Sir, Recently, while visiting London, I asked for 18 first-class stamps in a well-known store on The Strand.
 Alarmed by my request, the assistant informed me that they only sold books of six.

Oh, go on then, I'll have three of them.
Yours,
DAVID CARTER,
Stoke on Trent. June 19

Unsex me here?

From Mr Ken Brotherhood
Sir, A female *Richard III* (First Night, review and photograph, later editions June 12 and earlier editions, June 13)? Whatever next? *Titus Androgynous?*
Yours sincerely,
KEN BROTHERHOOD,
Stockport, Cheshire. June 13

Rock on . . . and on

From Mrs Janet Babb
Sir, At the ripe old age of 46, I was considered too old by my elder daughter to attend the Isle of Wight pop festival with her and see Starsailor at the Saturday performance.
 Last night, just after 10pm, my younger daughter and I were treated to a raucous rendition of Bryan Adams's *(Everything I Do) I Do It For You* via her mobile phone.
 I am so envious! Roll on next year, I will be there.
Yours faithfully,
JANET BABB,
Warwick, Warwickshire. June 16

From Mr Ian Whitmore
Sir, In answer to Mrs Janet Babb, whose daughter thought her too old to attend the recent Isle of Wight festival, I speak as someone old enough to have attended the first such festival.
 When my son asked recently if I would attend a rock concert with him I agreed somewhat reluctantly, until I found that every member of the chosen group had been eligible for Saga membership longer than myself.
Yours faithfully,
IAN WHITMORE,
Lower Froyle, Hampshire. June 17

From Mrs Karen Bujakowski

Sir, My husband, aged 50, accompanied our daughter, aged 15, and friends to the V Festival of music last year, where he was approached by a young festival-goer who commented how nice it was to see an elderly gentleman enjoying such an event.

When asked about the possibility of supplying drugs, my husband was able to offer Panadol and Pro-plus.

Yours faithfully,
KAREN BUJAKOWSKI,
Warton, Lancashire. June 17

Morning glory?

From the Reverend Shamus Williams

Sir, Jane Shilling might have cited many a biblical passage in praise of early rising.

However, just as I feel sure that her article would be less likely to appear in winter, I have always had a sneaking suspicion that the Almighty might be less keen on early mornings if the Psalmist had experienced a few English grey, drizzly February mornings.

Yours faithfully,
SHAMUS WILLIAMS,
Guilden Morden, Hertfordshire. June 13

No stones unturned

From Mr Philip Carn

Sir, Like English Heritage and the National Trust, Richard Morrison misses the practical solution to the Stonehenge problem.

To obviate the necessity for a tunnel and re-routing of roads, and to allow more people to see the monument, surely it would be easier and less expensive to move it.

As they were able to bring Cleopatra's Needle from Egypt to the Thames Embankment in the 19th century and shift old London Bridge to an American desert in the 20th, it should not be too difficult to transfer the ancient stones to, say, Wandsworth Common in the 21st.

Yours faithfully,
PHILIP CARN,
Cranleigh, Surrey. June 16

From Mr Patrick Loobey

Sir, Mr Philip Carn suggests that Stonehenge be resited on Wandsworth Common. I can assure him that members of the Wandsworth Historical Society and also Wandsworth Museum would be delighted at the prospect of getting the stones here.

The only fair exchange I can think of is to transplant Wandsworth Prison to Salisbury Plain.

Yours faithfully,
PATRICK LOOBEY
(Vice-chairman, Wandsworth Historical Society), Streatham, London. June 20

Royal Ascot style

From Mrs D. E. Pincott

Sir, For many years my husband has readily and freely offered me advice on clothes that would hopefully enhance my far-from-perfect figure.

Having seen some of the fashions worn at Royal Ascot, I am pleased that his schoolmaster's salary would never have allowed me to employ a personal stylist.

Yours faithfully,
KAY PINCOTT,
Bristol. June 18

A weak solution

From Mrs Anne Cowan

Sir, To paraphrase Groucho Marx, I don't care to do a crossword which, like today's main puzzle, can be solved by people like me in 20 minutes.

Yours faithfully,
ANNE COWAN,
North Berwick, East Lothian. June 17

Just when I thought . . .

From Mr Stephen Chittenden

Sir, Having now finally seen the back of David Beckham I discover that Jeffrey Archer is to be visited upon us again.

Could Real Madrid be persuaded to put in a bid?

Yours faithfully,

STEPHEN CHITTENDEN,
Chellaston, Derby. June 19

Cabinet reshuffle

From Dr Fred Haslam
Sir, Our little parish church operates in the gift of the Lord Chancellor, or at least it did until last week.
Are we now a Constitutional Affair?
Yours faithfully,
FRED HASLAM
(Churchwarden, St Swithun's, 1998–2003),
Martyr Worthy, Hampshire. June 19

From Mr Nicholas Matheson
Sir, Should the Department for Constitutional Affairs be known as Decaff as, like its counterpart, it lacks any stimulation?
Yours faithfully,
NICK MATHESON,
Wimbledon, London SW19. June 16

Life under Labour

From Mr D. A. Brooks
Sir, In view of the shift to presidential-style politics, is it not time for additional honours to be added to the list currently available?
I suggest, in ascending order of importance: the KB (Knows Blair); the KBW (Well); the KBVW (Very Well).
Yours faithfully,
D. A. BROOKS,
Cranleigh, Surrey. June 17

From Mr Francis Barnard
Sir, Mr D. A. Brooks suggests a new high honour of KBVW (Knows Blair Very Well), but surely Lord Falconer of Thoroton (report, June 18) qualifies for the even greater honour of BF (Blair's Flatmate).
Yours faithfully,
FRANCIS BARNARD,
Sevenhampton, Cheltenham. June 22

Double trouble

From Mr Christopher Holroyd
Sir, TV Review (T2, June 18): "Joe Joseph is away."

Parliamentary Sketch (main paper, June 18): Joe Joseph, writing on the anomaly of ministers doing two jobs.
Yours faithfully,
CHRISTOPHER HOLROYD,
London SW15. June 18

Tax on high earners

From Mrs Tressa Parker
Sir, My five-year-old nephew has just returned from his local primary school with, amongst others, the following spellings to learn: wealth, health and stealth.
Could this have been a government directive?
Yours faithfully,
TRESSA PARKER,
Tonbridge, Kent. June 18

Surprise party

From Mrs Jenni Hall
Sir, You report today about problems at a summer solstice party in Hampshire.
The party is described as an annual event.
Well, blow me down.
Yours faithfully,
JENNI HALL,
Bramhope, Leeds. June 23

Higher purpose

From Dr Sue O'Hare
Sir, A letter from the consumer council Postwatch in response to a recent complaint contained the "hope that this levitates your concerns".
I feel my burden has been lifted already.
Yours faithfully,
SUE O'HARE,
Sandhurst, Berkshire. June 24

Magic moments

From Mr Robert O. Green
Sir, Harry Potter is now 15 years old and he "doesn't understand how girls' minds work" (Interview, T2, June 20).
I have been married to the same "girl" for almost 50 years and have two daughters and

I still don't know how girls' minds work. Perhaps I am a slow learner.

Yours faithfully,
ROBERT O. GREEN,
Killamarsh, Sheffield. June 21

From Mr Neil Murray

Sir, "It's my turn now!"

"No, it's not. You had it for half an hour, and I've only had it for 20 minutes."

"Dad! It's not fair!"

In my household, this would normally signal another children's squabble over a video game, time on the computer, or possession of the TV remote control.

But this time it is over a book.

Outside our house, I heard two of the neighbours' children discussing it, each inquiring of the other how far they had got through it, and dissecting the plot.

If the Government wants to attract children back to the magic of books, I suggest that it finds a useful post in the Ministry for Education and Skills for J. K. Rowling.

Yours faithfully,
NEIL MURRAY,
Sutton, Surrey. June 26

From Dr Peter Jennings

Sir, Mr Robert O. Green notes that he lacks insight into the female mind. In our household, at least, this is not reciprocated.

On the few occasions when I have been able to resist an application for a "loan" from my daughter, her understanding of my mental processes has been rapid and sweeping: "Mum, Dad's stressed again."

Yours faithfully,
PETER JENNINGS,
Burgh-by-Sands, Cumbria. June 26

Match points

From Mrs Jean Martland Binner

Sir, At this time of year I wonder if it is possible to divorce someone just because he likes to watch Wimbledon with the sound turned off.

Yours faithfully,
JEAN BINNER,
Horsham, West Sussex. June 25

From Mr Alan G. Heaton

Sir, Although I sympathise with Mrs Jean Martland Binner, the divorce judge may find that Mr Binner had just cause to watch Wimbledon with the television sound turned off; after all, Greg Rusedski might be playing.

Yours faithfully,
ALAN G. HEATON,
Teddington, Middlesex. June 27

Iraq dossier, BBC and the truth

From Mr Bill Torrance

Sir, I was amused to read in "Creme" of today's date that Mr Terry Waite is "still an Anglican with Christian connections".

In the present climate this, I fear, must render him almost unique.

Yours,
BILL TORRANCE,
Bromley, Kent. June 25

Politics off the shelf

From Mrs Anne Edwards

Sir, For 18 years I shopped at the supermarket where Roy Hattersley (Thunderer, June 21) used to be assistant manager.

Prices were high, the product range was limited and the management often appeared inflexible to consumer demand.

In spite of these shortcomings, I remained loyal until new Labour opened a store near me, offering friendly service, competitive prices and a manager who listened.

Oh, and my favourite brand of soap powder was still on the shelves, in a bright modern package.

Somehow I don't think I'll be shopping at the old place any more.

Yours,
ANNE EDWARDS,
Cheltenham, Gloucestershire. June 25

Shared graves

From Mr Geoffrey Woodward

Sir, Running out of burial spaces (T2, June 23)? The records at Bunhill Fields Burial

Ground in the City show that in grave number 209 are:

Catherine Mary Woodward 1791 at a depth of 13 feet; Alice Woodward 1798 at 11 feet; Charles Woodward 1819 at 9 feet; Robert Woodward 1830 at 7 feet.

I think this gives a new slant to the phrase "nearest and dearest".

Yours, etc,
GEOFFREY WOODWARD,
Worthing, West Sussex. June 24

Food for thought

From His Honour Judge Anthony Rumbelow, QC
Sir, I have just returned from an alumni weekend at my Cambridge college.

In the students' dining room, one serving dish bore the words:

Smoked Haddock (Fish)

And they want top-up fees?

Yours,
A. RUMBELOW,
Littleborough, Lancashire. June 25

From Mrs Bernice Foreman
Sir, Judge Anthony Rumbelow was amused by the explanatory "fish" on the plate of smoked haddock at his Cambridge college. My experience of dining with my student son at Cambridge is that any explanation is welcome, as the food is unrecognisable as fish or fowl.

This does not apply, however, to the excellent fare provided in Hall, where the students dine but rarely.

Yours,
BERNICE FOREMAN,
53 Wolmer Gardens, HA8 8QB. June 27

Making a 'horlicks'

From Wing Commander Derek Martin, RAF (retd)
Sir, "Horlicks" in the context of a mess (report, later editions, June 25) was in use towards the end of the Second World War.

The instigator of "a proper horlicks" was sometimes considered to be "Harpic", or clean round the bend.

Yours, etc,
DEREK MARTIN,
Marlow. June 26

Calculating a long life

From Mr Jon Ritman
Sir, You report today that failing to take regular exercise for 20 minutes a day can knock 1.4 years off my life. But, by my reckoning, in a 75-year lifespan it would take over a year to take the exercise. If you take into account the extra high-stress work needed to pay for gym fees it doesn't seem worth rising from my armchair.

Yours sincerely,
JON RITMAN,
London N8. June 23

From Mr Bernard Tierney
Sir, By adding up minus points for unhealthy living (eg, failing to floss teeth regularly, indulging in risky sex) and deducting that total from the current average life expectancy for men of 75 years, I have discovered that I should have been dead as of August, 1994.

Thanks heaps.

Yours sincerely,
BERNARD TIERNEY,
Binham, Norfolk. June 23

Index of Letter Writers